The Europeanisation of Whitehall

MANCHESTER
1824

Manchester University Press

European Policy Research Unit Series

Series Editors: *Simon Bulmer, Peter Humphreys* and *Mick Moran*

The European Policy Research Unit Series aims to provide advanced textbooks and thematic studies of key public policy issues in Europe. They concentrate, in particular, on comparing patterns of national policy content, but pay due attention to the European Union dimension. The thematic studies are guided by the character of the policy issue under examination.

The European Policy Research Unit (EPRU) was set up in 1989 within the University of Manchester's Department of Government to promote research on European politics and public policy. The series is part of EPRU's effort to facilitate intellectual exchange and substantive debate on the key policy issues confronting the European states and the European Union.

Titles in the series also include:

Globalisation and policy-making in the European Union   Ian Bartle

The power of the centre: Central governments and the macro-implementation of EU public policy   Dionyssis G. Dimitrakopoulos

Creating a transatlantic marketplace   Michelle P. Egan (ed.)

The politics of health in Europe   Richard Freeman

Immigration and European integration (2nd edn)   Andrew Geddes

Agricultural policy in Europe   Alan Greer

The European Union and the regulation of media markets   Alison Harcourt

Mass media and media policy in Western Europe   Peter Humphreys

The politics of fisheries in the European Union   Christian Lequesne

The European Union and culture: Between economic regulation and European cultural policy   Annabelle Littoz-Monnet

Sports law and policy in the European Union   Richard Parrish

The Eurogroup   Uwe Puetter

EU pharmaceutical regulation   Govin Permanand

Regulatory quality in Europe: Concepts, measures and policy processes   Claudio M. Radaelli and Fabrizio de Francesco

Extending European cooperation   Alasdair R. Young

Regulatory politics in the enlarging European Union   Alasdair Young and Helen Wallace

The Europeanisation of Whitehall

UK central government and the
European Union

*Simon Bulmer
and Martin Burch*

Manchester University Press
Manchester and New York
distributed in the United States exclusively by Palgrave Macmillan

Published by Manchester University Press
Oxford Road, Manchester M13 9NR, UK
and Room 400, 175 Fifth Avenue, New York, NY 10010, USA
www.manchesteruniversitypress.co.uk

Distributed exclusively in the USA by
Palgrave Macmillan, 175 Fifth Avenue, New York,
NY 10010, USA

Distributed exclusively in Canada by
UBC Press, University of British Columbia, 2029 West Mall,
Vancouver, BC, Canada V6T 1Z2

British Library Cataloguing-in-Publication Data
A catalogue record for this book is available from the British Library

Library of Congress Cataloging-in-Publication Data applied for

ISBN   978 0 7190 5515 7 *hardback*
ISBN   978 0 7190 5516 4 *paperback*

First published 2009

18 17 16 15 14 13 12 11 10 09   10 9 8 7 6 5 4 3 2 1

Typeset
by Graphicraft Limited, Hong Kong
Printed in Great Britain
by CPI Antony Rowe, Chippenham, Wiltshire

Contents

List of boxes

List of figures

List of tables

Preface

In 1973 the United Kingdom (UK) acceded to the European Communities (EC), now known as the European Union (EU). Over the subsequent thirty-five years of membership the European issue has remained the subject of controversy within the party-political arena and amongst public opinion. Nevertheless, UK central government – officials and ministers alike – have had to contend with the demands of membership. How have they adapted to engagement with this increasingly important tier of governance? Has their adaptation been as controversial as that of the political parties? Our study explores the Europeanisation of British central government with a view to answering these questions. We argue that the impact of the EU on the work in, and working practices of, Whitehall has been considerable. We offer an analytical framework for understanding the adaptation of UK central government and of national institutions more generally and comparatively.

The main body of our analysis is centred on the situation prevailing under the Major and Blair governments. This was the period during which our research was undertaken and we have been able to obtain a detailed picture of the evolution of the impact on Whitehall of EU membership from the implementation of the Maastricht Treaty in 1993 through to the resignation of Tony Blair in May 2007. However, we have complemented this research with some archival and interview-based work so that we are able to present the first comprehensive view of central government's adaptation over the period since the first application, made in 1961.

Just as Britain's relationship with the EU has been highly controversial, so academics have not been exempt from expressing value judgements about the desirability of integration. No work can be completely value-free, of course, but we embrace explicitly one normative presumption in this study. It is that, having joined the integration process, British positions will be most effectively represented by ministers and officials if they learn to adapt their political behaviour and strategies to the multi-tiered system of governance that is the EU.

Methodology

In carrying out the analysis we undertook extensive elite interviewing over the period from 1996 to 2006. Our interviewees covered all central government departments including the Scottish, Welsh and Northern Ireland Offices, as well as the United Kingdom's Permanent Representation to the EU in Brussels (UKREP). In later projects we conducted further interviews in the devolved executives, the 'hub' and inner core departments of Whitehall. As part of the original project we also interviewed in both Houses of Parliament and in the European Union institutions in order to gain rather different, more distanced and critical appreciations of how UK civil servants and ministers have performed on the European stage. Our analysis also included interviews with retired ministers and officials who had been practitioners at the time of failed attempts at accession as well as, more importantly, the successful accession of 1973. This historical dimension was complemented by analysis undertaken in the Public Record Office and informs Chapter 4 of our study. Some of our interviewees, including for the contemporary component of research, helpfully provided us with documentation to augment the material that is on the record. All our interviews were conducted on an unattributable basis, and this is reflected in our referencing of them. Our project was funded by the UK's Economic and Social Research Council (ESRC) under its Whitehall Programme award no. L 124251001.

Acknowledgements

We must acknowledge first of all the help given by our many interviews and the financial support of the ESRC. We are particularly appreciative of the officials and diplomats who opened up the Cabinet Office European Secretariat, UKREP and the Foreign and Commonwealth Office to us, affording widespread access. The Council Secretariat in Brussels helpfully provided some data for tables in Chapter 3. Rod Rhodes, as Director of the Whitehall Programme, was an important intellectual and organisational support. A number of academic colleagues were very helpful to our work: Ian Bache, Jack Hayward, Andrew Jordan, Brigid Laffan, Alberta Sbragia, Handley Stevens, Helen Wallace and the late Vincent Wright. We were participants in a study group, organised by Stephen George and then Ian Bache, on the Europeanisation of British politics and were able to benefit from the papers and discussions within that framework. Christian Lequesne and Philippe Rivaud wrote a project paper on the French coordination system, and we are grateful to them for that work. Our collaborators on the subsequent devolution projects – Caitríona Carter, Ricardo Gomez, Patricia Hogwood and Drew Scott – must also be acknowledged. We acknowledge the exchanges that we have had with our University of Manchester Ph.D.

students working on closely related topics, namely Chen-Yu Huang and Scott James. We also had assistance of various kinds from Christine Agius, Kay Green, Charlie and Leslie Farnell, Adrian Jarvis and Cathryn Jones. Simon Bulmer drafted some work while holding a Spanish government scholarship at the Universitat Autónoma de Barcelona and carried out his part of final editing while a Visiting Professor at the Stiftung Wissenschaft und Politik in Berlin. He acknowledges the financial and intellectual support offered during both stays.

We gave seminar or conference presentations in a range of venues and benefited from the feedback offered, which we acknowledge with thanks. Seminars were given at the universities of Bradford, Edinburgh, Essex, Loughborough, Manchester, Nottingham, Sussex, Salford, Konstanz, at the Scottish Office and to two 'Westminster Explained' conferences of practitioners. We also presented our findings at a Whitehall Programme seminar to EU policy-makers from central government, hosted by the Chartered Institute of Public Finance and Accountancy (CIPFA), and would like to thank the Cabinet Office for publicising this event within its European network. Conference presentations were given within the Whitehall Programme at Birmingham, at the American Society for Public Administration (in Philadelphia), the University Association for Contemporary European Studies (UACES) (Budapest), the European Union Studies Association (Austin, Texas), a CONNEX (Connecting Excellence on European Governance) Framework 6 workshop in Oslo, an Economic and Social Research Council (ESRC)/Joint University Council of the Applied Social Sciences research training conference in York, a UACES/Jean Monnet conference on constitutionalism at Queen's University Belfast, and to a workshop of the ESRC/UACES Seminar Group on the Europeanisation of British Politics as well as its concluding conference at Sheffield Town Hall. We are, of course, responsible for any errors or omissions.

We would also like to thank our colleagues in the University of Manchester's Department of Government for offering an excellent intellectual context within which our research was undertaken. And finally we wish to thank our partners, Helen and Annie respectively, for their patience and support during the research and drafting of this book.

February 2008

List of abbreviations

AE	Approach to Europe committee (ministerial)
AE(O)	Approach to Europe (Official committee)
BERR	Department for Business, Enterprise and Regulatory Reform
BoT	Board of Trade
BRE	Better Regulation Executive
BSE	bovine spongiform encephalopathy (mad cow disease)
CAP	Common Agricultural Policy
CATS	Article 36 Committee
CEECs	central and eastern European countries
CFP	Common Fisheries Policy
CFSP	Common Foreign and Security Policy
CIVCOM	Committee on Civilian Aspects of Crisis Management
CMN(O)	Common Market Negotiations Committee (Official)
CMN(O)(L)	Common Market Negotiations Official Legal Committee
CMN(SC)	Common Market Negotiations Steering Committee
COES	Cabinet Office European Secretariat
COEU	Cabinet Office European Unit
COLA	Cabinet Office Legal Advisers
COPS	Political and Security Committee
COREPER	Committee of Permanent Representatives
CRO	Commonwealth Relations Office
DBERR	Department for Business, Enterprise and Regulatory Reform
DCA	Department for Constitutional Affairs
DCE	Departmental Committee on Europe (MAFF/DEFRA)
DCLG	Department for Communities and Local Government
DCMS	Department for Culture Media and Sport
DEFRA	Department of the Environment, Food and Rural Affairs
DETR	Department of the Environment, Transport and the Regions

DfES	Department for Education and Skills
DfID	Department for International Development
DG	Directorate General
DH	Department of Health
DHSS	Department of Health and Social Security
DNE	detached national expert
DNH	Department of National Heritage
DoE	Department of the Environment
DoT	Department of Transport
DfT	Department for Transport
DSS	Department of Social Security
DTI	Department of Trade and Industry
DWP	Department for Work and Pensions
EAD	Eastern Adriatic Directorate (in FCO)
EC	European Communities
ECJ	European Court of Justice
ECOFIN	Economic and Financial Affairs Council
ECSC	European Coal and Steel Community
EDF	European Development Fund
EEA	European Economic Area
EEC	European Economic Community
EFS	European Fast Stream
EFTA	European Free Trade Association
EMS	European Monetary System
EMU	European Monetary Union
EP	cabinet committee on European Policy (in UK context)
EP	European Parliament (in EU context)
EPC	European Political Cooperation
EPG	Environmental Protection Group (Department of the Environment)
EPSED	Environment Protection Strategy and Europe Division (DoE)
EQ	European Economic Association Committee (ministerial committee)
EQ(O)	European Questions official committee
EQ(S)	European Questions (steering) committee
ERM	Exchange Rate Mechanism
ESDP	European Security and Defence Policy
ESRC	Economic and Social Research Council
ESU	European Staffing Unit
ESPRIT	European Strategic Programme of Research and Development in Information Technology
EU	European Union
EU-I	European Union Directorate (Internal)

EU-X	European Union Directorate (External)
EUD	European Union Directorate (FCO)
EUF	European Union Finances (team in the Treasury)
Euratom	European Atomic Energy Community
EUR(O)	Official committee on the approach to Europe
EUR(M)	Ministerial committee on the approach to Europe
EUR(S)	Steering committee on the approach to Europe
EUROPES	European Public Expenditure Survey
EUS	European Strategy (cabinet committee)
EUSB	European Union Staffing Branch
FCO	Foreign and Commonwealth Office
FER	Fundamental Expenditure Review
FO	Foreign Office
FRG	Federal Republic of Germany
GAERC	General Affairs and External Relations Council
GORs	Government Offices in the Regions
HO	Home Office
IGC	Intergovernmental Conference
IT	Information Technology
JHA	Justice and Home Affairs
JMC	Joint Ministerial Committee
JMC(E)	Joint Ministerial Committee (Europe)
LCD	Lord Chancellor's Department
MAFF	Ministry of Agriculture, Fisheries and Food
MAG	Ministry of Agriculture
MEP	Member of the European Parliament
MINECOR	Interdepartmental ministerial group on European policy
MoD	Ministry of Defence
MTG	Medium Term Group
NATO	North Atlantic Treaty Organisation
NAW	National Assembly for Wales
ODA	Overseas Development Administration
ODPM	Office of the Deputy Prime Minister
OECD	Organisation for Economic Cooperation and Development
OEEC	Organisation for European Economic Cooperation
OMC	Open Method of Coordination
OSI	Office of Science and Innovation
OST	Office of Science and Technology
PES	Public Expenditure Survey
PHARE	Poland, Hungary: Aid for the Re-Structuring of Economies
PM	Prime Minister
PMPU	Prime Minister's Policy Unit
PRO	Public Records Office
PSA	Public Service Agreement

QMV	Qualified Majority Voting
RDAs	Regional Development Authorities
SCA	Special Committee on Agriculture
SCIFA	Strategic Committee on Immigration, Frontiers & Asylum
SE	Scottish Executive
SEA	Single European Act
SECPOL	Security Policy Group (FCO)
SGCI	Secrétariat Général du Comité Interministériel
SGAE	Secrétariat Général des affaires Européennes
SNA	Subnational authority
SNP	Scottish National Party
SO	Scottish Office
SOS	Secretary of State
SPD	Social Democratic Party (Germany)
TEU	Treaty on European Union
TSol	Treasury Solicitors
UK	United Kingdom
UKDEL	UK Delegation to the European Communities (pre-accession)
UKIP	United Kingdom Independence Party
UKREP	UK Permanent Representation to the EU
UN	United Nations
WEU	Western European Union
WGE	Working Group on Europe
WO	Welsh Office

1

Setting the scene

The United Kingdom's relationship with the European Union (EU) has been complex and troublesome. The relationship itself is multifaceted: open to historical, political, economic and legal analysis. A comprehensive examination of the political relationship alone would need to take into account the interaction between the EU and British political forces, the system of government and public policy. Our study is rather more restricted, though of key importance to the political relationship. It centres on the interaction between British central government and the EU. Our concern is thus with how central government has adapted to EU membership and with its response, broadly understood, to the need to engage in the policy-making process centred on Brussels. In an extensive literature on Britain and the EU this is a subject-matter which has almost escaped detailed study (but see Wallace 1973; Gregory 1983; Forster and Blair 2002). However, it has been covered in comparative context (see in particular Kassim *et al.* 2000a; Kassim *et al.* 2001; Wessels *et al.* 2003; Jordan and Schout 2006).

In this chapter we set the scene. First of all, we set out our research objectives. We then review the key events in Britain's relationship with European integration. Thirdly, we highlight the controversies in Britain's relations with the EU and how they bear upon the central focus of the book, namely adaptation in central government. We then examine the different component parts of the relationship by looking at aspects of the reception of European integration in the British polity, and the very different task of projecting British politics into the European arena. This review reveals the different facets involved in the adaptation of the British political system to integration. We conclude by outlining the structure of the book and how we relate the specific question of central government's relations to the EU within the broader context.

Our research objectives

Our aim in this study is to provide an authoritative account of the impact of EU membership on the practice of government in Whitehall: that is to say, the UK machinery of executive government. Our approach to the subject matter is to examine the impact upon Whitehall over the period since the first application to join, made under the Macmillan government in 1961, up to and including the Blair governments. This long-term view therefore covers a period of over forty-five years, although our main focus will be upon the governments of John Major (1990–97) and Tony Blair (1997–2007). The time-frame has been chosen deliberately, for we argue that some of the key characteristics of UK central government's adaptation to European integration predate accession in 1973. Significant changes have occurred only rarely but they also took place under the Blair government. In part the Blair reforms were linked to broader organisational changes and constitutional reform at the heart of UK government. A second aim of the study is to capture the temporality of UK central government's adaptation to integration. What have been the critical junctures in its adaptation: not only on a government-wide basis but also in individual ministries? In order to offer an analysis over such a time-period we relate our research to two analytical approaches, namely Europeanisation and historical institutionalism. The former is broadly concerned with the impact of EU membership within the member states and, in the present context, upon the machinery of government. Historical institutionalism assists with the analysis of temporality. It can help identify the differing patterns of adaptation: some which are incremental in nature; others which represent significant change. In line with an institutionalist approach, we focus in particular on the organisational arrangements made within Whitehall to adapt to the EU but take a relatively 'thick' understanding of institutions so as to include procedures, norms and culture. An important part of our analysis is to attempt to disentangle the impact of the EU upon Whitehall from a myriad of other variables that impact upon central government's handling of European policy, including the changing pattern of domestic governance within the UK and the impact of domestic political actors. Finally, we aim to understand UK adaptation in comparative context. All member states – from founder members through to Romania and Bulgaria, which acceded in January 2007 – have had to respond to the demands of EU membership. The prevailing view in the academic literature is that each member government has adapted its machinery in a manner consistent with its domestic traditions (see Kassim *et al.* 2000b). The distinctive character of UK adaptation can, we believe, be best profiled when seen in comparative context.

Historical overview

An outline of the key phases in the UK's European policy over the post-war period is necessary to provide the context for this study. Put starkly, we cannot explore the impact of the European Union upon UK central government without recognising the highly contested political nature of the

European issue in British politics. The story begins with the national policy responses to the postwar settlement. These responses were crucial since
they distinguished the approach of the UK (and of some other states) from
that followed by the original six members. Thus, whilst France came to
recognise that the German problem was a crucial security concern, for the
UK the principal concern was initially defence against Germany (reflected
in the 1947 Dunkirk Treaty and the 1948 Brussels Treaty Organisation)
before attention shifted to the developing Cold War. At the same time, and
having emerged from the Second World War as a victor state, the UK was
not disposed to reducing its status from a global to a regional power. Imperial
concerns still loomed large, while the Anglo-American wartime alliance
was continued into the postwar period, with involvement in the design of
international economic institutions, such as the International Monetary Fund
and the World Bank. By contrast, France sought innovative European
solutions to co-existence with Germany. The enthusiasm for such solutions,
expressed from various quarters at the Congress of Europe in May 1948,
ran into the difficulty that British participation in such bodies seemed
inevitably to steer them towards traditional intergovernmental organisations,
where the nation state remained key. That much became clear with the resultant emergence of the Council of Europe, whose statute was agreed in London
in 1949.

The French response to the divergent goals of the European states was
the Monnet method, set down most clearly in the May 1950 Schuman
Plan. The guiding principle was that France and Germany would pool their
coal and steel reserves, and their sovereignty over these resources, through
a system of governance which would transcend the nation state. Other states
were invited to join but the offer was only taken up by the Benelux states
(Belgium, the Netherlands and Luxembourg) and Italy. The British government was ill-disposed towards such forms of international organisation
and, having recently nationalised its coal and steel sectors, refused.

This development was to be a key branching point in the history of
European international organisations. An inner core of states pursued the
'Monnet method' of integration, starting with the European Coal and Steel
Community (ECSC), which came into operation in July 1952. In doing so
they started the construction of a set of rules, procedures and values from
which the UK was detached until accession to the European Communities
in 1973. As Michael Charlton puts it, 'Britain lost the more or less controlling influence it had managed to exercise until then over the evolving
character and extent of European unity' (1983: 89). While France and,
gradually, West Germany came to set the agenda of integration, the UK
remained part of a wider and looser grouping of states that was prepared
to work towards European trade liberalisation in the Organisation for
European Economic Cooperation (OEEC), facilitated by Marshall Aid from
the United States. Many of these states were also prepared to cooperate on

matters of defence, notably within the Atlanticist framework of the North
Atlantic Treaty Organisation (NATO).

This broad pattern of Europe's international organisation was to continue until 1973. The 'Monnet method' of seeking to transcend the nation
state (supranationalism) suffered setbacks and advances during the 1950s.
The abortive European Defence Community was the principal setback
(rejected by the French national assembly in 1954) but the Messina Conference of 1955, at which the UK was not represented, paved the way for
the establishment of two further supranational communities: the European
Economic Community (EEC) and the European Atomic Energy Community (Euratom). Embodied in the Treaties of Rome, which were signed in
March 1957, they came into effect at the start of the following year. The
final setback was of a different nature. It came as a result of the collapse
of the French Fourth Republic and General de Gaulle's assumption of the
presidency. His view of the European Communities (EC) was much more
instrumental: how to use them to rebuild the *grandeur* of the French
nation state. Under his influence supranationalism was weakened, and his
attempt to exploit the integration process for national ends had mixed
results.

British interest in supranational integration remained that of a spectator.
The Conservative government sent an observer, Russell Bretherton, a civil
servant (Under-Secretary) at the Board of Trade, to the post-Messina talks,
held in Brussels and otherwise attended by foreign ministers (see Young
1998: 86–98). Bretherton was 'withdrawn' from this process (known as the
Spaak Committee) in November 1955. Anthony Nutting, junior minister
with responsibility for European affairs at the Foreign Office subsequently
put it thus, 'I think it was the last and the most important bus that we
missed. I think we could still have had the leadership of Europe if we had
joined in Messina' (quoted in Charlton 1983: 167). The British government's
response to the gradual realisation that the Messina process was likely to
lead to a successful outcome, namely a customs union, was to propose the
kind of arrangement with which it was happy, namely a free trade area
that had no implications for national sovereignty. The resultant 'Plan G',
initiated in 1956 by Peter Thorneycroft, the President of the Board of Trade,
envisaged a free trade area, in industrial goods only, but was proposed
as an alternative to the emergent EEC. In fact, the momentum of the
Messina process was such that this proposal only secured the interest of
six other states which were not participants in the EEC. The result was the
European Free Trade Association (EFTA), established in 1958.

The turning point for British diplomacy was the failed military intervention (with France) in 1956 in response to the Egyptian government's
nationalisation of the Suez Canal. This debacle dealt a serious blow
to the global aspirations of British foreign policy (see Box 1.1). In addition, it created divisions between the UK and the USA and within the

---

**Box 1.1 Observations of Lord Garner (former Permanent
Under-Secretary at, and historian of, the Commonwealth Office)**

In my view, there's absolutely no doubt there were two major events which
changed the British attitude. The first I would say unhesitatingly, was Suez
. . . I think Suez more than anything punctured that Great Power illusion once
and for all. We showed ourselves – we showed the world, which was more
important – that we could not operate on this sort of scale. This was a great
shock. But we accepted it and we drew the conclusions . . . Point number two
was the Messina Conference which, we thought, stood a poor chance of getting off the ground. But by the post-Suez era it was clear that not only did
the Common Market exist, it was enormously successful. It was prosperous
and it was going ahead. And the question therefore faced us, what were we
going to do!

Source: Charlton 1983: 219.

Commonwealth: two of the three circles of British foreign policy according to Churchill's formulation. Under the new, post-Suez Prime Minister,
Harold Macmillan, a tilt took place towards the third circle, namely
Europe. Macmillan's bolder move was his application for membership of
the European Communities in 1961 (see Chapter 4). However, the striking aspect about the decision to apply for membership was the role played
by a committee of officials, headed by Sir Frank Lee from the Treasury. In
view of the Treasury's consistently rather sceptical position on European
policy, the influence of Lee's committee on the decision to apply for membership was remarkable. Like many subsequent démarches in relation to
European policy, the move was politically contested both within the major
parties and between them. Despite an apparently supportive position for
applying, the Labour leader, Hugh Gaitskill, eventually declared to his
party's conference in October 1962 that membership would mean 'the end
of Britain as an independent state' and 'the end of a thousand years of British
history' (quoted in Young 1998: 163). In fact, Hugo Young argues that
Gaitskill should be recognised as the first 'Euro-sceptic' (1998: 161). In any
event, the application came precisely at the time when President de Gaulle
wanted to exploit the Communities for French gain, and the UK's membership would have challenged that. De Gaulle's rejection of the application
followed in January 1963. The same fate followed the application made
by Harold Wilson's Labour government in 1967. British accession was out
of the question while de Gaulle retained the French presidency.

Following de Gaulle's retirement and the election of Georges Pompidou
as his successor, European integration could be re-launched. The re-opening
of enlargement negotiations was one of the key components of the agreements reached at the 1969 summit of heads of government and state at

The Hague. Accession negotiations under the Heath government, elected in 1970, were eventually successful and at this point British domestic politics became centrally concerned with the issue of integration. Ratification of the Treaty of Accession was highly contested, with divisions evident in both the leading parties. The Labour Party was only able to resolve its internal divisions on the matter by adopting a policy of opposing the 'Tory terms' and by promising in its 1974 election manifesto to re-negotiate the terms of entry ahead of a referendum on continued membership. Thus the internal party divisions were externalised into the EC following Labour's election victories in 1974. The extent of the divisions was no more apparent than with the June 1975 referendum on EC membership, where collective cabinet responsibility was suspended during the campaign because of deep-seated divisions between ministers. Thus a tone was set for Britain's relations with the EC/EU: consisting internally of intra- and inter-party divisions, on the one hand, and externally of an abrasive pattern of diplomacy.

The internal divisions over integration have been latent throughout the subsequent period. Examples have included: intra-party divisions at the time of the 1975 referendum over continued membership; the Labour Party's shift following its election defeat in 1979 to a policy of withdrawal from the EC (prompting a split in 1981 and the creation of the Social Democratic Party); the emergence within the Conservative Party of tensions over substantive matters of European policy from the mid-1980s, including the resignation of Michael Heseltine (1986), Nigel Lawson (1989), Nicholas Ridley (1990) and Sir Geoffrey Howe (1990); the contribution of the style of Mrs Thatcher's European diplomacy to her replacement as prime minister at the end of 1990; the warfare within the Conservative Party over the ratification of the Maastricht Treaty; and the ramifications within the Conservative Party of sterling's departure from the Exchange Rate Mechanism (ERM) of the European Monetary System (EMS) (Black Wednesday) in September 1992. Only with the election of the Blair government in May 1997, and with a large majority, did the internal debate over integration subside somewhat. The Conservative leaders, William Hague (1997–2001) and Iain Duncan Smith (2001–3), had severe difficulties seeking to resolve intra-party differences over the UK's relationship to the single currency. Their successor, Michael Howard (2003–5), avoided problems by the expedient means of trying to keep the issue off his agenda. David Cameron (2005–) has already experienced intra-party tensions in seeking to disengage Conservative Members of the European Parliament (MEPs) from the European People's Party. And despite its efforts to develop a more constructive and active engagement with the EU and partner states, the Blair government adopted a defensive position in response to public opinion and a Euro-sceptic print media by promising referendums on the single currency and the Constitutional Treaty.

Externally, the UK's diplomatic record in the EC/EU has been mixed. A willingness to challenge the accepted rules and policies of the game – the so-called *acquis communautaire* – was revealed in re-negotiation of the terms of entry (1974/75) and Mrs Thatcher's pressure for re-writing the rules governing contributions to the EC budget (1979–84). A reluctance to engage with the continental European policy agenda has led to a number of cases where UK governments have not signed up to specific European initiatives: the European Monetary System (1978/79); the Social Charter (1989); the Maastricht Treaty's social policy provisions (1991); and its provisions for monetary union (1991), the last two by means of opt-outs. The Major government's efforts to place Britain at the heart of Europe eventually subsided into a very damaging period of diplomacy with European partners. The two key issues were: its obstructionism over EU treaty reforms in 1996–97; and the spring 1996 policy of non-cooperation with the EU, the government's response to the EU's handling of the public-health ramifications of 'mad cow disease'. Both of these policy positions were closely connected with internal divisions within Major's party. Weighed against these flash-points, UK governmental successes in promoting economic liberalism in the EU, notably through the single market programme, or in promoting financial discipline have been overshadowed. The Blair governments also witnessed successes in the pursuit of a constructive European policy, such as in the advocacy of security and defence cooperation. However, Tony Blair's support for US President George W Bush's invasion of Iraq represented a more Atlanticist turn in his policy and created tensions with some key partners, notably France (Smith 2005). It is small wonder that books on Britain's involvement in integration have had such titles as 'An Awkward Partner' (George 1998) or 'Missed Chances' (Denman 1996).

Not all of the controversy of British European policy has been located directly within the government. Nevertheless, there have been indirect ramifications for government, for the political context surrounding Whitehall's interaction with European integration has rarely been consensual over the period since 1973. Ministers are not mere metronomes ticking away in time with the rhythms emanating from Brussels. In many cases they have had strongly held personal views on the desirability of European integration. During the ratification of the Maastricht Treaty in an unguarded moment with a political journalist, John Major, then prime minister, famously 'questioned the parentage' of four cabinet ministers because of their views on European integration. The views of government ministers, whatever their attitudes towards integration, set the tone of the work of their department. It is quite possible, therefore, to have, as one senior official put it to us, 'a Rolls Royce machinery but with a lunatic at the wheel'.[1] Thus, ministers and, for that matter, prime ministers matter. And we will endeavour to take into account the wider political context within which they and the machinery of government operate in the analysis which follows.

European controversy and UK central government

What are the political factors that have impacted upon government's adaptation to the EU? How do they impact upon the role of central government's conduct of European policy?

The historical divisions over whether the UK should participate in supra-national integration have left legacies within the political parties and public opinion. Those within the parties are striking because the legacies of conflict persist for a generation. Thus, the divisions within the Labour Party at the time of the 1975 referendum, when combined with other internal party disputes, culminated in a policy of withdrawal from the EC: the party's manifesto position for the May 1983 general election. Only when the party's broad manifesto had rendered it unelectable for a decade, and at a time when the Conservative government's own divisions on the issue revealed an open flank for partisan attack, did the divisions over the EU subside within the developing 'New Labour' under Tony Blair (see Holden 2002). During the Major governments the Conservative Party was split on European policy and the legacies of those divisions are present to this day within the party.

Intra-party divisions on European policy have affected all governments from Edward Heath's onwards, although under the Blair governments they were irrelevant to parliamentary arithmetic and more a matter of emphasis particularly between Blair and his Chancellor of the Exchequer, Gordon Brown. Nevertheless, the political context still matters, since ministers set the tone for their department. In addition, the conflictual nature of the British party system often makes ministers defensive on European policy for fear that the opposition seeks to take electoral advantage. Thus, as a result of intra- and inter-party politics Westminster has represented a potential veto point in the formulation of European policy (Armstrong and Bulmer 1996; Aspinwall 2000). Where a government has had a small parliamentary major-ity and a Euro-sceptic minority, such as Labour for much of the period 1974–79 and the Conservatives 1992–97, rituals of adversarial politics may compound intra-party dissent. The result has been controversy in domestic politics and spillover into the EU negotiating arena itself.

While Westminster's impact on European policy can be significant at times, the House of Commons was for much of the period from 1973 ill-adapted to the detailed scrutiny of EU business, a situation it shares to some degree with many national parliaments. Its debates are often symbolic in nature and, until parliamentary modernisation under the Blair government, it lacked the powers to even scrutinise some parts of EU activity (Carter 2001; Giddings and Drewry 2004). Nevertheless, there are important procedural require-ments placed on government to keep parliament informed of developments in the EU.

Support for integration amongst public opinion has been low in the UK by comparative EU standards. Amongst the contributory factors have been the divisions over integration in the party-political arena; confrontations with EU partners; 'Euro-scepticism' in the press for much of the period since 1973 (Wilkes and Wring 1998); and a reluctance or unwillingness on the part of successive governments to explain the UK's role in the EU to the public. The real impact of membership has been swept under the carpet, while there has been little consistent attempt to see integration as part of a constructive political agenda. Elite groups such as industrialists, while often instrumental or constructive Europeanists themselves, have sought to keep their heads below the parapet even when British governments have pursued diplomacy inimical to their interests. None of this has created a climate conducive to central government's own ease at handling European policy. The contrast is striking with the Federal Republic of Germany whose adaptation to Europe was achieved by the mid-1950s, that is, well within a decade of becoming a (founder) member of the (ECSC). By that time, industry, trade unions, government elites and the two principal party-blocks had formed a pro-integration consensus.

On a wider scale, the congruence of the UK's political system with that of the EU historically has been low. The first-past-the-post electoral system; adversarial ritual within Westminster; the British doctrine of parliamentary sovereignty; the limited constitutionalisation of rights; governmental secrecy; and the extent of political centralisation: these long-standing features of UK politics find limited resonance in the EU itself or in its member states. To see the challenge of integration as extending to the fundamentals of the constitutional order has traditionally been the argument of nationalist 'Euro-sceptics'. Indeed, no British government has ever made it clear that the constitution might have to adapt in response to Europeanisation. Nevertheless, the EU is one factor behind the constitutional modernisation pursued from 1997 by the Blair governments.

The ability of governments to contend with European policy has been qualified by these characteristics of the political context: party divisions, adversarial politics, lukewarm public support for integration and hostility in the print media. At times the domestic context has forced ministers to adopt a confrontational approach in the EU. This situation has made other EU states less willing to form longer-term bilateral alliances with the UK, and hampered the government's pursuit of a constructive European policy agenda – certainly in the period prior to 1997. As Andrew Gamble has put it: 'Europe is the issue that never goes away' (1998: 11).

Dissecting Britain's relations with European integration

A feature fundamental to our study is the *inter*active character of Britain's relations with the EU. The EU affects the United Kingdom; the UK government (and other actors) seek to influence the EU. Neat, positivist social-scientific methodologies of independent and dependent variables encounter the more complex relationships between structure (the EU) and agency (the British government), where the latter is itself an aggregation of ministers and officials. Beyond the world of political science analysis lies the more complex real world of intensely interactive relations between multiple administrative units within the British and EU levels of governance. Even so, we can disaggregate the relationship into a two-stage process, each stage of which has involved the need for adaptation in British government.

The 'reception' of European integration in the UK

British relations with the EU are in no small measure shaped by the initiatives emanating from Brussels, although initiatives may also come from other member governments, as important Franco-German initiatives demonstrated in the 1980s and 1990s. It is symbolic to look at EU's impact on the UK first of all, since for the first decades of membership it was relatively infrequent that British governments pursued pro-active policies in the EU. The conversion to European integration with the decision in 1961 to make an application for membership of the European Communities was also reactive in nature. The predominant pattern has been one of Britain 'backing into' Europe. On a more day-to-day level the reception of EU business in British central government is of key importance to understanding the relationship. In a manner quite distinct from domestic decision-making, on European policy the rhythm of business is determined overwhelmingly by the EU's timetable. Whitehall and Westminster do not control the all-important temporal aspect of the policy process. This situation presents a clear challenge to British central government to adapt its conventional practices.

How can the difficulties associated with the 'reception' of European integration within the British political system be dissected?

First, European integration has triggered divisions within *British domestic political forces* (see Bache and Jordan 2006a: Chapters 8–11). As already noted, the issue of integration notably has been the source of major intra- and inter-party conflict right from 1960, when prime minister Harold Macmillan first flirted with making an application to the European Communities but was blocked by opposition from within his cabinet (Tratt 1996: 113–27). Latent divisions existed thereafter, periodically re-emerging: initially during the accession process in the early 1970s; then in connection with substantive policy issues, treaty revisions or similar major developments in the European arena. European integration came to be regarded as a 'poisoned chalice' in the party political arena (to use the title of a BBC television series on the subject). The divisions have extended beyond the party arena to public opinion more widely, where support for the integration process has been relatively cool (see Nugent 1992). Interest groups within the UK have also been forced to adapt. Apart from some initial difficulties, notably on the part of trades unions, who originally boycotted attending EC committees (Butt Philip 1992: 159–60), they have proved to be adept in attuning their tactics and strategies to the emergence of a new locus of power in the EU institutions.

Secondly, European integration has presented significant challenges to the *institutional structure of UK governance* (see Bache and Jordan 2006a: Chapters 3–7). The English Common Law system has been challenged since accession in 1973 by the introduction, indeed incorporation, of continental legal doctrine via European Community law. A new hierarchy has been established in the court structure, with the European Court of Justice at its apex in certain key policy areas. In matters such as equal opportunities, rights have become more formalised and juridified via the EU. The constitutional doctrine of parliamentary sovereignty has been tested by the supremacy of EC law (Page 2004: 39–44). Parliamentary procedure has been challenged to find a means whereby British parliamentarians can express their voice on European legislation through the traditional Westminster route. Central government departments have been obliged to respond organisationally and procedurally to the EU's activities. Further, European integration has had a significant impact upon the territorial dimension of government. The EU has impacted upon the de-concentration of UK executive power through the Scottish, Welsh and Northern Ireland Offices. With devolution in 1999 central government and the new authorities had to rethink their handling of EU policy. Integration was a factor behind the establishment, during John Major's premiership, of Government Offices in the English regions and, under Labour, of Regional Development Agencies and the Greater London Authority. The EU has had major implications for the work of local government, with the emergence of new funding opportunities for them or through their responsibilities for the implementation of some areas of EC law. Finally, the EU structural funds have prompted a partnership approach to subnational policy-making (Burch and Gomez 2002: 770; Bache 2008). In short, the British system of governance has been subject to key challenges as a result of participation in European integration.

Thirdly, the EU has had significant *policy impact* (see illustrative cases in Bache and Jordan 2006a: Chapters 12–16). Right across government and beyond, EU policy has brought in new requirements in terms of legislative compliance, health and safety procedures, environmental impact assessments and such like. These requirements have a broad impact. Within government it also had some rather unexpected impacts, which we can illustrate by reference to the Ministry of Defence (MoD). Prior to the development of a European Security and Defence Policy from 1999 the EU's impact on the policy work of the MoD had been quite limited. But more mundane, administrative consequences were felt, as three brief illustrations reveal. The impact of EU environmental legislation upon the MoD as one of the UK's biggest landowners was significant. So was EU equal opportunities policy: the dismissal of servicewomen on the grounds of pregnancy was found to be in breach of EC law, with a series of expensive court cases on compensation ensuing for the MoD. Finally, and paradoxically, given the Euro-sceptic views of John Major's Secretary of State for Defence, Michael Portillo, the British opt-out from social regulation under the Social Chapter did not apply to civilian personnel working for the MoD in Germany. Thus, the ministry had to be fully aware of the implications of EU for three important areas of its work.[2]

Our interest in policy impact within this study focuses on the policy-making function of ministries rather than their need to undertake administrative compliance to EU policy. Some policy areas, such as foreign trade, are now essentially EU policies. Domestic policy discretion scarcely exists in such domains. Instead, the UK has to make its voice heard in the policy process in Brussels. Once policy has been agreed, British public authorities have to put the legislation into practice, but normally with some discretion as to *how* the policy is put into effect. Some key areas of domestic policy remain relatively unaffected: the provisions of the welfare state, for example. Until the mid-1990s security and defence policy was unaffected except indirectly by the EU's foreign and security policy decisions, for instance on Bosnia. However, it has now become much more affected by the EU with the development of a common European Security and Defence Policy (ESDP), agreed at the Cologne European Council in 1999 and confirmed in the 2001 Treaty of Nice. Whilst this development is relatively recent, the EU's salience for the Department of the Environment, Food and Rural Affairs (DEFRA) has been long-term and pervasive. Whitehall-wide, therefore, the policy consequences of EU membership have been extensive. And the numbers of officials who have had to deal with EU policy as part of their routine governmental business has grown very significantly since 1973.

The reception of European integration in the British political system has left few political forces, institutions or policy areas untouched. The impact of European integration upon British governance, furthermore, has not been confined to concrete procedural or institutional impacts but has also extended into the realm of ideas about politics, governance and policy. Corporatism, christian democracy, multi-level governance and subsidiarity, cohesion, partnership: these are amongst the ideational influences that have flowed from the EU and its member states with consequences for politics in the UK. For some parts of the party-political spectrum, integration has prompted a response of resistance: ideas and practices emanating from the EU and its member states have been opposed as a matter of principle. This situation was expressed most clearly by the United Kingdom Independence Party (UKIP), which secured 16 per cent of the vote in the June 2004 European parliament elections in mainland Britain. Elsewhere in the political system a more utilitarian response has been engendered, as in the trade unions embracing Jacques Delors' vision of a social Europe in the late 1980s, during the period of marginalisation from the Thatcher government's policies (see Rosamond 1998). The continuing party-political divisions over the European issue have in turn had major implications for the projection of British politics and policy into the institutional arena of the EU.

The 'projection' of British politics and policy in the European Union

The British record in diplomacy within the European Union is also a contributory factor to its reputation as a troublesome member. Periodic diplomatic stand-offs have developed between UK governments of different political stripes and the EU. Some of the bitterest disputes have developed where the UK has challenged the *acquis communautaire*, such as over contributions to the European Community budget 1979–84 or reform of the Common Agricultural Policy (CAP). Other stand-offs have been heightened because of domestic political disagreement. Thus, re-negotiation of the terms of entry (1974–75) or the 1996 policy of non-cooperation with the EU in connection with the BSE crisis have entailed substantive policy disagreements exacerbated by the transfer of domestic discord into the European arena. Such stand-offs are all part of the description of the UK as 'an awkward partner' in the EU (George 1998). But as the originator of this terminology on the UK's diplomacy, Stephen George himself has also been at pains to argue that British policy in the EU has not been unremitting awkwardness (George 1998).[3] Indeed, Anthony Teasdale has made the case that Britain has had a number of important successes in its European diplomacy over the period since 1973 (Teasdale 1998). These successes have been enlarged under the Blair governments (Smith 2005; Kassim 2004). The single market, the ESDP and the Lisbon Strategy on economic competitiveness are notable areas of UK influence.

It is important to consider the different aspects of projecting British politics and policy on the EU stage. What is 'the UK' here? Is it a single 'agency'? Is even the government a single agency in its dealings with the EU structure? In reality there are multiple channels and multiple dimensions to the projection of the UK in the EU arena. The channels for projecting the UK into the EU arena may be broken down into a fourfold categorisation.

First, governmental and non-governmental agencies are involved in projecting the UK into the European arena. We will leave aside governmental actors for the moment, since they can be further sub-divided. However, it is important to bear in mind that there are other actors of considerable importance. Governments cannot act as the 'gatekeepers' of national interests in the manner which was possible when the EC more closely resembled an intergovernmental organisation. In the EU of today there are multiple access points to the decisional process: the Commission (especially important for lobbies at the agenda-setting stage before formal legislative proposals are drafted); the European Parliament (EP), with its important legislative powers; and lesser institutions such as the Economic and Social

Committee or the Committee of the Regions. These access points are open to transnational interest groups, of which most British interest groups are constituent members; to individual major corporate actors, such as British Airways; and sometimes to key national interest groups as well. The political parties also have some direct access, most notably through the election of MEPs, who are then organised into party groups within that body. Thus, during especially the later years of Conservative government, Labour MEPs used their strength in the Group of the Party of European Socialists to try to influence EU policy decisions. A further channel of influence came to be exploited, namely the meetings of leaders of the main European party families held prior to sessions of the European Council, the regular agenda-setting summits of EU heads of state and government. Thus, as leader of the opposition – and later when prime minister – Tony Blair met his counterparts from other EU states, including those in power in their member state, and could seek indirectly to shape the broad terms of debate at the summits (Hix and Lord 1997: 183–8). Conservative leaders/ prime ministers generally have a weaker position in utilising such channels because of their poor match with continental party families. To summarise this point: governments do not have a monopoly of access to the EU arena.

If we turn, secondly, to 'government', we find that this term encompasses a multitude of actors. Gary Marks and others have argued that integration from the mid-1980s has been characterised by the emergence of a form of multi-level governance (Marks *et al.* 1996). We will not consider their argument in full here but they contend, *inter alia*, that 'the state' is far too loose a construct to be of much value in assessing member state-EU interaction.[4] To take the vertical dimension of the state alone, subnational government has become much more engaged in EU policy-making with the growth of EU spatial policies from the 1980s. In the UK it was initially local government which was affected in this way. From 1999 onwards devolved authorities in Scotland, Wales, Greater London and Northern Ireland have given this notion of multi-levelled governance much greater currency in the UK than ever before. However, for other member states with a federal constitution, such as Germany, Belgium or Austria, subnational government has an established tradition of strong involvement in EU decision-making (Jeffery 1997; 2000).

Thirdly, what of central government itself? Is it a unitary actor? We shall argue that UK central government is relatively cohesive in its European diplomacy but it is important to be aware that this cohesion is far from assured. The German federal government is usually considered to be at the opposite end to the UK on a scale measuring coherence of governmental positions (Bulmer *et al.* 2000: 28; also see Chapter 9 below). But in any member government there is scope for sectorisation to the extent that one ministry can pursue its 'mission' within the EU independently of another or of a coordinated governmental line (Kassim *et al.* 2000b: 7–8).

As we shall see in Chapter 6, the Treasury has exercised a considerable amount of autonomy within Whitehall on European policy. Inevitably a government's record on policy coherence will affect, but not determine, its performance at projecting its interests into the EU arena.

A further consideration in connection with dissecting 'government' relates to the distinction between the political and official levels of government: a distinction which differs in nature in those member states, for instance the Federal Republic of Germany (FRG), where senior officials are appointed on political grounds or on the basis of party-political allegiance. In the UK the constitutional understanding is that politicians, i.e. ministers, determine the policy line and officials are expected to carry it through in EU official-level intergovernmental fora. Of course, in reality the position is much less cut and dried than the constitutional understanding implies and officials do on occasions need to make decisions, if only to keep the line of business flowing, and they certainly in most cases significantly shape them. Nevertheless, in theory it is ministers who hold the initiative. Particularly pertinent in this connection is the way in which the same set of officials, who were negotiating in the Inter-Governmental Conference 1996–97, made the transition from prosecuting an obstructionist policy towards institutional reform under the Major government to a constructive one following the election of Tony Blair in May 1997. Thus, the official level of machinery in central government may be highly organised for developing and coordinating European policy. However, it is in many cases only as good at projecting government policy as ministers allow it to be. If policy is embroiled in political divisions (within government or the ruling party), or is given an impractical political direction, its effectiveness will be hampered.

Behind this account of the projection of British politics and policy into the EU arena lies an analytical debate. The dominant account of the articulation of national interests in the EU is the liberal intergovernmentalist one (see Moravcsik 1993; 1998 for an exposition). The essence of this approach is that, mindful of the need to secure re-election, member governments mediate between competing domestic interests in order to define those national interests which are to be represented at EU level. Liberal intergovernmentalism represented an advance on some of the earlier international relations literature, notably realism, whereby states' interests were considered as constant, to be 'read off' according to their position in the international system. Instead, Moravcsik identified how state interests could change over time. Nevertheless, contrary to our empirical dissection, member governments are seen by liberal intergovernmentalists as the predominant actors in shaping the EU and its policy debates. Hence it is worth spelling out the contribution of competing approaches.

New institutionalist analysts of the EU argue that the interplay of governments at EU level is also shaped by the institutional rules and norms of the supranational institutions (Aspinwall and Schneider 2001). Some institutionalists were critical of the notion that action within the EU was simply a clash between competing national governments. Rather, the EU institutions had developed norms and values about the conduct of diplomacy which would modify governments' behaviour. As Andrew Jordan has pointed out (2002: 7), the liberal intergovernmentalist position assumes that central governments are monolithic and highly coordinated; individual ministries and interdepartmental relationships are of little importance. When applied at the domestic level, an institutionalist approach by contrast posits that the domestic structure of government is important in two respects. It mediates the pressures of interests emanating from within the domestic arena. Thus domestic structure may privilege certain actors within government and privilege certain non-governmental actors as well. Secondly, therefore, the institutional structure shapes the interests that are projected into the EU.

Institutionalism is not a single approach (Hall and Taylor 1996; Aspinwall and Schneider 2001). Rational choice institutionalists would explore how political actors take a rational calculating approach in responding to the British central government structure and articulate their interests accordingly. Those holding a 'thicker' understanding of institutions would emphasise the informal rules of British central government. Habitual practices such as information-sharing within government; 'singing from the same hymn-sheet', compliance with the EU deadline for implementing directives within the UK: these are institutional norms which transform central government from a neutral referee of domestic interests into an agent in its own right. Sociological institutionalists and constructivists place even more emphasis upon culture, ideas and identity as key factors influencing political behaviour. Patterns of member state diplomacy may also be influenced by these sociological factors, which are often expressed in the language of policy. The discourse of civil servants using an expression such as 'singing from the same hymn-sheet' to characterise Whitehall's approach to European policy, or that of politicians in referring to Britain 'punching above its weight' in international relations, express embedded norms and values. The attention of successive UK governments to American policy on international events, sometimes at the expense of collective EU positions, as in the case of intervention in Iraq in 2003, reflects another deep-seated policy value that impacts on European diplomacy but which does not emerge from a competition amongst domestic interests in line with liberal intergovernmentalism.

Institutionalists and constructivists thus challenge the assumption that national governments are neutral referees arbitrating amongst competing domestic interests and the pre-eminent architects in EU governance. The implications of these competing views of domestic policy-making for our assessment of the UK government's efforts at projecting policy into the EU arena are significant. They bear upon any evaluation of the effectiveness of central government in projecting British policy. First, policy interests change. For example, attitudes towards EU environmental policy may change with the passage of time and the emergence of new information, as they did during the course of Conservative rule, notably when first Chris Patten (1989) and then John Gummer (1993) took over as Secretary of State and pursued a 'greener' policy (Jordan 2002: 40–2). An important consequence of the degree of embeddedness of member states in the EU is the fact that their ' "national interest" comes to be (co-)defined by European policy and context' (Hanf and Soetendorp 1998a: 10). Secondly, the institutions of central government or Parliament may place their own imprint upon British interests. For instance, if British European policy were simply the product of the preponderance of domestic interests, as liberal (or liberal intergovernmentalist) theorists argue, then British European policy under John Major would not have been influenced by the views of a small number of Euro-sceptic backbenchers.[5] In reality, the institutional characteristics of the British parliamentary system disproportionately enhanced these backbenchers' influence (Aspinwall 2000).

Thirdly, deep-seated values and norms need to be identified and monitored. For example, 'singing from the same hymn-sheet' may well be an embedded norm of British central government's EU policy-making but analysts must avoid using this criterion as the key one in evaluating policy success. If central government has a coherent European policy, that is laudable enough but the real test is the effectiveness of that policy within the EU itself. Similarly, if British negotiators deploy the robust adversarial style of political behaviour engendered by the UK's majoritarian system, that may not prove to be the route to securing effective results in the EU. Finally, identity must also be part of the account of how British government projects its wishes into the EU arena. British governments have tended to see themselves in global terms and, particularly on matters of foreign policy cooperation, regard the EU as but one arena for diplomacy; others being the United Nations or bilateral action with the United States. The notion of 'punching above one's weight' on the international stage is doubtless influenced by British diplomatic history. It entails going beyond a purely European framework for diplomacy where necessary. By contrast, UK governments have seldom endorsed enthusiasm for political integration as an end in itself in the way that their German or Italian counterparts have. Rather, the tendency has been to regard such enthusiasm as 'cheap talk' designed to camouflage real interests. Following the arguments of Marcussen *et al.* (1999) these different approaches are reflective of different social beliefs within various member states. The distinctive beliefs within the UK explain why politicians of both major parties have come to accept inward economic investment with open arms, while intrusions into political sovereignty have been unwelcome or rejected (Wallace 1986). Indeed, the symbolic issue of sovereignty has been a dominant discourse in the debate about integration (Larsen 1997). Thus British European policy has been conducted against the backdrop of a domestic normative context, illustrated particularly by ideas about integration.

It should be clear from our review of the political context of Britain's relationship with European integration, and from our dissection of the character of the relationship, that membership of the EU brought about a fundamental change to British foreign policy and domestic politics since 1945. The significance of accession was played down by the government at the time. The subsequent period has been characterised by a largely incremental process, punctuated by a number of step-changes such as the Single European Act (SEA) and the Maastricht Treaty. Nevertheless, the ramifications have been pervasive. David Allen has argued that the institutions of British government have adapted to the requirements of membership but the wider political system has failed to provide a political consensus to support that (Allen 1988; 2005). His argument resonates with our own findings. Indeed, in a number of our interviews government officials pointed to the way in which the political line of government had affected the projection of British interests in the EU.[6]

To summarise this section, we underline the interactive nature of UK central government's relationship with the EU. The challenge for Whitehall has thus been not only to find effective ways of dealing with the flow of business from the EU institutions, but also to devise effective mechanisms of engagement with supranational policy-making process. Naturally, the consequent adaptation has been bound up with the political context outlined earlier and specifically with the wishes of ministers and prime ministers over time. A key issue to be examined within this book is whether adaptation has served to integrate EU business into the conventional patterns of Whitehall governance, or whether there has been a shift towards the patterns of policy-making that are more characteristic of the EU.

Structure of the book

In order to understand the notion of adapting to European integration – both within government and in the wider political system – we need to develop a conceptual framework. In Chapter 2 we do that through reference to 'Europeanisation' and institutionalism. Europeanisation dissects the phenomenon of adapting to integration. We augment Europeanisation by using historical institutionalism to explore, over time, the adjustments of UK central government to the EU. We thus set up a framework that is designed to evaluate change in central government. Before exploring the change empirically, we examine in Chapter 3 the character of EU governance. What are the rules of the game at EU level? Where do national governments fit in with EU policy-making? What are the pressures emanating from the EU system of governance that impact upon British central government? This chapter is designed to reveal the rules and norms at EU level within which British central government has to operate. Chapter 4 then commences the study of adjustment within UK central government. It examines the process of coming to grips with integration: from the early 1960s, when the Macmillan government applied for membership of the EEC, up to accession.

Subsequent chapters concentrate on the period of the Major and Blair governments, examining the coordination of policy across Whitehall at the hub of policy-making (Chapter 5), within the core departments (Chapter 6) and within those parts of government that are more peripheral to European policy (Chapter 7). In these chapters we look at the patterns of adjustment to Europeanisation in a more fine-grained manner. In Chapter 8 we take stock of the Europeanisation process across the board by evaluating the degree and extent of change that has taken place in Whitehall in the light of our institutionalist approach. We then advance a model of Europeanisation to explain the character of adjustment that has come about. In other words, we move from mapping and evaluating the character of adaptation to explaining it. In Chapter 9 we compare UK adaptation with that of other EU member states. Finally, we conclude by reflecting on the key characteristics of the response in Whitehall and on the strengths and weaknesses of Whitehall's adaptation.

Notes

1 Interview, Home Office, 23 November 1996.
2 Interview, Ministry of Defence, 5 December 1996.
3 Attempts to develop a debate around the strengths and weaknesses of the term 'awkward partner' as an analytical tool have not been entirely fruitful: see the critique by Buller (1995) and the response by George (1995).
4 These authors are critical of the work of such commentators as Moravcsik (1994) and Milward (1992), who have argued that 'the state' is strengthened by European integration.
5 For the defining statement of liberal intergovernmentalism, see Moravcsik (1993). For a thorough application, see Moravcsik (1998).
6 This line was evident in particular in those interviews conducted in the last year of the Major administration.

2

The Europeanisation of UK central government: analytical challenges

Introduction

This chapter is designed to provide an analytical basis for our study of how British central government has come to terms with European integration. It rests on two elements which are examined in the chapter: Europeanisation and new institutionalism. Our initial concern is to locate the study in the context of the Europeanisation literature. In doing so, we place the adaptation to the EU of the UK generally, and of Whitehall specifically, within a comparative context. While our concern is principally with the UK, notwithstanding the comparison in Chapter 9, placing our study in the context of Europeanisation is designed to give a comparative dimension and avoid the pitfalls of a purely Anglo-centric approach. Europeanisation itself is principally an organising concept and is normally operationalised by deploying a supporting analytical model. Typically, the models deployed derive from new institutionalism. In the second half of the chapter we set up an institutionalist framework for analysing change in British central government. Historical institutionalism is particularly suited to examining the temporal dimension of adaptation that forms the basis of our study. In Chapter 8 we take our analytical apparatus further and suggest a framework for explaining change.

Europeanisation: adapting to integration

The literature on Europeanisation has been growing in recent times and has included detailed consideration of how to define the concept as well as the specification of research designs for exploring its empirical features (Börzel 1999; Radaelli 2000; Knill 2001; Risse *et al.* 2001; Featherstone and Radaelli 2003; Graziano and Vink 2007). First, we consider what Europeanisation refers to in empirical terms; then, we consider the conceptual and analytical dimensions; finally, in this first part of the chapter we look at evaluating the outcomes of Europeanisation.

The scope of Europeanisation

If national political life consists of politics, polity and policy, it is likely that all three of these domains are affected by Europeanisation. A study of the impact of integration on member state *politics* in these terms would be concerned typically with the effect on parties and interest groups but also upon public opinion. For parties and interest groups Europeanisation poses the dual challenge of organisational adaptation and exploiting EU channels of action. Europeanisation poses methodological challenges when examining the impact of the EU upon member state *policies* because of the difficulty of isolating an 'EU-effect' from the consequences of, say, globalisation. Thus the Europeanisation of national telecommunications policies, to take an example, cannot be seen in isolation from global trends in the regulation of that sector. Nevertheless, the EU has had an important effect across the whole policy spectrum of member states, especially on agriculture or trade policy, where competences have been transferred to a significant extent to Brussels. The development of EU policy competences, such as through treaty reforms in the SEA or the Maastricht Treaty, may also be seen as a key dimension of Europeanisation. Also relevant is the introduction of new techniques of EU governance, of which the most notable in recent times has been the Open Method of Coordination (OMC), with its emphasis on horizontal methods, such as peer review or benchmarking (Wallace 2005: 85–7). These developments also have implications for Europeanisation, as will be discussed below.

Europeanisation of the *polity* also comprises a variety of impacts. If we interpret 'polity' widely, to encompass the constitutional order, a wide range of effects is discernible. The concerns of this chapter are with a narrower notion of the institutions of government: how governments handle European policy at home and conduct European policy abroad. Thus, Europeanisation impacts upon the political and administrative responsibilities for policy, on the handling of policy issues, on executive–legislative relations and on the territorial distribution of power within the state. What are the kinds of impacts that are felt in this domain of political life? In essence, civil servants and ministers have to take EU business into their stride, as it becomes a routine part of their work. All the member governments need to find 'translator devices' (Genschel 2001: 98) so that business emanating from the EU can be converted into the domestic pattern of governance.

In assessing the impact of the EU upon the institutions of government the nature of the Europeanisation effect is rather indistinct. There is no overall European principle of organisation: there is no single pattern of practices, style or culture likely to spread with increased interaction (Olsen 1995: 25). All that can be said is that the EU is more in keeping with continental rather than British administrative traditions, with an emphasis on legal rules, codes, technical specialisms and departmental distinctiveness.

In Johan Olsen's view national administrative diversity has co-existed with ever-closer European political integration, suggesting that each member state has found suitable translator devices. This view is borne out by the findings of several surveys of member state response to EU membership (for example, Rometsch and Wessels 1996a; Hanf and Soetendorp 1998b; Kassim 2003; Wessels *et al.* 2003). Rather than European integration prompting major reform of governmental structures, it may be handled by adapting the existing structures of government in the member states. This situation explains why the evidence of institutional convergence on the part of the member governments towards a common model – a stage beyond Europeanisation according to Rometsch and Wessels (1996b: 36) – is so limited.

Europeanisation: concept and analysis
When working with Europeanisation it is important to clarify three aspects: the conceptual dimension; the associated use of analysis and theory; and the methodology deployed to investigate the phenomenon empirically.

Taking the conceptual dimension first, the immediate challenge is to arrive at a workable definition of Europeanisation. There are competing definitions and understandings available in the literature (for discussion of variants, see Olsen 2002: 923–4). We focus on what is understandably at the core of Europeanisation and is termed by Johan Olsen the 'central penetration of national systems of governance'. More elaborately Claudio Radaelli understands Europeanisation as:

> Processes of a) construction, b) diffusion and c) institutionalization of formal and informal rules, procedures, policy paradigms, styles, 'ways of doing things' and shared beliefs and norms which are first defined and consolidated in the EU policy process and then incorporated in the logic of domestic discourse, identities, political structures and public policies. (2003: 30)

This definition is encompassing; it incorporates both relatively 'hard' institutional changes, such as rules and procedures, but it also introduces the cognitive dimension by capturing beliefs, discourse and identities. We understand the term 'EU policy process', as employed in Radaelli's definition, to incorporate the full range of techniques of governance: from those policies following the 'community method' where the Commission is powerful through to those associated with the OMC, where the EU provides an arena for exchanging policy ideas (for reviews of policy types, see Wallace 2005: 77–89; for a different typology in the context of Europeanisation, see Bulmer and Radaelli 2005). As our study is concerned with the impact upon government, we also include the multiple bilateral diplomatic relations between national governments that are part and parcel of EU membership.

Europeanisation is not, of itself, a theory. However, it has been very closely associated with the new institutionalist literature. It is also associated to a lesser degree with constructivism, which regards reality as socially constructed rather than 'objectively given' (Rosamond 2000: 119). An institutionalist understanding of political science is frequently deployed to provide the explanatory variables behind the Europeanisation process. Institutionalism's predominance arises because Europeanisation is normally understood as entailing a domestic adjustment process, and member state institutions are typically seen as amongst the intermediating variables in this process. This view is to the fore in the work of those who see Europeanisation as a process arising from some kind of 'misfit' with the policies and practices of the EU (see Börzel 1999; Risse *et al.* 2001). This 'fit/misfit' approach is not without its critics. However, the critics have also been working within an institutionalist framework. For instance, Christoph Knill has argued that 'misfit' does not represent a 'necessary condition for domestic change' (2001: 13). Similarly, Héritier and Knill have found cases of domestic reforms taking place in response to the EU despite an absence of misfit (2001). To take another example, Markus Haverland (2000) has drawn attention to the importance of institutional veto points in explaining the adjustment to adaptation pressures. According to him it is not just misfit but the presence/absence of veto points that explains the mechanisms of Europeanisation. These debates, then, are being conducted firmly within the institutionalist literature (see Bulmer 2007).

Constructivism is introduced – albeit implicitly – where analysts interpret Europeanisation as bi-directional. Implicitly, they recognise that Europeanisation is not just out there as a given but is in large part the product of member state 'construction' at the stage where European policy or institutional arrangements are first being drawn up. Working within an institutionalist framework, Tanja Börzel has seen Europeanisation as 'uploading' and 'downloading' (2002). Uploading and downloading are, of course, inter-related. Hence policy leaders or pace-setters who successfully upload their policy or institutional model to the EU level may reduce their adjustment processes at the later stage of Europeanisation, when EU policy has to be put into domestic effect. Constructivism explicitly addresses the situation where social learning is introduced to national policy-makers via European engagement (see, for instance, Checkel 1999). Constructivism also chimes with bringing discourse within the remit of Europeanisation studies (on discourse generally, see Diez 1999a; on its usage in the UK, see Diez 1999b). For example, the discourse deployed by politicians at national level in the discussion of the impact of the EU entails social construction of the European issue. In the UK the European Communities often used to be referred to as the 'common market' in the early years of membership (Diez 1999a: 602). Similarly, the prevalence of national and parliamentary sovereignty in Britain's European policy discourse contrasts with the situation in other member states and reflects the way in which the British political elite has 'constructed' the European issue (see also Larsen 1997).

The methodological challenge of Europeanisation is to ensure that one's research strategy can derive sound results and reasonable inferences about causality (Bache and Jordan 2006b: 29). One of the ways in which this challenge can be met is through a comparative case-study approach (for instance, Cowles *et al.* 2001). Another potential way of meeting the challenge is by adopting an historical perspective: the approach followed here. A potential methodological pitfall for any Europeanisation study is the tendency to attribute domestic change exclusively to Europeanisation, thereby screening out other causes. Thus, Klaus Goetz has warned that research should consider the *relative* impact of Europeanisation in comparison to other causes or rival hypotheses (Goetz 2001; Radaelli 2003: 50). Except where evidence is gathered by survey data, formal *measurement* of Europeanisation is problematic.

In focusing on the Europeanisation of domestic governance arrangements, it is easier to isolate the causation flowing from the EU than is the case with policy studies. In the case of the latter, Europeanisation in some instances may turn out not to be an independent variable at all. EU policy may be following international developments, for instance by transposing an international environmental agreement at EU level. Alternatively, it may be attempting to *mediate* global trends, such as by reinforcing European regulatory standards against global pressures. Moreover, and regardless of which of these two circumstances apply, the Europeanisation effect might be constructed discursively in order to make globalization more palatable domestically (see Hay and Rosamond 2002). But it is still not easy to isolate causation in the Europeanisation of the polity. One of the problems is the fact that the 'object' – in this case UK executive government – has not been static. Indeed, over the period of nearly half a century that we are concerned with in this volume, there have been many changes in UK central government that have been quite unrelated to Europe. Moreover, some of the impact upon government may be the result of the UK government's attempts to 'upload' policy solutions to the EU level in line with Tanja Börzel's understanding of Europeanisation (2002).

How, then, do we deploy Europeanisation – as defined above – in this study? A first point to note is that our methodology in what follows will not be to use a comparative case-study approach but, rather, will compare change over time: from the 1960s onwards, but with particular reference to the contemporary period. The rationale for this examination of Europeanisation over a long time-period is reasonably straightforward. If member states' patterns of governance have adjusted in distinctive ways to the long-term effects of Europeanisation, as the existing literature suggests, it is only through a developmental perspective that we can account for patterns of Europeanisation. Comparative snap-shot analyses, for instance, exploring the impact of the Maastricht Treaty on several governments, may not yield the real dynamics of the Europeanisation process. More concretely, by examining British central government's adjustment over the long haul, we will be able to come to a clearer judgement as to whether the way in which EU business is handled derives from a functional logic as to how to deal with membership of the EU, or whether Europeanisation is understood in terms of an internal dynamic of UK government's organisation.

Secondly, we are using Europeanisation initially as a device to organise an empirical review of change in UK central government over time. In essence, we are exploring the proposition that *European integration has brought about significant change in the character of UK central government*. Our task in Chapters 4–7 is to make sense of the changes that have occurred. In reviewing the findings in Chapter 8 we then try to develop a model accounting for the effects of Europeanisation over time. In Chapter 9 we explore the utility of this model for explaining developments in a selection of other member states. Hence the initial use of Europeanisation to organise our empirical account is designed to assist analysis.

Thirdly, in order not to fall into the trap of attributing all change to a Europeanisation-effect, we acknowledge that domestic reform efforts have intersected with the process of adapting to Europe. Their intersection may have facilitated adaptation to the EU or impeded it: that is for our empirical account. In it we shall be trying to identify instances where Europeanisation pressures, whether 'vertically' from the EU or horizontally through the dense network of bilateral relations that are intrinsic to EU membership, have been the primary force behind institutional change.

Europeanisation and outcomes

The conceptual literature has devoted some attention to the outcome of change in response to Europeanisation. In the context of institutional adaptation a helpful classification is offered by Tanja Börzel and Thomas Risse (2003: 69–70; for different sets of criteria on change, see Hall 1993). They identify absorption, accommodation and transformation as the possible outcomes of domestic change. These represent low, modest and high degrees of change respectively.

In theory all three of these outcomes are possible in the context of UK governmental adaptation to the EU. However, the empirical picture is potentially quite differentiated across both time and activity. Temporal differentiation may arise from the time-frame that is taken for assessing the impact of Europeanisation. This is perhaps not surprising in view of the fact that the process of European integration has been fitful, with gradual evolution punctuated over the last couple of decades by constitutional reforms. If domestic change were simply a function of those changes at EU level, then adjustments might be expected to take place according to those dynamics, albeit with a time-delay as the full implications of treaty implementation take effect. Differentiation across activity is likely to be present because the EU's policy competences are not evenly spread. The EU has only explicitly come to activity on defence policy since 1999 and on home affairs cooperation since the Maastricht Treaty, implemented from November 1993. Hence the impact across government is likely to vary between departments as regards both the absolute impact and the timing and tempo of the impact.

What are the potential outcomes of Europeanisation in British central government in line with the three categories of Börzel and Risse identified above, namely absorption, accommodation and transformation (2003: 69–70)?

- *Absorption* would represent a minimalist approach: the ability to 'process' proposals and intelligence emanating from Brussels within the existing institutions, processes and norms associated with the Whitehall model of government.
- *Accommodation* would be a more significant, though still modest, form of adaptation: the adjustment of the institutions, processes and norms of Whitehall so as to be able to play an active role in the EU. Such adaptation would entail British government deploying traditional Whitehall patterns in order to play an active role in EU governance.
- *Transformation* would involve greater adaptation. This adaptation would either entail substantial reform of the existing Whitehall institutions or fundamental change to their features and/or the norms embedded within them.

In the context of our study we use an additional terminology for explaining responses to Europeanisation, namely *reception* and *projection*: terms which were already utilised to organise Chapter 1 (Bulmer and Burch 2000). This terminology is distinct from the three categories above and is advanced to capture the nature of governmental response. The Europeanisation of the polity sets up a potential conflict between the logic of EU governance and that of domestic governance. Translator devices need to be able to channel EU governance into the logic of domestic governance. However, just as Tanja Börzel (2002) has understood the Europeanisation of policy as bi-directional, so it is important that domestic governance has suitable institutional arrangements and procedures in order to be able to channel its policy interests into the logic of EU governance. Thus reception is concerned with judging how domestic governance structures handle EU initiatives and policy, whereas projection is about the ability of those structures to facilitate the conduct of European diplomacy abroad. The logics of EU and domestic governance are in creative tension, but it is vital that a balance is struck so that both logics are catered for. Thus, the Europeanisation of components of the polity also involves bi-directionality. The terms reception and projection allow us to capture important characteristics of the institutional response in British central government, and they also facilitate a discussion of institutional effectiveness (see later in this chapter).

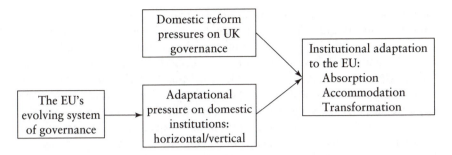

Figure 2.1 Europeanisation and domestic institutional adaptation

Summary
Thus far we have discussed how Europeanisation comes about and how it may be evaluated in the context of impact upon government institutions. The EU generates adaptation pressures from above, but also horizontally through bilateral relations with EU partners. This adaptation pressure is not the only source of domestic institutional change in British government, since separate, domestic challenges, such as new public management, bring their own adaptation pressures. We depict our propositions in terms of Europeanisation in the form of a simple model (see Figure 2.1). It is a simple model because it assumes that domestic institutions adapt in direct response to shifts at EU level. We will return to the model in Chapter 8, modifying it in the light of empirical observation. However, it is to the point already at this stage to identify some of the insights of institutionalist analysis and how they relate to UK government's adaptation to the EU. Given our temporal focus on governmental adaptation, we draw on historical institutionalism in order to explore the pattern of development in governmental machinery.

Europeanisation and institutional theory

New institutionalism has been identified as comprising three variants. Each sheds different light on empirical evidence (Hall and Taylor 1996; Aspinwall and Schneider 2001). Rational choice institutionalists adopt a rather narrow rule-based understanding of institutions and assume that actors respond in a strategic manner to their institutional environment. In the present context of Europe, national governments should, according to this view, respond strategically to new opportunities in the EU *unless* domestic veto points present insuperable obstacles to such a response (see also Börzel and Risse 2003: 70). At the other end of the institutionalist spectrum sociological institutionalism adopts a different approach compared to the logic of *consequentialism* that is central to rational choice institutionalism (March and Olsen 1989: 160–2). Following a logic of *appropriateness*, institutional actors will not respond strategically but by reference to embedded norms and culture. There may be scope for learning new practices but the extent of change is presumed to be modest or minimal unless there is fundamental upheaval brought about by a crisis of some kind (Olsen 1996; Börzel and Risse 2003: 70). Most historical institutionalists also share this view of institutions being sticky and resistant to change (see in particular, Pierson 2004: 17–53). Historical institutionalists are especially concerned with the role of time: how policy trajectories and institutional structures may become 'frozen', out-living their original purposes or becoming sub-optimal in respect of their original objectives.

In describing and evaluating the Europeanisation of UK central government we develop and apply ideas derived from historical and sociological institutionalism. These approaches share an assumption that institutions matter: they serve to channel and prioritise choices; shape actors' behaviour, objectives and values: and thus affect outcomes. They provide a way of linking deeper, structural factors such as those located in the economy, society and wider polity on the one hand with human agency on the other. This linkage is essential in any effective application of these approaches and throughout our account of Whitehall's response to Europe we refer to the wider pressures which have shaped UK policy.

There are three aspects of institutional theory which need to be given attention. These concern the characteristics of change; the contributions of significant actors; and institutional effectiveness. We now consider each of these points and indicate how we operationalise them, beginning with the characteristics of change.

Europeanisation and the characteristics of institutional change
The process of Europeanisation is an iterative one. It involves examining institutional adaptation and change over six decades. In seeking to make sense of these changes, we draw out and develop three propositions from the historical institutionalist literature.

First, we hold, along with other historical institutionalists, that in settled and stable societies, pressures for change, whether generated externally or internally, usually lead to the adaptation of existing institutions rather than the creation of wholly new ones (Skowronek 1982: 12; Thelen and Steinmo 1992: 16–18; March and Olsen 1996: 256; Pierson 2004: 17–53). We refer to this situation as *incremental change*. Significant transformations may occur, though these tend to be infrequent (Krasner 1988; Collier and Collier 1991). We call this *radical change*. However, there is a third way of understanding change. That is when the outcomes of incremental change have accumulated and crystallised to such an extent that what has become established is something distinctly and qualitatively different from that which previously existed (see Bulmer and Burch 1998: 605; 2001: 81; Héritier 2007: 1). We call this *incremental-transformative change*. We hold that while institutional change is usually incremental it is useful to distinguish moments of qualitative change within the incremental pattern.

Second, historical institutionalists also hold that institutions change not only in line with existing institutional formats, but past choices also restrict subsequent actions. As Pierson notes, 'actors find the dead weight of previous institutional choices often seriously limits their room to manoeuvre. Coordination around alternatives may be difficult, and veto points may present formidable alternatives' (Pierson 2004: 152). Change is thus often referred to as path-dependent in that initial choices determine later developments and once a particular pathway is selected alternatives tend to be constrained thereafter. We are concerned to explore the extent to which institutional change has been path-dependent.

Third, like other historical institutionalists, we find it useful to concentrate on key points of institutional choice and change when departures are made from established patterns (Thelen and Steinmo 1992: 27). These are the moments when new patterns and processes are set. Collier and Collier (1991: 29) use the term 'critical juncture' which they define 'as a period of significant change . . . which is hypothesised to produce distinct legacies' (see also Hall 1986: 66). Indeed we go further by distinguishing a critical moment from a critical juncture. A 'critical moment' is when a *perceived opportunity* arises for significant change. That is, an event takes place which raises a general expectation that significant change will follow. It may, for example, emerge within elite groups, it may come to dominate or define media debate, or it may register substantially among public opinion or indeed involve a mixture of these manifestations (Burch *et al.* 2003: 8). Such opportunities may not be realised and exploited but, if they are, the outcome is a 'critical juncture' at which there is a clear departure from previously established patterns. Critical junctures create branching points at which institutional development moves on to a new trajectory or pathway which is then followed incrementally until a new critical moment arises, and (potentially) a new critical juncture follows and a new direction is taken. In theory, at each critical moment the opportunities for institutional innovation are at their widest. Timely interventions by actors at these critical moments may make a difference to the subsequent development of the institution. Also at these points, actors, or the interests they represent, can gain an advantage in the future game of power (Rothstein 1992: 35). Conversely, at each such moment, various alternative pathways are not taken – either because they were considered and rejected, were addressed but unsuccessfully, or actors were not aware of them.

In order to be able to identify when institutional change is not simply incremental, it is necessary to have some way of mapping the extent of change. In order to do this, we break the institutional structure of British government into distinct parts. We define institutions here as abiding patterns of organisation and practice surrounding a particular purpose, activity or task (see Burch *et al.* 2003). The activity at issue is the handling of UK European policy both at home and in the EU. Working from these general points we distinguish a number of *dimensions* along which institutional change can be examined and assessed (see Bulmer and Burch 1998; 2000; 2001; Bulmer *et al.* 2002). We distinguish four of these plus a fifth dimension which applies to all of them. These are:

- changes in the *system*: affecting the constitutional rules and the framework of the state and government;
- changes in *organisations*: affecting the formal structure of offices and key positions, and including the distribution of formal authority and resources of money and staff;
- changes in *processes*: affecting the means whereby business is handled, information distributed and policy decisions determined, and including the networks established to fulfil these tasks; and
- changes in *regulation*: affecting rules, guidelines and operating codes and also the capacity for strategic guidance (i.e. the means to ensure that tasks are fulfilled and that forward thinking is undertaken).

In addition to these, change in the *cultural* aspects of institutions – the norms and values affecting activities across all these dimensions – must be taken into account. Many institutionalist theorists, namely sociological institutionalists and some historical institutionalists, hold that 'ideas' and/or cultural elements play a significant role in political processes, although there is less agreement as to how and why this is so (for discussion, see March and Olsen 1989: 159–62; Hall and Taylor 1996). In practical applications of such institutionalist approaches, cultural aspects may concern, for example, accepted values about how processes should work, which actors should be involved and which excluded in this or that activity, what rules and conventions should apply to which activities and so on. While such values may be slow to adjust, change in value systems may come about through new interpretations of widely accepted norms. New values, or new understandings of values, may come about through generational change in politics, or through a change of government. The result may be a change in the terms of reference of a particular policy activity arising from communicative action (Risse 2000), advocacy coalitions (Sabatier 1998), epistemic communities (Haas 1992) or double-loop learning (Argyris and Schön 1978; for an application, see Jordan 2003). The impact of developments at EU level, such as the application of the subsidiarity principle and efforts to introduce new governance techniques, for example benchmarking, all entail an impact upon British government. As does the gradual socialisation of ministers and officials into the EU way of doing things as a result of substantial and sustained engagement in policy-making in Brussels and across the member states. In addition British government is also experiencing changing norms, generated largely in the domestic arena, in terms of the new public management and public service delivery. These elements, not to mention the cultural shift accompanying moves towards greater decentralisation of the political system, all feature in our empirical account.

The purpose of dissecting the above dimensions of governance is to develop a means of measuring change qualitatively. Namely, we argue that a critical juncture may be identified where change is detected across a majority of the five dimensions.

Europeanisation and significant actors

Institutional analyses tend to allow limited space for the effect of particular actors on institutional change and development. Indeed sociological institutionalism would seem to deny that individual actors are capable of acting in this way (Powell and Di Maggio 1996). According to this variant of institutionalism actors are seen as derivative, their values are primarily shaped by the institution to which they belong and they pursue its interests and goals. While we would see the individual as both constrained and conditioned, there are evidently instances when the personal impact of an individual can prove critical in moving matters forward. In many cases change simply would not happen or at least at the time that it does happen without the intervention of such actors. Consequently an analysis of Britain's approach to Europe that fails to give recognition to the role of key actors – whether they are ministers or officials – would be a partial and restricted account. Moreover, as we have already mentioned, critical moments open up opportunities for actors to exercise influence.

The problem is that it is difficult to generalise about the effect of 'significant actors'. This is partly a matter of isolating particular instances, for the impact of an individual will obviously vary according to the nature of the opportunity arising and whether and how he or she chooses to exploit it. In this book, however, we are able to identify from comments in interviews and other sources those who practitioners regard as significant: that is, people that they feel made a difference in their own right. Such an approach also requires that some attention be given to determining whether an actor's intervention, as opposed to his or her reputation, was significant in that it actually made a difference to either the timing or content of what happened. We return in Chapter 8 to this notion of significant actors – individuals who have had a *lasting effect on the institutions for handling EU policy making in Whitehall*. Defined in these terms significant actors are not to be distinguished simply as a consequence of the positions they hold. It is more a matter of how they use that position, if and when opportunities for change arise, and whether they bring their own individual stamp to that change.[1]

Europeanisation and institutional effectiveness

We are also concerned to examine the effectiveness of UK central government's response to Europeanisation. We regard a concern with the evaluation of the practical working of institutions to be an essential part of institutional studies. In the concluding chapter of our analysis we consider the strengths and weaknesses of the British approach. In doing this we draw on the evaluation of practitioners and observers and studies of how EU policy is handled in other states. We go further than this in terms of developing criteria for judging the effectiveness of member states' approaches to reception, projection and pro-active engagement.

In our view *reception* is effective when a national government is able to absorb, handle and reach decisions on material transmitted from the EU. Here evaluation centres on such matters as: the speed of response to EU initiatives; how widely information is distributed to relevant players within the system of government; how comprehensive that information is; the extent of the capacity to examine and analyse the input received; the effectiveness of procedures for scrutiny and oversight both within the bureaucracy and within parliament; and the ability to reach a coordinated and agreed view in preparation for negotiations with other member states – either bilaterally or in EU fora. A related aspect is performance in respect of transposing and implementing European policy.

The effectiveness of a member state's *projection* can be evaluated in terms of two central criteria: dependability and calculability. In practical terms these cover a number of factors including: the effectiveness of diplomatic representation and in particular the smoothness with which business is conducted and the clarity with which positions are presented; the extent to which a member government has an effective strategic capacity to think ahead; its general reputation for positive and constructive action in the EU; and its capacity to adopt and pursue tactics commensurate with effective bargaining in the multi-governmental context of the EU. This latter, tactical capacity depends on the nature of the decision-making rules that apply at the point of formal decision in the EU: the critical distinction being between situations in which unanimity and qualified majority voting rules apply in the Council. In the former case the ability to formulate and maintain an agreed national position is seen as effective. In cases where Qualified Majority Voting (QMV) applies, however, flexibility is paramount as allowing some leeway for exploiting the negotiating situation is essential to success. At its most successful, projection would result in the exporting of British domestic governance practice or policy models to the EU. In consequence, a British imprint would be placed on the governance of the EU. Of course, and especially in an EU of 27 member states, such success is contingent on securing the support of partner governments.

Conclusion: our analytical tool-kit

Having outlined our analytical approach, we conclude with a brief resumé of the key analytical points which are applied in this study of the impact of the EU on Whitehall. The concept of Europeanisation is central to our analysis. It provides purchase on the nature and extent of Whitehall's adaptation to the EC/EU. In the broadest sense we are concerned to evaluate our proposition that Europeanisation has taken place and whether the governmental response can be judged to have been characterised by absorption, accommodation or transformation. In order to reach some conclusions on this matter we examine the development of the Whitehall response over time. Our points drawn from historical and sociological institutionalism provide us with a means of describing and analysing change in Whitehall in relation to the effect of the EU. We also look at the extent of change by examining it across all four institutional dimensions – system, organisation, process and regulation. In addition, we consider the patterns of change since the 1950s by examining the extent to which critical moments have produced alterations of such a significance that they can be judged to constitute a critical juncture. Finally, we highlight, where appropriate, the importance of significant actors and explore matters concerning the effectiveness of the UK's approach to the EU.

Note

1 For detailed case study analyses applying an institutional approach to isolating and defining significant individuals see Burch and Holliday (1996: 150, 266–9).

3

The EU framework for UK policy-making

The purpose of this chapter is to offer a review of the EU framework within which UK central government operates. This EU framework is important for a range of reasons, but most centrally because it is the main source of Europeanisation effects. There are other sources of Europeanisation, such as the separate, Strasbourg-based Council of Europe, but we have excluded them from our study. Europeanisation and European policy are also closely bound up with a series of bilateral relationships with individual EU member states. Bilateral relations form an important context for European policy-making in the UK but our primary concern is the EU's institutions.

Why is it important to be familiar with the nature of the EU framework in order to understand how European policy is formulated in British government?

- As suggested earlier, the EU now generates a substantial amount of business across a wide range of policy areas for British central government. We need to review EU business in order to reveal the *amount* of activity that needs to be processed in Whitehall, *who* in government is affected by it, and *how* it is dealt with procedurally. In short, what is it that flows from the EU – the independent variable – that impacts upon British government?
- Moreover, in light of our historical institutionalist approach, it is important that we are aware of the historical trajectory of European integration. Has it developed incrementally or by step-changes? Have the adjustments in UK central government been straightforward responses to the timing of developments at EU level, as implied in our model (see Figure 2.1)? It is important to understand the key developments at EU level.
- Given our institutionalist approach, it is essential to have a good grasp of the character – formal, informal and cultural – of EU governance. We need such an understanding in order to appreciate the 'fit' or

congruence between the patterns in the EU and the UK. We also need to understand the character of EU governance in order to evaluate central government's strengths and weaknesses in engaging with the EU in terms of the twin tasks of reception and projection.

• A series of important multi-levelled linkages has been created between British central government and the institutions of the EU. Identifying the EU partners in these institutional linkages is vital to understanding where Whitehall 'fits in'. This aspect is especially important in understanding the 'projection' role of UK central government in the EU.

The chapter is divided into three parts. The first simply explores the key stages in the EU's evolution in order to set out the landmarks in integration. The second part reviews the EU's policy portfolio in order that the impact upon UK central government may be judged. Thirdly, we explore the contemporary system of EU governance that ministers and civil servants must engage with if they are successfully to project UK interests.

Historical context

When the UK applied for membership of the European Communities in 1961 they were still at an early stage of development. By the time of the second application in 1967 their shape had become more complex. Politically, the supranational characteristics of the EC had been placed in question by President de Gaulle's empty-chair policy in 1965, and by the emphasis on reaching consensual decisions that was enshrined in the consequent Luxembourg Compromise of January 1966 (Teasdale 1993). On the face of it, this development placed limitations on the potential impacts for national sovereignty that would ensue from EC membership. In terms of legal integration, however, developments had proceeded in the opposite direction. The European Court of Justice (ECJ) had begun to develop its case law. By the mid-1960s it had already established such supranational principles as the direct effect and supremacy of EC law, both of which had major implications for EU–member state relations in the judicial domain (Dehousse 1998: 36–46). Also of major significance was the growth of EC legislation in the intervening period (see Table 3.1). The regulatory apparatus associated with the Common Agricultural Policy was being established. The removal of tariffs and quotas had also proceeded apace such that the Common External Tariff was in effect in 1968, ahead of schedule. Elsewhere, progress on putting the EC treaties into effect was more mixed but the *acquis communautaire* had taken on a significant size by this stage. Moreover, the three Communities were in the process of merging their institutions following a treaty agreed in 1965 and put into effect in July 1967.

When the application for membership was revived by the Heath government the political structure was unchanged, but the *acquis communautaire*

Table 3.1 Output of binding decisions by EC/EU institutions (1961–98)

	1961	1973	1978	1983	1988	1993	1998
Council Directives	1	30	66	43	56	66	54
Council Regulations	4	375	428	409	458	315	231
Council Decisions	13	16	26	20	37	46	43
Total Council binding decisions	18	421	520	472	551	477	328
Commission Directives	0	8	20	20	26	52	44
Commission Regulations	3	582	753	887	1066	1062	2619
Commission Decisions	81	134	462	396	377	532	594
Total Commission binding decisions	84	724	1235	1303	1469	1646	3257
ECJ judgments	11	80	97	151	238	203	254

Note: Calculations by Council Secretariat.
Source: Celex database.

had grown still further. As Hugo Young puts it, 'There had been an immense accumulation of Community rules and precedents, even though half the decade had been spent, thanks to de Gaulle, in a condition of stasis' (Young 1998: 227). It was the replacement of de Gaulle by President Georges Pompidou in 1969 that brought an end to the stagnation. Thus, at a summit in The Hague in December 1969 the six heads of state or government agreed to relaunch integration by: re-opening the issue of EC enlargement to all applicants; coordinating economic and monetary policy; re-opening the question of an 'own resources' budget; and commissioning a report on foreign policy cooperation.

Against this background the accession negotiations were essentially a matter of accepting the *acquis communautaire*, which was non-negotiable even if it was not to British taste. Acceptance would imply a clear Europeanisation effect, including any disadvantages arising from policy misfit. The report of Sir Con O'Neill, the chief official UK negotiator, states that: if the UK had been a founding member, 'we would never . . . have allowed a situation to develop which made it so difficult, for instance, to ensure fair arrangements for New Zealand dairy products or developing Commonwealth sugar, or to create a situation of equity in respect of our contributions to the Budget' (O'Neill 2000: 355). These issues together with fisheries were the main subject-matters of negotiation and the concessions concerned transitional arrangements rather than re-negotiation of the policies.

By the time the UK acceded in 1973, the EC had also made progress in respect of all four of the commitments made in The Hague. While enlargement was self-evidently successful, the first efforts at economic and monetary integration were less so; sterling lasting a mere three months

(March–June 1972 – before actual accession) in the exchange-rate system known as the Snake. The 'own resources' budget had been agreed and was being phased in during the 1970s. That its mechanisms did not reflect British interests was clear during the accession negotiations but was to become particularly manifest during Margaret Thatcher's premiership. Finally, European Political Cooperation (EPC) represented a new strand of activity in diplomatic relations between the member governments, initially kept distinct from the EC institutions, but which increased the frequency of contacts between foreign ministries. Hugo Young again: 'as a result of the British not being there from the start, the fresh enactments they had to address amounted to some 13,000 typewritten pages' (1998: 227). However, once the UK acceded to the EU, government became a policy-*maker* rather than a policy-*taker*.

European integration in the remainder of the 1970s was sluggish due to the continued adherence to the intergovernmental spirit of the Luxembourg Compromise. The key policy innovations were the creation of the European Regional Development Fund in 1975; faltering efforts to develop social and environmental policies; and the creation in 1979 of the European Monetary System (EMS). In institutional terms the key developments were the creation of the thrice-yearly summit meetings, known as the European Council, from 1975 and the introduction of direct elections to the European Parliament in 1979. Ratification of direct elections created internal problems for the Labour government (see Burch and Holliday 1996: 172–8). Full UK participation in the EMS was ruled out at its establishment for political reasons (Ludlow 1982).

The early 1980s saw further incremental development of the EU whilst integration more broadly was blocked by the Thatcher government's dispute with partners over budgetary contributions. However, out of the acrimony of this dispute, settled at the Fontainebleau European Council in 1984, there emerged a Community in which a number of key politicians, notably President Mitterrand, Chancellor Kohl, Prime Minister Thatcher and Commission President Delors, were willing to forge a more strategic, outward-looking EC agenda to address some of the important economic challenges of the era. The single-market programme was the key policy development but was linked with flanking measures, such as social policy, the structural funds, research and technology policy, and initial renewed momentum towards EMU. The single-market programme generated a significantly increased legislative programme but had a much wider impact in dynamising integration (Armstrong and Bulmer 1998). The dynamism was further facilitated by the linked EC treaty reforms contained in the Single European Act (SEA), signed in 1986 and implemented from July 1987. The spirit of the Luxembourg Compromise was ended as the practice of Qualified Majority Voting (QMV) increased in the Council of Ministers. Moreover, the EP's legislative powers were increased in certain policy areas.

For British central government the consequences were essentially threefold. More Whitehall departments had to contend with the significantly increased business flowing from Brussels. Secondly, the government embarked on an awareness-raising programme on the single market to alert the industrial and service sectors to its implications. Finally, as regards coordinating European policy within Whitehall, the government had to be mindful that the national veto could no longer be applied in certain policy areas. The implication of this development was that negotiating tactics might need to change.

Already in 1981 the EC had enlarged to take in Greece but Spanish and Portuguese accession in 1986 led to a more noticeable tilt towards 'the south'. Alliance-building became more complex and the emergence of the 'Club Med' states, with Ireland as an honorary member, led to a major enhancement of the structural funds. By the late 1980s the EC's agenda had run ahead of what Mrs Thatcher's government was prepared to countenance, with Delors' social dimension, moves towards monetary union (EMU) and a smaller group of states removing border controls and combating crime through the Schengen Accord. The end of the Cold War offered no let-up in the dynamic of integration, as France and Germany sought to deepen integration through binding their interests still closer together in European integration. The resultant Maastricht Treaty did not have the programmatic legislative content of the single market but the commitment to a single currency was to become no less significant later in the 1990s and early 2000s. The emergence of a three-pillared European Union also created a new architecture for integration. Apart from the EMU commitment the EC pillar was strengthened by means of a further move towards QMV, additional powers for the EP and the granting of a small number of extra competences to the supranational level. The foreign policy cooperation process, EPC, which had developed incrementally outside the treaties over the period since 1970, became the second pillar of the EU and was re-named the Common Foreign and Security Policy (CFSP). Finally, cooperation in Justice and Home Affairs (JHA) became the third pillar. The last of these areas of cooperation had been given new momentum by the removal of border controls in the single market, by the dynamics of the Schengen Accord and by the new internal security agenda following the end of the Cold War. It is worth noting that the Conservative government of John Major secured opt-outs from EMU, the social policy changes (the 'Social Chapter') and did not participate in the Schengen Accord.

The new momentum of the Maastricht Treaty was far from immediate, for the ratification process was problematic, most notably with the initial Danish rejection of the Treaty in June 1992. Indeed, these difficulties were amongst the contributory factors to a new concern with the so-called subsidiarity principle. Its test, namely to ensure that the EU level of government was best placed to deliver effective policy, contributed to a decline in the quantity of Council legislation following completion of the single-market programme in 1992 (see Table 3.1). JHA activity, however, became a growing area even if there were initial problems in achieving concrete results. According to Ludlow in 1997 'approximately one-third of all the documents processed by the Council Secretariat and one-fifth of all Council meetings (including working groups) dealt with Pillar III issues' (Ludlow 1998: 576–7). JHA activity introduced dialogue, mutual assistance, joint effort and cooperation between the police, customs, immigration services and justice departments of the member states. JHA work extended the impact of Europeanisation by drawing in government departments which had traditionally been marginal to the integration process, thus raising new coordination challenges. Home affairs and justice began to be Europeanised.

The Maastricht agreement included a commitment to further treaty reform. These negotiations got under way after the 1995 enlargement, which had brought in Austria, Finland and Sweden. The obstructionism of the Major government, due to internal divisions on European policy, cast a shadow over the work of the Intergovernmental Conference (IGC). However, after its election in May 1997 the incoming Blair government took a more constructive approach to negotiations in the six-week period leading to the Amsterdam European Council. Traditional protagonists of integration – such as the German government of Chancellor Kohl – were content to settle for an 'interim service' of the treaties in light of the parallel project of EMU. The resultant 1997 Amsterdam Treaty lacked the core policy impact of its predecessors. Only the commitment to 'an area of freedom, security and justice' had such potential but the provisions were messy and entailed a five-year transition phase as well as special arrangements for the UK (plus Ireland and Denmark). Some JHA work – but excluding police and judicial cooperation – moved to Pillar One of the EU, thus enabling EC legislation to be used, much as elsewhere, as well as QMV to be introduced at the end of the transition period.

Stimulated chiefly by the institutional challenges anticipated by major future enlargement of the EU, in 1999 the process got under way for a further revision of the treaties. Once again the process was one of convening an IGC to prepare a draft treaty to be agreed by government heads and then submitted to the relevant national ratification procedures before implementation. This process, which culminated in agreement at the Nice European Council in December 2000, and the 2001 Nice Treaty, was even more restricted than the Treaty of Amsterdam. The only significant policy change was the creation of a European Security and Defence Policy (ESDP). The other changes were institutional (for a review of the Nice Treaty, see Galloway 2001). Because of the large number of central and eastern European countries (CEECs) that had applied for membership, along with Cyprus and Malta, there were significant reforms needed: on vote weightings in the Council, numbers of MEPs and commissioners for each member state, as well as provisions to enable 'enhanced cooperation' amongst smaller groups of the member states. Enlargement took place in May 2004, when ten new states – eight CEECs plus Cyprus and Malta – acceded to the EU. The combined effect of the Nice Treaty and this round of enlargement has made a big impact upon the EU. The Franco-German alliance is no longer so central to the EU because the latter has become much more diverse and coalition-building on decisions more complex. Successive UK governments have supported enlargement; its achievement has changed the Europeanisation-effect on the UK from mid-2004 onwards. Romania and Bulgaria joined in January 2007, bringing membership to 27 states.

In the 2000s there has been a protracted constitutional debate designed to consolidate the existing treaties. This process began through a different process, namely with a more broadly composed Convention on the Future of Europe, chaired by the former French president, Valéry Giscard d'Estaing (see Norman 2003). It drew up a draft treaty before governments moved into a more central negotiating role. The culmination was the Constitutional Treaty, signed in 2004. The resultant ratification process was punctuated by adverse referendum results in France and the Netherlands in 2005 and the European Council's June 2005 call for a 'pause for reflection'. This period ended when, in June 2007, the German presidency secured agreement in the European Council on a somewhat less ambitious treaty that certain member governments – notably France and the UK – hope will not need to be submitted to a domestic referendum. The Portuguese presidency in the second half of 2007 has had the task of overseeing a further IGC to finalise this new treaty (the Lisbon Treaty). We will not consider the impact on the UK of this protracted period of constitutional debate in detail, since the process had not reached a conclusion at the time of writing and the impact on UK central government will not be felt until the ratification process has been completed. Nevertheless, there will be some significant institutional and policy reforms with an impact upon the UK, assuming that ratification is successful.

One other significant development is worthy of mention regarding the EU's development in the early 2000s. Developing chiefly out of an initiative in employment policy and confirmed in the 2000 Lisbon Strategy for enhancing European competitiveness, a new form of governance has gradually taken shape: the so-called Open Method of Coordination (OMC) (Borrás and Greve 2004). Utilised in a range of policy settings, including competitiveness, research policy, social inclusion, innovation and asylum policy, the process is essentially horizontal. The objective is policy learning through exchange between member governments and other policy stakeholders. As Bulmer and Radaelli put it: 'The idea is to use the EU as a transfer platform rather than a law-making system' (2005: 349). The OMC has introduced additional diversity in the EU system of governance. This is a particularly important development as the OMC is of crucial importance to the Lisbon Strategy which, re-launched in early 2005 under the headline 'Growth and Jobs', is a key priority of Commission President José Manuel Barroso.[1] A final development to be noted was that on 1 January 2002 the Euro became the currency of twelve member states of the EU (sixteen as of January 2009).

To sumarise these developments we can see that an increasing number of policy areas has become Europeanised. It is also clear that the membership has increased from 9 states to 27 in the period 1973–2007, thus impacting on alliance-building within the EU and tactical considerations for the UK government. The number of bilateral relationships relating to EU business has also increased greatly. The balance of the EU's interests has shifted as a result of the enlargements. The EU has become more supranational as the veto mentality has been marginalised to a small number of policies: areas of treaty reform, and aspects of CFSP, ESDP and home/judicial affairs issues. However, the EU has also shifted towards a neo-liberal agenda and away from the greater economic interventionism of the 1970s; the looser horizontal approach of the OMC reflects this shift. Contradictory as they are, all these developments have profound implications for British central government.

A final observation on the EU's historical evolution concerns the time, timing and tempo of integration. A pattern has emerged whereby episodes of treaty reform have punctuated periods of relative equilibrium in the EU's development. The SEA and the Maastricht Treaty in particular represented critical junctures in the EU's development. However, the periods of relative equilibrium must not be ignored. First, there is the separate judicial dynamic to European integration. Path-breaking decisions by the European Court of Justice can impact significantly on individual policy areas or system-wide. Their timing is quite independent of the political dynamics of treaty reform. Secondly, after every IGC there is a period of bedding down. Policies develop incrementally; new institutional opportunities arise from new rules governing the EU institutions and so on. The effect of Europeanisation is the combination of these different dynamics. And it is further shaped by the shifting power balance amongst the member states, depending on the importance individual government heads give to European policy, national electoral cycles and so on.

In the next section we turn to the range of policies for which the EU has competence and how their Europeanisation-effect varies.

The EU's policy repertoire

The EU's policy responsibilities can be defined in two ways: where does the EU have policy competence; and what type of competence? However, both tasks are problematic. The EU treaties currently in force have not produced a catalogue of policy competences. Fligstein and McNichol (1998) drew up a listing on the basis of the EEC Treaty and its subsequent reform by the SEA and the Treaty on European Union (TEU: or Maastricht Treaty). They then ascribed legislation passed over the period 1958–94 and assigned it to the twenty different competences identified in their classification (Fligstein and McNichol 1998: 80–1; see also Maurer and Wessels 2003: 46). Rather unsurprisingly, agriculture represented the largest category with 44.4 per cent of the legislation, followed by external relations at 10.3 per cent, and industry/internal market (7.8 per cent). Their evaluation was confined to Pillar One and was further limited by not including non-legislative indicators which are particularly important for measuring activity on the structural funds.

Competences

For brevity we depart from our default position of not considering the incomplete constitutional process that culminated in the 2007 Lisbon Treaty. However, the treaty includes a list of competences that correspond in broad terms to the status quo. They were drafted mainly as a way of codifying existing practice and can serve as a useful guide to summarising the UK policy areas that are affected by the EU and to the extent of the impact (see Box 3.1). It should be clear from the listing that not many domestic policy areas are left untouched: the welfare state and health care, for example, although each of these is affected in a minor way by the EU. However, there are two caveats. First, the Lisbon Treaty has not yet been ratified by all member states, so the listing has no formal status as yet. Secondly, there is no quantitative component to the listing – unlike Fligstein and McNichol's analysis – and that is needed for a definitive picture of the EU impact on UK public policy.

Type of competence

There are two ways in which it is possible to comment on the qualitative nature of EU competence. One relates to the extent to which member governments retain domestic autonomy; the other to the character of governance in the policy domain. The former can be deduced from the categories in Box 3.1. Four categories of EU competence have been identified:

- areas of exclusive competence, where only the EU may legislate and adopt legally binding acts;
- areas of shared competence, where both the EU and member states may legislate, but the latter may only do so where the EU is not itself active;
- areas of policy coordination, where the EU adopts policy guidelines; and
- areas of supporting, coordinating or supplementary action.

Foreign, security and defence policy are listed separately. A further feature of EU competences that must be noted is provision for deeper integration by 'pioneer groups', that is where smaller groupings of states move ahead

Box 3.1 The EU–member state balance of policy competences

Areas of exclusive competence
Customs union
Competition rules for the internal market
Monetary policy for those states in the euro-zone
Conservation of marine biological resources under the common fisheries policy
Common commercial policy
Where an international agreement is necessary to enable the Union to exercise its internal competence.

Areas of shared competence
Internal market
Aspects of social policy
Economic, social and territorial cohesion
Agriculture and fisheries (except marine conservation – see above)
Environment
Consumer protection
Transport
Trans-European networks
Energy
Area of freedom, security and justice
Aspects of public health safety
Technological development and space
Development and humanitarian aid

Areas of policy coordination
Member states' economic policies
Member states' employment policies
Member states' social policies

Areas of supporting, coordinating or supplementary action
Protection and improvement of human health
Industry
Culture
Tourism
Education, vocational training, youth and sport
Civil protection
Administrative cooperation

The common foreign and security policy
'The Union shall have competence . . . to define and implement a common foreign and security policy, including the progressive framing of a common defence policy.'

Source: Summarised from Articles 2A and 2B of the Treaty establishing the European Community as revised by the Lisbon Treaty (*Official Journal of the European Union* C 306, 17.12.2007: 46–8).

of the pack but on the understanding that the latter can later opt in at a later stage. The Schengen Accord and the Euro-zone are both examples of such developments.

Much EU activity, and especially in areas of exclusive and shared competence, is undertaken through legislation, which can take two forms. Legislation by Directive permits member states to achieve policy goals by the means each deems appropriate, whereas legislation by Regulation does not permit such discretion. Member governments have to initiate legislation to transpose Directives. Domestic authorities have to implement most EC legislation, since the EU lacks field agencies. In the contemporary UK, significant policy responsibilities are devolved, for instance in agriculture, and may result in differential application within the UK. The EU's impact is also not simply on UK government – central or devolved – but also upon regulatory authorities and government agencies that largely fall outside the scope of this study. The Financial Services Authority, the Competition Commission, the Office of Communications and energy regulators illustrate the former; the Environment Agency and the Countryside Agency illustrate the latter. There has been little quantitative analysis of legislative impact on the UK. Ed Page conducted one such exercise over the period 1987–97 to establish what proportion of UK Statutory Instruments could be attributed to European legislation; his finding was 15.8 per cent (Page 1998).

The character of EU governance is quite diverse. Bulmer and Radaelli (2005) distinguish between hierarchical modes of governance and horizontal ones, such as OMC. The former are more intrusive in their Europeanisation-effects than the latter, since they depend on legislation and European law, whereas the latter are more intergovernmental, reliant on policy exchange and give greater discretion to member states. Other analysts have suggested that there are more modes of governance in the EU. Helen Wallace (2005: 77–89) suggests there are five modes: the traditional Community (or Monnet) method; a regulatory mode (for instance, in the single market); a distributional mode (notably the multi-level governance of the structural funds); policy coordination (OMC); and intensive transgovernmentalism (covering intense horizontal exchange between governments, such as in CFSP or JHA).

What can be anticipated from this survey and from Box 3.1 is that few areas of UK central government and, indeed its agencies and regulatory bodies, have been undisturbed by the European Union. The impact of Europeanisation has been pervasive across British public policy. However, this impact has been highly differentiated, meaning that the adaptation pressures are quite different for individual policy areas. As Bulmer and Radaelli have argued (2005), the impact of the EU on national policy is quite differentiated, with different mechanisms of adaptation pressure depending on the character of governance in the policy area and issue concerned. The picture presented here has been one for the contemporary

EU. However, since membership, the nature and form of the EU's competences has evolved considerably. For example, in November 2004 home affairs cooperation moved to greater use of qualified majority voting on asylum, immigration and border control issues as a result of The Hague Programme.[2]

Engaging with the EU: the institutional challenge for Whitehall

We now explore the challenges posed for the structures of domestic government in greater detail. The most important point for a national government to recognise, in interacting with the EU, is that the institutions of the EU set the context for European policy-making within the member states. In what follows we look at the following aspects:

- the broad characteristics of EU policy-making;
- the institutional arrangements, especially those which impact upon Whitehall;
- where the UK institutions engage at EU level; and
- the norms and culture of EU policy-making.

Broad characteristics

A first, general point to make is that the EU style of policy-making and administration, inasmuch as there is one, has only recently become institutionalised. We can perhaps characterise its general features as fluid, open, network-based, rule-guided, sectorised and subject to significant inter-institutional bargaining.[3] Brigid Laffan highlights the 'dense institutionalisation' of EU governance, its 'continuous system of negotiations' and 'high degree of functional differentiation', with a 'rhythm of control that is *beyond the control of any one member state*' (2007: 128–9, italics in original). The policy process is fluid in the short or medium term because it is characterised by 'uncertain agendas, shifting networks and complex coalitions' (Mazey and Richardson 1996: 54). It is also fluid in the long term because of episodic constitutional changes within the EU from the SEA onwards. In the same way, potential alliances have shifted as successive enlargements have taken place. The policy process is also open in that the Commission is surprisingly receptive to external thinking by comparison with national executives. It draws heavily upon the ideas and expertise of national officials and of interest groups.

The EU policy process is network-based. The openness outlined above encourages the cultivation of personal contacts. So does the fact that multinational meetings like those in the EU can confront the newcomer as if entering a bazaar. As a result, good inter-personal skills are helpful for successful networking in the EU. All manner of networks exist in Brussels, as habitué(e)s of Brussels bars can attest. For instance, several interview partners spoke approvingly of the ability of the Irish to work networks through their more 'touchy-feely' approach than the sometimes more patrician Brits (or, perhaps, the English). Certainly, there are Scottish and Welsh networks in Brussels: the latter known as the 'taffia'. Making scientific judgements about the importance of such networks is highly problematic but networking has become part of the culture of EU policy-making.

Traditionally, the EU policy process has been particularly rule-bound and rule-governed. Its legalism follows the continental tradition. In addition, there are strong imperatives for regulation because of the lack of shared institutional culture and trust in what is an immature, multinational polity. The creation of a supranational body of law, and of the European Court of Justice to oversee it, reflected a wish to develop new forms of trust, confidence and legitimacy in the European integration process. The EU policy process places a premium upon legal expertise.

The EU policy process is sectorised. Horizontal coordination between Directorates General (DGs) of the Commission has historically been poor. They often operate according to different 'missions', although a more coordinated approach has been developed of late (Jordan and Schout 2006: 224). Coordination also tends to be poor between the different functional Councils of Ministers. The introduction of three different pillars of activity under the Maastricht Treaty, i.e. the EC, Common Foreign and Security Policy (CFSP) and Justice and Home Affairs (JHA) pillars, introduced further differentiation into the policy rules. The EU may have one single, overarching institutional framework but the devil is in the detail.

EU policy and its policy process introduce certain requirements into the domestic arena. Of particular note are two that the structural funds have brought in: namely the principle of partnership and incentives to organise on a regional basis. Because of the financial incentives offered by the structural funds local and regional actors in the UK and elsewhere mobilised in order to secure support from the EU (see Burch and Gomez 2002; Bache 2004; Bache 2008). The OMC, by contrast, has encouraged a more bilateral form of working with other member governments (but also with non-governmental organisations).

Inter-institutional rules have become increasingly complex and procedures more byzantine. This development was one impulse for constitutional reform in order to simplify matters. Differing parliamentary procedures and their intersection with unanimous or qualified majority voting in the Council create a complex set of rules of engagement. In consequence, alliance-building is potentially both inter-state and inter-institutional in character. It is imperative for officials and ministers to understand what the rules are for the matter at hand! The EU's small but increasing variable geometry, whereby not all states participate in all policy activities, has added further complexity. If variable geometry may operate through 'pioneer groups', it can also operate through opt-outs and the UK has utilised the latter on several occasions.

In sum, EU policy-making resembles no national pattern. External to member states, it has its own timetable, flow of business and norms. Finally, the policy process is open and potentially unpredictable in the sense that the EU institutions have some autonomy of action. It is a multinational institution and thus a 'melting pot' of different national outlooks and practices. Getting to grips with these characteristics is a key challenge for UK central government.

Institutional arrangements

The main institutions within which the UK government – ministers and officials – participates are those which are composed intergovernmentally, namely the Council hierarchy. However, whilst government is able to use its voice in the European Council, the Council of Ministers, the Committee of Permanent Representatives, Council working groups and so on, seeking to influence the Commission, the Parliament or the European Court structure is not excluded. So, how does UK central government interface with the EU institutions?

The European Council

The European Council is a key institution. Although only established in 1975, and with something of a mixed record in terms of its results, the regular summit meetings, held anything between twice and four times per annum, offer important opportunities for national governments. The European Council's significance lies in the following functions (see Hayes-Renshaw and Wallace 2006: 165–85):

- it is the EU's overall agenda-setter;
- it can give the EU strategic direction;
- it can give direction to individual policies;
- it has also been a 'court of appeal' for governments with a grievance of some kind, normally about Europeanisation-effects in their state.

Since 2004 all meetings have been held in Brussels; previously most meetings were held in a major city of the country holding the Council presidency (see Westlake and Galloway 2004: 423–5).

The wide-ranging functions of the European Council derive from the fact that it is the institution which straddles all EU activity. It is therefore the most suitable forum for agenda-setting. The advantage held by the European Council is that ideas endorsed by it command greater national support and are thus likely to be translated successfully into EU (legislative) action. As the single market programme demonstrated, the Commission is most effective as an agenda-setter when it has first received the European Council's endorsement of overall goals, as it did at the 1985 Milan summit. If there is a 'battle of ideas' within the EU, it is played out within the European Council. These battles are best engaged in coalition with one or more partner-governments, as the success of Franco-German initiatives attests (Cole 2001: 56–82). The European Council is the forum in which the key initiatives on integration have been launched: EMU (both as an idea and then specifically, in May 1998, the launch of Stage III), the single market, all rounds of treaty reform, enlargement and so on.

Apart from overseeing these examples of the EU's 'constitutive politics' the European Council also oversees more programmatic, strategic decisions, for example the EU's seven-year 'financial perspectives', last agreed in December 2005 to cover the budgetary period 2007–13. The European Council's position at the apex of the Council hierarchy uniquely enables it to coordinate across the EU's pillars of activity and across the range of individual policy areas. Increasingly, the government heads have also taken an interest in individual policy areas, wishing to retain some control over policy direction. Thus major démarches in the CFSP are overseen in summits, as are initiatives in home affairs cooperation. An annual spring summit now deals with the Lisbon Strategy on competitiveness. Finally, the European Council may also be a 'court of appeal' for governments who regard some aspect of Europeanisation to impose intolerable adaptation pressures, such as the UK argued in the early 1980s regarding its budgetary contributions.

The meetings themselves are supposed to be small, consisting of heads of government (or state for presidential systems, such as France), the foreign ministers, the Commission president and a vice-president (Hayes-Renshaw and Wallace 2006: 167–8). There is a small secretariat and translators but also a rule that no more than one official for each member state may enter the conference chamber as a messenger at any time. Outside the chamber, however, there are many officials ready to give advice on any issue that may come up in discussions. Officials are not required in the meeting because decisions taken are political rather than legal in nature. On the fringes of the summits there is a media 'circus' which feeds off rumour, news, press conferences and so on.

For the British government, European Council sessions have numerous implications. The Prime Minister and the Foreign Secretary are the key participants and must be briefed. Their key advisers must be available in the conference venue. The presence of the media has inevitably brought in the prime minister's official spokesman, to handle the press. At official level the European Council is carefully stage-managed. In Brussels logistical preparations are carried out by middle-ranking diplomats from the permanent representations in Brussels and the Commission. Known collectively as the Antici Group, these officials prepare the agenda meticulously. It is they who sit in an ante-room of the European Council chamber and take messages to/from their head of government and multiple national advisers elsewhere at the venue (Westlake and Galloway 2004: 210–11). The European Council is an institution which was characteristically informal but proceedings have become more routinised, especially with the increase in participants following the 2004 enlargement (Tallberg 2007). Its composition of political 'chief executives' means that personalities and inter-personal relations matter rather more than normal. Tony Blair's ability to 'work the room' was an asset in this respect. Reflecting the summits' importance, from the mid-1980s there have also been informal meetings of government heads from the key party families ahead of some European Council sessions, facilitating party-political agenda-setting.

Increasingly government heads have come to recognise that bilateral meetings can be a useful adjunct to their diplomacy in the European Council. They are an important opportunity for shaping the policy ideas of counterparts. They are especially valuable for the 'projection' response to Europeanisation. Putting across national interests in the form of a constructive European diplomacy necessitates the support of counterparts. For example, the 1998 bilateral summit on defence at St Malo between Blair and Chirac was intrinsic to moving European defence cooperation onto the EU's agenda at the European Council in Cologne and Helsinki in 1999, culminating in the commitment to a European Security and Defence Policy (ESDP). Much of the agenda at bilateral summits, for instance with German, French, Spanish or Italian counterparts, is taken up with EU issues.

European Commission

In formal terms it is the European Commission that is the initiator of EC legislation, even if it is sometimes specifically invited to do so by the European Council or Council of Ministers. This role as initiator gives the Commission authority, especially in the many areas where the Council decides by QMV. Here, only Commission proposals may be decided by QMV. If they are to be amended, consensus is normally required in the Council, and that is more difficult to achieve. What this means, then, is that if one's ideas and interests can be insinuated into the Commission's proposals there is a good chance of them being influential. But how does this happen, given that the Commission is supposed to be independent of the national governments? The answer lies in the Commission's consultative nature, its scarce informational resources and lobbying.

There are two ways in which national governments may get their ideas across, although there may be 27 states competing at this game as well as numerous interest groups! The more formal channel is through Commission advisory groups, which discuss legislative proposals. As one insider's guide puts it:

> The earlier you get your views across, the more chance you have of influencing the debate, so try to keep abreast of thinking in the Commission on future proposals and the initial preparation of proposals. The meetings of national experts . . . should be taken seriously. You should also build up personal contacts with colleagues from other Member States: these are **absolutely vital**

[bold in original] and should be cultivated whenever possible to help your negotiating effort and also to make the process more enjoyable. (Humphreys 1996: 92)

Here is an opportunity for agenda-setting by national officials, and where networking (and foreign language) skills are valuable. Furthermore, it is important to recognise that the vast majority of these advisory groups are attended by home civil servants rather than diplomats, thus indicating how Europeanisation affects even the most technical of policy areas. Humphreys' guidance for officials working on environmental policy is again instructive, 'The UK position for Commission working groups should be thought through and expressed . . . carefully . . . including tactics and fall-backs.' Reflecting the characteristic Whitehall approach of active information-sharing, he adds that as 'part of the team-working approach UKREP and Legal [the relevant ministry's legal service] should be copied in on notes of meetings and papers on the dossier in general' (Humphreys 1996: 94).

The second way of getting views across is at a slightly later stage in inter-nal Commission deliberations but has to be used sparingly.[4] All proposals are prepared within the so-called services of the Commission, in one of its 23 policy-based directorates-general. At this point the proposal is passed up to the responsible commissioner, who has the job of securing its for-mal adoption in the College of Commissioners. Each commissioner has sworn an oath of allegiance to the EU and is not a national representative; hence the occasional accusation of a British commissioner 'going native'. Each commissioner has a *cabinet* of political advisers who owe their current appointment to the patronage of the respective commissioner (for more, see Donnelly 1993; Ross 1994; 1995).[5] Commissioners can speak on any issue they like at the College, and not just on their own area of respons-ibility. Hence within each commissioner's *cabinet* advisers will take responsibility for monitoring all policy areas alongside the more detailed activities on the commissioner's portfolio. Let us say that a policy proposal is reaching maturity within the College on some aspect of agricultural policy. As part of the build-up to a College decision a meeting is held of the 'special chefs', bringing together from each commissioner's *cabinet* the political adviser who is responsible for agriculture, and chaired by an adviser from the agriculture commissioner's *cabinet*. At this point it is pos-sible for the UK commissioner's agricultural 'special chef' to intervene, just as – at the level of the College – it is possible for the UK commissioner to do so. This potential policy veto-point has been utilised by those member states which are efficiently organised and well coordinated, and the UK is well-placed on these criteria. Lobbying of the *cabinets* of the UK commis-sioner has become part of the policy process, and is normally undertaken by UKREP officials. On a highly politicised issue such as the EU's decision in 1996 to place a beef-export ban on the UK, the *cabinets* of the then UK commissioners Neil Kinnock and Sir Leon Brittan, were regarded as important channels for trying to head off adverse policy proposals.[6] As decisions in the College are adopted by simple majority amongst the commissioners, success is by no means assured but does not prevent the effort being made!

This second, unofficial, channel – of utilising national contacts in the British commissioner's *cabinet* – is mostly used to try and block unwelcome proposals, since it is rather late to shape them positively. 'Cabinets and commissioners can insist on substantial changes to proposals or even return them to DGs for complete revision' (Humphreys 1996: 94). This method of influence, often under-explored in the academic literature, has its own unwritten rules; for instance, ministers contact commissioners, whereas officials contact those in the Commission services or in the *cabinet* (Humphreys 1996: 20).

There is one other way that the national card may be played, and that is through the strategic placing of British personnel in the Commission. One example is through seeking to secure a Commission portfolio of strategic value to the UK. Examples include achieving the appointment of Lord Cockfield, a former trade minister in the Thatcher government, to the single market portfolio in the aftermath of the 1985 decision to prioritise that goal (see Cockfield 1994) or Christopher Tugendhat's tenure as commissioner responsible for the budget during Mrs Thatcher's efforts to secure a re-negotiation of British contributions. There is no guarantee of this strategy succeeding because one or two commissioners can achieve little without the assent of the College as a whole. Moreover, the scope for such action has been reduced by two developments: the greater autonomy given to the Commission president to assign portfolios; and the reduction in the number of UK-nominated commissioners (from two to one) as of 2005 following the Nice Treaty reforms. Nevertheless, Tony Blair would doubtless have lobbied for a key portfolio, and Peter Mandelson's external trade responsibility is one of the key areas of EU competence. The practise of *parachutage* is the counterpart at official level. It relates to the parachuting of appointees into senior positions contrary to the usual route whereby officials work up the grades. *Parachutage* can have a distinct nationality dimension: to increase national representationat top level, or to secure a particular appointment (see Page 1997; Stevens and Stevens 2001: 83–7).

Lobbying the Commission through these different routes is an important part of the 'projection' function of UK central government. Given the multinational nature of the Commission's senior officials, UK civil servants may find it useful to cultivate contacts in Brussels in order to understand the best channels for lobbying. The relationship between UK officials and the Commission is not confined to this kind of lobbying. The Commission administers a number of areas of policy through detailed regulation that does not need ratification in the Council, such as the CAP, competition and trade policy. In many of these areas the Commission is again reliant on national officials. The resultant work – known as comitology (see Hayes-Renshaw and Wallace 2006: 196–7; Docksey and Williams 1994) – may bring together the same people to deal with a specific policy issue as had been brought together in an advisory committee at an earlier stage. However, in comitology administrative decisions are being taken, so UK officials have to ensure the 'right' decision is made at this stage. As Hayes-Renshaw and Wallace (2006: 196) note, 'In 2003, there were 1,024 meetings of comitology committees, delivering 2,981 opinions, and the Commission adopted 2,768 implementing measures in its 256 comitology committees.'

The Commission also acts as guardian of the treaties, making sure that the member states are putting EC law into practice. Specifically, there are three tasks for national governments: to ensure that EC legislation is transposed into national law (as needed in the case of EC legislation by directive); to notify to the Commission that transposition has occurred; and, thirdly, to ensure the legislation is properly implemented. Within Whitehall these tasks have numerous implications, such as introducing any necessary domestic legislation before parliament, promulgating statutory instruments or overseeing the implementation of policy by central government agencies or local authorities. Transposition and implementation may be further complicated by the need for different arrangements in different jurisdictions: England/Wales, Scotland (including Scots law), Northern Ireland and, in some cases, Gibraltar.

Civil servants in the UK are charged with responsibility for ensuring compliance or, failing that, for the subsequent process, namely action under Article 226 of the EC Treaty. A three-stage process may follow: a letter of inquiry from the Commission; followed by a reasoned opinion from the Commission legal service; and, finally, full reference to the European Court of Justice. At each of the first two stages the government may opt to secure proper implementation. All British governments have encouraged the proper transposition and implementation of EC law, and its record on infraction proceedings is generally the best of the large states (see data in Mittag and Wessels 2003: 438). As Humphreys notes, this is 'a record which ministers take very seriously' (1996: 115). Ultimately, failure to transpose or implement correctly can result in the government being fined. On this provision Humphreys notes: 'It is a key UK objective that this provision is not used against us' (1996: 123).

The European Commission is a supranational actor, and we certainly do not wish to give the impression here that it is somehow merely the tool of member governments. Its authority is at its greatest for EC (Pillar One) business. The Commission is a key part of the policy-making machinery that Whitehall cannot neglect. Indeed, the government also has an interest – institutionalised in the Cabinet Office's European Union Staffing Branch (see Chapter 5) – in securing high-quality UK recruits as permanent officials and in encouraging high-flyers to take a temporary posting or that of a detached national expert (DNE) (on which, see Stevens and Stevens 2001: 19–22). Whitehall may indeed seek to 'cultivate' Brits who hold permanent posts in Brussels at a later stage, although some are understandably resistant to such approaches.

The Council of Ministers

The main institutional structure with which ministers and civil servants interact is the Council hierarchy (see Figure 3.1). At its apex is the European Council. Beneath is the Council of Ministers proper, whose business was rationalised at the 2002 Seville European Council into nine different formations.[7] However, several of these formations are umbrella terms; for instance, the General Affairs and External Relations Council (GAERC) would most likely be attended by the Foreign Secretary but the agenda might conceivably entail attendance by a UK minister with responsibility for trade, development aid or even defence. There then follows the top level of preparatory bodies, the Committee of Permanent Representatives (COREPER). At middle level is a set of functionally specific committees, such as the Special Committee on Agriculture or the increasingly important Political and Security Committee (COPS). At the bottom level is an array of Council working groups, of which there are some 250 (Hayes-Renshaw and Wallace 2006: 72). At all levels meetings are composed of member government delegates, but with the Commission also represented. Also present are representatives of the Council Secretariat to oversee the smooth conduct of business, including through distribution of papers, recording the minutes and offering legal advice. The chairing of meetings and a number of other functions like representing the Council before the European Parliament are assured by the country holding the six-month presidency of the Council, a task which fell to the UK government in the first semester of 1998 and the second semester of 2005.[8]

The Council of Ministers is responsible for taking decisions (subject to the applicable procedural interaction with the EP). Although there are nine formations of the Council, bringing together all functional Whitehall departments, the Council is officially a single body and thus any business can be signed off by any formation.[9] Its business tends to be divided into those matters where it rubber-stamps agreement reached lower down the hierarchy, so-called 'A' points, and those dossiers where ministers need to thrash out agreement, 'B' points (Hayes-Renshaw and Wallace 2006: 52). A national delegation is typically comprised of a minister, a senior diplomat from the UK Permanent Representation, such as the ambassador or the deputy ambassador, and a senior home-based official from the lead Department in Whitehall. There are typically three other seats in a second row for more junior officials, e.g. a desk officer from UK Permanent Representation to the EU (UKREP) (Humphreys 1996: 9). Given that the agenda might be quite mixed, other officials may sit in a kind of overflow

Figure 3.1 The Council of the European Union: key components

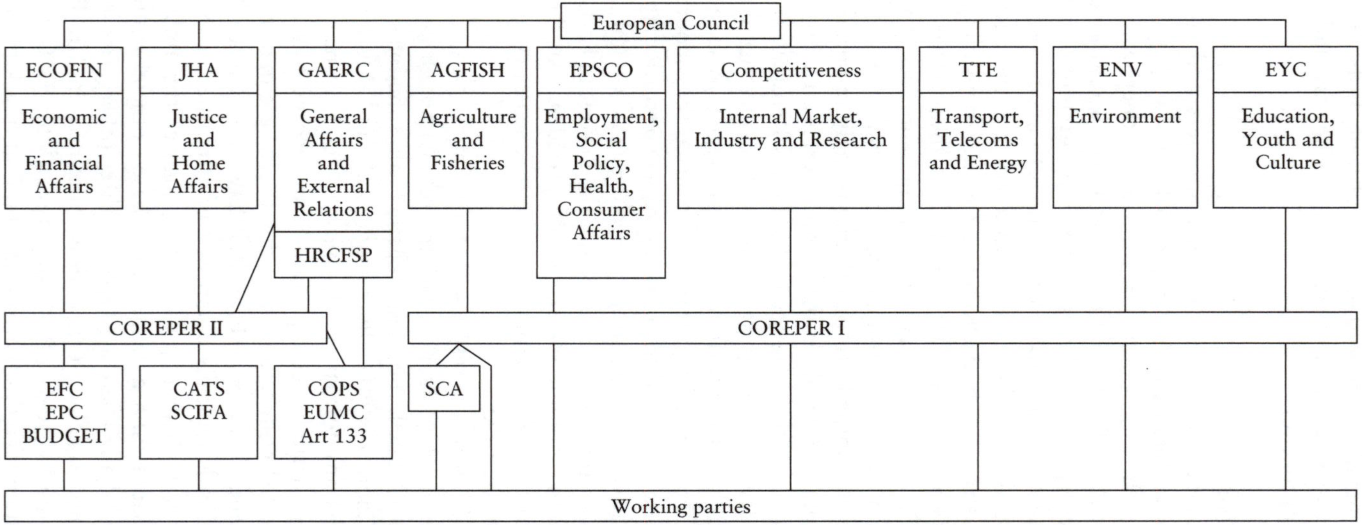

Key: Art 133: Article 133 Committee; BUDGET: Budget Committee; CATS: Art 36 Committee; COPS: Political and Security Committee; COREPER: Committee of Permanent Representatives; EFC: Economic and Financial Committee; EPC: Economic Policy Committee; EUMC: EU Military Committee; HRCFSP: High Representative for the Common Foreign and Security Policy; SCA: Special Committee on Agriculture; SCIFA:Strategic Committee on Immigration, Frontiers and Asylum.

Source: Adapted and simplified from Table 3.1 in Hayes-Renshaw and Wallace (2006, 71).

room, the *salle d'écoute*, where they can follow proceedings until they replace another delegation member. The composition can become complicated, for instance if a Scottish minister is also in attendance (see Chapter 7). The formations of the Council that have met most regularly over the past, namely approximately monthly, have been: General Affairs (foreign ministers), Agriculture and Ecofin (Economics and Finance). Over twenty different formations have met over the years (see Table 3.2). Following the consolidation into nine formations, and with the development of CFSP and ESDP, GAERC has become the dominant one (see Table 3.3).

Table 3.2 List of formations of the Council (1993–98), and their frequency of meetings

Formation	1993	1998	Total 1993–98	N/year (1993–98)
Agriculture	11	12	68	11.3
Budget	2	3	13	2.2
Civil Protection	–	–	2	0.3
Consumer Affairs	2	2	12	2.0
Culture and Audiovisual	2	2	13	2.2
Development	2	2	13	2.2
Econfin (Econ./Finance Ministers)	11	14	63	10.5
Education	2	1	11	1.8
Energy	2	2	14	2.3
Environment	5	4	25	4.2
Fisheries	5	4	26	4.3
General Affairs (Foreign Ministers)	19	14	90	15
Health	2	2	13	2.2
Industry	5	2	20	3.3
Internal Market	6	5	22	3.7
Justice and Home Affairs	1	4	18	3.0
Others or Joint Sessions	3	3	9	1.5
Research	5	4	21	3.5
Social Affairs	4	5	26	4.3
Telecommunications	3	3	18	3.0
Tourism	–	–	2	0.3
Transport	4	4	24	4.0
Youth	–	1	5	0.8
As Heads of State/Government	–	1	1	–
Total	96[a]	94	529	88.2

Note: [a] The number of formations was reduced in 2002 (see Figure 3.1 and Table 3.3).
Source: Data supplied by Council Secretariat, January 1999.

Table 3.3 Council formations and meetings (2006)

Formation	No. of meetings in 2006
General Affairs and External Relations	22
Economic and Financial Affairs	11
Justice and Home Affairs	6
Employment, Social Policy and Consumer Affairs	3 (+ 1 extraordinary)
Competitiveness (Internal Market, Industry and Research)	5
Transport, Telecommunications and Energy	6
Agriculture and Fisheries	11
Environment	4
Education, Youth and Culture	3
European Council[a]	1
Total meetings	72

Note: [a] If the European Council makes legal decisions, which it does very occasionally, it is considered to be a formation of the Council, meeting as Heads of State or Government.
Source: *Bulletin of the European Union*, 2006.

Much of the preparatory work for the Council is conducted in COREPER, in so-called senior or Council committees or in more specialised working groups (see Figure 3.1). COREPER meets in two formations: I and II. COREPER II consists of the ambassadors, i.e. the British Permanent Representative and his counterparts. It is responsible for preparing the General Affairs and External Relations Council, the Ecofin Council, the Justice and Home Affairs Council and the European Council. COREPER I consists of deputy ambassadors and deals with the other Councils. COREPER meetings are not attended by UK-based officials. At the next level there are various specialised senior or coordinating committees. The Special Committee on Agriculture (SCA) prepares agricultural business (but *not* fisheries) for the 'AGFISH' Council. The Political and Security Committee (COPS) is a very important coordinating body at the heart of foreign, security and defence policy and is attended by a senior official from each permanent representation, by the High Representative for CFSP, currently Javier Solana, as well as Commission delegates (often Commissioners). COPS meets twice per week. Where ESDP matters are discussed, the chair of the European Union Military Committee may attend. This committee comprises the Chiefs of Defence of each member state (for full details see Hayes-Renshaw and Wallace 2006: 82–6). Amongst other specialised functional committees at the next tier are the Article 133 Committee (trade policy), the Economic and Financial Committee and two Justice and Home Affairs committees: the Strategic Committee on Immigration Frontiers and Asylum (SCIFA), which deals with home affairs business located in Pillar One of the Treaty and the Article 36 Committee (whose acronym is CATS), which deals with police and judicial cooperation located in Pillar Three. At the lowest level are the Council working parties, of which there were 162 in 2005, with 121 sub-groups (Hayes-Renshaw and Wallace 2006: 70). Working parties are attended either by attachés from the permanent representations or by UK-based officials. Because there are so many working groups it follows that it is at this official level that the bulk of UK negotiating takes place in the EU. Working parties, the coordinating committees and then COREPER form a pyramid seeking to provide agreement ahead of the Council itself. By the time of a COREPER meeting policy should be readied for either decision or for thrashing out politically.

Council decisions can take various forms. In the EC pillar they can take different legal forms – Regulations, Directives and Decisions – but they can also be non-binding in legal terms, i.e. political decisions. In the CFSP and police and judicial cooperation pillars decisions are almost invariably in this last category because EC law is not normally utilised. The decisions can be arrived at in different ways. In the EC pillar QMV is available on many policy issues, although it is not always used.[10] However, unanimity is the norm on most business in the other two pillars. QMV and unanimity have different implications for national delegations. Under QMV there is no facility to rely on a national veto, so ministerial and official negotiators need to think carefully about alliances with other governments to push through a majority or in order to form a blocking minority. Sometimes outright opposition is the only politically acceptable position for a government. However, where such a principled form of opposition is not needed, the best strategy may be at the 'tipping point'. There, the delegation may be able to secure important concessions in return for moving to facilitate the formation of a pro-agreement majority. As Humphreys puts it: 'Those in outright opposition will be discounted: those firmly inside the majority will be taken for granted; those in-between will be courted and offered concessions to come aboard' (1996: 105). Depending on the dossier, therefore, the delegation 'must weigh up the options, make a firm choice of strategy, but remain ready to change it (but not too often: those who keep changing tack will be abandoned by other delegations as too unreliable to do deals with) (Humphreys 1996: 106). Where unanimity applies, the delegation can 'play harder to get' but excessive use of this approach through 'Canute-like' tactics may create ill-feeling over the longer term and damage European diplomacy on unrelated dossiers, as occurred most evidently during the Major government's policy of non-cooperation during 1996 (Westlake 1997).

We have outlined the principal forms of intergovernmental meetings within the Council hierarchy. However, two others are worth a brief mention.

First, there are meetings of Intergovernmental Conferences (IGCs), held inter-mittently since 1985 ahead of treaty reform. These meetings spawn their own hierarchy of preparatory committees (see McDonagh 1998; Galloway 2001: 34). Since the subject matter is wide-ranging they require more inten-sive preparation, from right across national governments.[11] Secondly, there has been a growth of informal Council sessions where ministers meet in 'awayday' mode, eschewing legal decisions in favour of more abstract dis-cussion. These meetings require a smaller negotiating team as a consequence, and the minister has a much greater chance to make a personal input into discussions if s/he is willing to seize the opportunity and feels comfortable about the situation. The meetings are always held in the country holding the presidency and participation is, according to Humphreys (1996: 11) 'limited to one or two policy officials expert in the theme of the informal; one or two coordinators; the UKREP attachés; and the Private Secretary to the Minister'.

The presidency of the Council rotates between member governments every six months (until ratification of the Reform Treaty triggers new arrange-ments). The presidency deserves mention because the incumbent state takes on additional functions: business manager in the Council; promoter of initiatives; package-broker; liaison point; and collective representative of the EU externally (e.g. in EU summits with the USA, Russia and China) and in inter-institutional negotiations (Hayes-Renshaw and Wallace 1997: 139–50; Westlake and Galloway 2004: 334–6). These functions impose huge additional burdens upon the state concerned, but especially smaller ones. Another burden is that ministerial representation may be doubled, with one minister acting as chair of the meeting and the other carrying out the normal representational duties. Since 2002 there has been an effort to create a multi-annual programming of Council activities, placing some limitations upon the scope for individual presidencies to influence the agenda.

The European Parliament

The European Parliament has significantly increased its influence in EU policy-making since the 1980s. This increase has come overwhelmingly in the EC pillar of activities, where it has become a co-legislator. The EP's links with individual national governments are weak: it is only when a government holds the presidency that its representatives may be called to account (or to conciliation over legislation), albeit on behalf of the Council. Nevertheless, the permanent representations are well aware of the fact that it may be advantageous to keep MEPs from 'their' national delegation informed of the government's viewpoint. Within UKREP one desk officer is responsible for liaison with the EP. Cabinet Office guidance reportedly *requires* officials to provide written briefing to MEPs on all Commission proposals (Humphreys 1996: 106). Separately, party-political channels may also be employed to try to influence MEPs to follow a particular line.

Under the Blair government certain Labour MEPs were designated as 'links' to Whitehall on specific policy issues.

Other policy-making institutions
The Economic and Social Committee and the Committee of the Regions are also made up of national delegations. Although nominated by national governments, the members come from a diverse set of backgrounds. This factor combines with the lesser influence of the two institutions to make them of much less interest to national governments for lobbying purposes.

Bilateral relations
We have already alluded to the importance of bilateral relations as supporting measures for developing alliances at EU level. However, it is worth noting that bilateralism is not simply a factor when (prime) ministerial visits are made to another member state. Rather, embassy staff in other member states will have ongoing responsibilities for providing information to London on the development of policy views on the full range of EU activity. Bilateralism adds to the issue-linkage across EU policy areas in placing a premium upon active coordination within member governments.

Norms and culture of EU policy-making
An outline of the EU's institutions can only give a rough idea of how policy-making works in Brussels. First of all, it is necessary to see how it all hangs together, and how members of the UK government (ministers and officials) participate. This joined-up picture is offered in Table 3.4, which shows the different stages from agenda-setting through to infringement procedures for faulty application of the law (also see Jordan and Schout 2006: 50–6). Secondly, the practice of policy-making has its own norms and values, which are unlike the traditionally centralised and non-coalitional patterns characteristic of Whitehall and Westminster. As one senior diplomat in UKREP told us, 'You can be perfectly competent in some parts of Whitehall work and find this [the Brussels context] very uncongenial'.[12] What are the distinctive features about practical negotiating in the EU?

Strong networking skills are needed because these may be decisive in breaking through the formal hierarchies in the EU institutions. Negotiators in Brussels – whether civil servants or ministers – must learn diplomatic skills swiftly. They are needed in order to gather information, to lobby and to secure acceptable decisions. Language skills may help. *Negotiating flexibility is needed.* As the same UKRep diplomat put it:

> You can be a brilliant rhetorician, a brilliant advocate, but if people have some agenda that is not susceptible to your argument, it won't work. So it's that capacity to empathise and to judge by intuition where the mood of a discussion is going to end up that distinguishes the ordinary negotiator from the good negotiator.[13]

Table 3.4 The participation of UK government officials and ministers in the EU policy cycle

Phase / Level	I Agenda-setting	II Policy initiation	III Decision-making			IV Decision implementation		V Control	
			Parliamentary consideration	Decision preparation	Decision-making	Transposition (where by member states)	Implementation (where direct by the Commission)	Execution	Verification and/or sanction
EU level arena or institution	European Council	European Commission: Commissioners, cabinets, directorate-generals advisory committees (ACs)	European Parliament: party groups, committees, individual MEPs	COREPER, coordinating committees, working parties	Council, European Parliament, Commission	Commission supervises calendar	Comitology committees	Commission monitors application of European law	Commission launches infringement proceedings; ultimately European Court of Justice adjudicates
Government participation from UK	Prime minister, foreign secretary, officials, bilateral contacts	Civil servants participate in ACs and may lobby Commission. Ministerial involvement is very selective	Government briefing for UK MEPs	UKREP and Whitehall officials (also occasionally from the 'devolveds'); bilateral intelligence-gathering and exchange	Ministers and officials; bilateral politicking (also occasionally from the 'devolveds')	Member state officials (including from the 'devolveds')	Member state officials	Member state administrations (including 'devolveds')	Legal officials of member state government; national courts

As a former UKREP attaché put it:

> the worst performance I ever saw in a negotiation happened to be where a
> DTI team was negotiating something with the Environment Council and they
> got a worse deal than they were offered by the Commission on the very first
> day of the negotiations because they believed that other member states
> would see the rightness of their position . . . that if they just sat there and
> said their piece . . . everyone would see it their way in the end.[14]

A further consideration is that *the negotiating process has to take second
place to securing the desired policy outcome.*

> One of the big problems of the British approach to the EU is that we are, in
> process terms, very introspective. In other words, we are very obsessed with
> beautiful reports, beautiful writing, beautiful briefs . . . being preoccupied by
> process and not by product . . . A very distinctive characteristic of Whitehall
> is that people's careers and their self-esteem [are] conditioned by their capa-
> city to service the process rather than to produce a product at the end . . .
> Where [this] affects us in negotiations is in nimble footedness because we
> have these massive coordinated briefs . . . and the capacity for any indivi-
> dual to shoot from the hip, or play it by ear, or to go with their instinct is
> not great.[15]

Much of the above commentary from negotiating insiders reinforces the
point made by Jeff Lewis (1998) that the 'hard bargaining' image of
defending national interests in the Council can be misleading. There is also
a 'collective rationality which transcends individual, instrumental rationality'
(Lewis 1998: 499). The whole Council hierarchy is Janus-faced in character:
individual negotiators are promoting a national line but collectively they
are seeking compromise and form part of the EU's administration (Egeberg
et al. 2006).

Conclusion: the imperatives of the EU process

This chapter has set out the EU context which impacts upon British central government in terms of Europeanisation. First, it set out the trajectory
of integration. Secondly, it set out the policy repertoire of the EU. And finally,
it gave an account of the character of EU governance. Each of these facets
of the EU is needed in order to grasp the implications for British central
government. To conclude, what must civil servants and ministers do in
order to adapt to the Europeanisation of their work? We summarise our
conclusions according to the two categories of reception and projection.

Reception
The spreading impact of Europeanisation across Whitehall (and to authorities in Belfast, Cardiff and Edinburgh) has had a number of impacts which
we now summarise.

- The EU has become an important dimension of every department's work. All departments must now 'organise for Europe'. They must organise themselves so as to be able to monitor and respond to developments in Brussels.
- Traditional divisions between international relations and domestic policy have been broken down. Home civil servants dealing with EU business are routinely engaged in negotiations that used to be considered the domain of the diplomatic service. European diplomacy is not the preserve of the FCO or even of a small number of departments; it is pervasive.
- Just as the Heath government deemed it inappropriate to have a Ministry for Europe, so it is also difficult within departments to have one desk dealing with all European business. A small team of, say, environment officials, may be able to advise on broad issues of conducting business in Brussels. However, wildlife issues, airborne pollution, water pollution, environmental impact assessments and so on all require different detailed expertise. The impact within many departments, therefore, is similarly pervasive.
- It is important to recognise that the EU policy process is different from that of the UK. It is not possible to behave in the same way as when putting together a departmental team to pilot legislation through Westminster. The process is multinational and has become much more subject to co-decision with the European Parliament. Agenda-setting cannot be controlled by the UK government, and the timetable of business is controlled by others: the Commission and the Council presidency. Also as Christoph Knill indicates, 'New legislation may necessitate administrative change: new domestic structures, new regulatory processes or new coordination requirements' (2001: 3).
- The important legal dimension must be taken into account, not least because of compliance requirements in different legal systems: England and Wales, Scotland, Northern Ireland, even Gibraltar as well as because of the dynamics of devolution.

Projection
If the response to EU membership is simply one of reception, the experience is likely to be problematic. The EU is an opportunity structure for solving intractable domestic and international policy problems. However, the projection response is obviously conditioned by the politics of the European issue in the UK. Thus, since 1973 UK diplomacy has run the full range from a period of non-cooperation with EU partners during the Conservative government of John Major in 1996, through re-negotiating terms of membership during 1974–75 under two governments headed by Harold Wilson, to an explicit attempt to set the EU agenda under the governments of Tony Blair from 1997.

- An active and successful diplomacy at the agenda-setting, initiation and decisional stages of the process (see Table 3.4) is assisted by pro-active coordination. Supportive bilateral diplomacy with key partners is an important co-requisite.
- Civil servants and ministers must also be able to 'play the EU game' by negotiating in a manner appropriate to securing their political goals at the supranational level. A premium is placed on the acquisition of key skills by home civil servants and diplomats alike. The most important skills are a practical understanding of how the EU works and an ability to 'network' with other policy-making participants. European training needs to be taken seriously amongst a wide range of senior officials.
- The Westminster 'cockpit' of political debate can also encourage a robustness of approach that is not always appropriate to EU negotiations. Sometimes robustness is needed, for example when Margaret Thatcher was trying to re-negotiate an unfair budgetary system in the early 1980s. However, too much robustness can result in intervention fatigue and allow other national delegations to 'slipstream' behind the UK without incurring any of the negative consequences (Humphreys 1996: 96–7).
- Above all, officials and ministers need to feel 'at home' in Brussels (or Luxembourg). Being there on sufferance is unlikely to be conducive to securing optimal results for the national interest in what is, after all, an extension of the UK policy process.

In sum, the requirements of reception and projection mean that civil servants and ministers need to 'think and act European': not out of a craven attitude to Brussels but because the EU is an integral part of the UK policy process. In the next four chapters attention shifts to the patterns of UK central government's adaptation in response to the developments outlined here. In the next chapter we turn the clock back and explore the UK's initial negotiations for membership of the European Communities, and the emergence of the framework for domestic European policy-making in the subsequent period.

Notes

1 For details of this policy priority, see http://ec.europa.eu/growthandjobs/key/index_en.htm, accessed 3 July 2007.
2 For details on these developments, see the justice and security dossier at www.euractiv.com, accessed 20 February 2005.
3 For broad reviews, see Wallace (2005), Armstrong and Bulmer (1998: 65–89), Humphreys (1996); Wright (1996: 150–3). For detailed institutional information, see Nugent (2006).
4 Excessive use of this tactic would risk undermining the Commission's supranational character.

5 Some, but not all, of the *cabinet* members are from the commissioners' own member state. Typically, UK *cabinet* members have had a European policy responsibility in a Whitehall ministry and may also have served in UKREP. Neil Kinnock's *chef de cabinet* as transport commissioner was Andrew Cahn, formerly a senior official in the Ministry of Agriculture, Fishereies and Food (MAFF) and then number two in the Cabinet Office European Secretariat (COES).

6 Interview, European Commission *cabinet* member, 19 March 1997.

7 This rationalisation was part of an attempt to streamline the Council's work in anticipation of a major expansion of the number of delegations following enlargement (Council of the EU 2002).

8 The presidency arrangements are projected to change if the 2007 Reform Treaty is ratified.

9 Lord Carrington, Foreign Secretary under Mrs Thatcher, is reported as demanding 'Who the hell has put pig-iron on my agenda'? quoted in Hayes-Renshaw and Wallace (2006: 34).

10 For an authoritative account of the nuances on the provision and practice of QMV, see Hayes-Renshaw and Wallace (2006: Chapter 10).

11 The 2004 Constitutional Treaty was prepared using a different procedure entailing a constitutional convention (Norman 2003).

12 Interview, UKREP, 20 March 1997.

13 Interview, UKREP, 20 March 1997.

14 Interview, Department of the Environment, 12 December 1996.

15 Interview, UKREP, 20 March 1997.

4

Approaching Europe: Europeanisation and accession

Introduction

In this chapter we examine adaptation in British central government in the period up to and including accession. We utilise the analytical toolkits of Europeanisation and historical institutionalism as set out in Chapter 2 to focus our empirical detail. Was accession in 1973 the critical juncture in adapting to Europe? That at least would seem to be an initial presumption, since Chapter 3 revealed that European integration had already developed a strong body of legislation and some supranational characteristics by the time the Heath government came to substantive negotiation of accession. By virtue of the UK having stood aside from the process of supranational integration in the 1950s that determined the scope and nature of the EEC (Camps 1964: 507), Europeanisation upon accession would seem the likely consequence.

In examining the adaptation of UK central government, we shall argue that Whitehall's adaptation to Europe began well before UK accession. In fact it was in the 1960s that the institutional forms and many of the practices and values which still apply today were established in line with traditional Whitehall ways. Thus in order to understand the present situation it is essential to delve back into this earlier history. In this chapter Whitehall's adaptation is charted from its beginnings in the 1950s through to full British membership in 1973. Four periods are considered: 1957–61, when the Conservative government made the policy shift culminating in the first application for membership; the first round of membership negotiations (1961–63); the second application (1966–69); the resumption of negotiations during the period 1969–71; and the period of preparation for accession (1971–73). A further section of the chapter utilises the five dimensions of institutional change, as set out in Chapter 2, in order to establish when any critical junctures occurred. The story is not just one of critical junctures, as we shall see considerable continuity in the patterns of British central government. In essence, the requisites of EC/EU membership were accommodated within the institutional logic of British central government and Whitehall rather than through making a conscious attempt to adapt Whitehall to Europe. This pattern of adaptation, overshadowed as it was by the political controversy associated with accession, set the tone for much of the subsequent period.

The big policy shift (1957–61)

The antecedents of the European policy machinery in Whitehall can be traced back to the year the Treaties of Rome were signed in 1957, and are inextricably linked with the change of policy leading to the first application for membership. The key institutional players in central government began to emerge at this time. The initial Whitehall European network was thus drawn from those ministries affected by the policies of the EEC and potentially involved in the European Free Trade Association (EFTA), an organisation which the UK advocated as an alternative, purely economic, grouping of western European states. Even leaving aside the question of whether EFTA could be seen as an agent of Europeanisation, the fact was that government departments were already affected by the European Communities prior to accession.[1] However, the impact at this stage was confined to reception, for there existed no opportunity for projecting views in the machinery of the EC until accession negotiations began. The departments involved were the Treasury and the Board of Trade (BoT), the Foreign Office (FO), Ministry of Agriculture (MAG), the Commonwealth Relations Office (CRO) and the Colonial Office.

At this point no department had a lead responsibility on the broad issue of European relations – a task which might have been expected to fall within the ambit of the FO. In fact, the Treasury was arguably the key player. Its importance derived from its centrality in two key respects: first, for coordinating economic issues across Whitehall and, secondly, from the characteristic British perception of European Community membership as an economic issue rather than a political one. The BoT was the key player in negotiations on EFTA, whereas the FO was on the sidelines. And it was the BoT which was largely responsible for UK participation in the Spaak committee which was set up following the 1955 Messina conference and led to the creation of the EEC. Indeed, as noted in Chapter 1, the Spaak committee meetings were attended, not by a minister, but by an official, Russell Bretherton, an Under Secretary from the BoT, who was under instructions to 'cooperate but avoid all commitments' and withdrew from the meetings in November 1955 (Denman 1996: 198; Young 1998: 88–91).

The emerging network of departments and positions was complemented by the development of a process for handling European business above the level of individual ministries. In typical Whitehall fashion a three-tiered structure of cross-departmental committees was developed, the antecedents of which can be traced back to January 1957.[2] The lower two tiers were made up of committees of officials: one at the Deputy Secretary level and below, dealing with matters of detail; and one at a higher level, dealing with broader matters of strategy and policy. These committees were co-ordinated by the Treasury and chaired by its officials. On the top tier was the European Economic Association Committee (EQ), a ministerial committee chaired by the Prime Minister (Treasury 1966: 75; Tratt 1996: 42–3, 61, 69 and Appendix III). It considered submissions drawn through from the official levels.

It was within the top level official committee, under the chairmanship of Sir Frank Lee, Joint Permanent Secretary to the Treasury, that the alteration in Britain's position in relation to Europe began to take place (Camps 1964: 280; Charlton 1983: 228–55). This committee, and especially its chairman, in reviewing Britain's relations with Europe between March and May 1960 managed to shift the terms of the debate away from seeking closer relations between EFTA and the EEC towards effectively seeking direct EEC membership (Tratt 1996: 91–100; Young 1998: 120). These moves were also accompanied by some departmental re-organisation, notably, in early 1960, the FO's European Economic Organisations Department was established, so that, for the first time, there was a section dealing with the EEC (Tratt 1996: 9 and 147).[3] This development assisted a change in the disposition of opinion in the Foreign Office and gave the issue more of a foreign policy perspective than had previously been the case.

Once Prime Minister Harold Macmillan was persuaded of the case for membership (Griffiths 1997: 48) he brought the matter to cabinet in July 1960 but failed to carry it through, though colleagues agreed to the commissioning of further studies and soundings (Tratt 1996: 123–7). Following a ministerial re-shuffle, discussion was kept at cabinet committee level until Macmillan was sure of the support of his ministers (Tratt 1996: 168–80; Ludlow 1997: 32–3, 37–8). Then, in April 1961, the cabinet endorsed the decision to apply for British membership of the European Communities. The problems over reaching this decision illustrate the deeply divisive nature of the European issue and the extent to which a degree of political manoeuvring was from the very start needed to see it through. What is also clear at this early stage is that two key aspects of the machinery for handling European issues had already emerged: a network of key players and a policy process centring on a hierarchy of cabinet committees. Both developments were wholly in keeping with Whitehall traditions. However, they indicated an important shift in the disposition of the machinery so that for the first time lines of communication and advice more favourable to a positive EEC stance prevailed in British central government.

The first negotiations (1961–63)

With the application for membership on the table the existing machinery was adapted to handle the negotiations during 1961–63. From September 1961, (EQ) was replaced by a smaller ministerial committee, the 'Common Market Negotiations Committee' which was chaired by the Prime Minster for the first two meetings and thereafter by R. A. Butler, the Home Secretary.[4] This committee was at the pinnacle of the whole process, it brought together the ministers directly concerned with the negotiations, and reported to cabinet as and when necessary. Again this was wholly in keeping with established Whitehall ways of proceeding. Adaptation at this point was, however, more significant than previously. Indeed, we argue that this may be seen as a critical juncture, since the essential components were put in place for coordinating governmental responses to Europeanisation. By seeking to join the EEC the UK government was for the first time actively drawn into the process of Europeanisation. It had moved from the status of observer to that of participant, albeit as a supplicant and not, as yet, a member. This shift in status required that the UK address both the reception/handling and the projection sides of European engagement. Thus it was during the first round of negotiations that the main outline crystallised of what was to become the Whitehall way of addressing Europe. As one key player put it to us, what emerged in 1961–63 'was the model T version of the Rolls Royce which one has today'.[5]

On the projection side what was required, for the very first time, was a mechanism to put the British case in the EC. This requirement was fulfilled through the arrangements made for the negotiations from which a number of features of the modern machinery have derived. On the ministerial side the negotiating team was led by Edward Heath (the Lord Privy Seal), who was located in the Foreign Office with a small secretariat of high flying junior officials: Christopher Audland and John Robinson[6] from the FO and Roger Lavelle from the Treasury. The official side was led by Sir Pierson Dixon, Ambassador to France, with Eric Roll from the Ministry of Agriculture as Deputy and a team of Deputy Secretaries from the FO, BoT, Colonial Office and the CRO plus an Under Secretary from the Treasury. The negotiating team were stationed in Brussels on average for three days a week, spending the rest of their time in London (Heath 1998: 212). They were serviced by the FO's representation in Brussels, which had developed from the four-person delegation to the ECSC in Luxembourg, established in 1955, into the UK Delegation (UKDEL) to the Communities in 1958. UKDEL was specially augmented for the negotiations.

On the reception/handling side in Whitehall, Lee chaired an official steering committee (CMN(SC)), composed of Permanent Secretaries, which had oversight of activity and was responsible for considering the major issues of policy and for arranging for reports to be submitted as necessary to ministers. The main body of detailed work, however, was carried out by an official committee (CMN(O)) under the chairmanship of Arnold France, a Third Secretary, who headed a coordination section in the Treasury (Treasury 1966: 4 and 75).[7] Members of the official delegation occasionally attended meetings of both these committees when they were back from sessions in Brussels. Ad hoc meetings were arranged to deal with special items of business. A particular problem was the lack of specialist knowledge in Whitehall on the legal implications of entry. To explore these matters, an expert advisory committee, the Common Market Law Advisory Committee, chaired by the Attorney General, was in operation between January and July 1962. Reporting to it was a committee of officials, chaired by the Treasury Solicitor, which undertook a detailed examination of Community law and its potential impact on government departments (Newman 1997: 121). An official committee, the Common Market Negotiations Official Legal Committee (CMN(O)(L)), was also established, in February 1962, to begin drafting the necessary legislation and a White Paper on the impact of entry on the UK legal and legislative systems (Treasury 1966: 73).[8]

Already the general outline of today's machinery was in place.

- On the projection side, the Whitehall European network and policy-making process had been extended into Brussels and facilitated through the UK's diplomatic representation. Also, the principle had emerged of FO lead on broad institutional and procedural questions, with relevant home departments leading on other matters.
- On the reception/handling side, the policy process had been further clarified. Policy coordination was assured by one ministerial committee and two tiers of official committees; departmental positions were distinguished (the FO coordinated the negotiations, while oversight of coordination within Whitehall lay elsewhere, for the time being in the Treasury); the role of the FO as the main reception point for material from the EEC was established; close involvement of key departments had begun; and the need to draw on legal expertise and advice was recognised.

The second application (1966–69)

After the first attempt to join was vetoed by President de Gaulle in 1963, the machinery fell into abeyance. For specific parts of Whitehall the Europeanisation process continued, as the EU's agricultural and trade policies developed and impacted upon UK interests. No central oversight was needed, however, until the Labour government of Harold Wilson made a further application. Preparations had begun for handling this at official level in May 1966 and by November an 'Official Committee on the Approach to Europe', EUR(O), was established at Deputy Secretary level and reported to a steering committee of permanent secretaries.[9] Once the cabinet agreed to apply for membership in May 1967 a ministerial committee on the approach to Europe, EUR(M), was created, chaired by the Foreign Secretary, to oversee the negotiations and to which the two tiers of official committees, and their sub-committees, related.[10] This development set the precedent that it is the Foreign Secretary who chairs the Ministerial Committee on European policy. The report on the legal implications of entry, that had been formulated in 1962, was updated.

In effect the same structure of machinery as had been used in the previous negotiations was re-activated. The Wilson government, however, made one significant change: it shifted the locus of the machinery and responsibility for policy coordination from the Treasury to the Cabinet Office and set up a European Unit in the latter. This unit prepared papers, serviced the relevant committees, and attempted to pull together the negotiation issues and discussions across central government (Wilson 1974: 495). It was headed by a second permanent secretary, (Sir) William Nield, who had been involved in the earlier negotiations. He chaired the EUR(O) committee while the permanent secretaries' steering group, EUR(S), was chaired by the cabinet secretary, Sir Burke Trend.

The Cabinet Office unit was to prove an important innovation. Its creation partly reflected Wilson's desire to use a 'neutral chairmanship' and to ensure that Cabinet Office and No. 10 'interests are well looked after'.[11] It was also in keeping with a change in the general operation of Whitehall in the late 1960s which involved a decline in the cross-departmental coordination role of the Treasury in favour of the Cabinet Office (Lee 1990; Burch and Holliday 1996: 22). It became the central point of the European network in Whitehall and its creation altered the disposition of European policy-making by enhancing the position of the Prime Minister and his/her advisers in No. 10 and the Cabinet Office.

Arrangements were also made for the negotiating team and the manner in which they would be deployed. Lord Chalfont, Minister of State in the FO, was selected to handle the day-to-day negotiations on the ministerial side with Con O'Neill from the FO[12] as leader of the official delegation and Nield and his unit in place to handle the Whitehall end.[13] It was decided that the negotiating team, consisting at the most senior level of deputy secretaries from the main departments involved (FO, the Commonwealth Office, Treasury, MAFF, Trade, Technology and Customs and Excise), would not be substantially based in Brussels but would go out when required and link into Whitehall through membership of EUR(O) Committee. This contrasted with the conduct of the first round of accession negotiations. However, as in the earlier negotiations, the team was to be backed-up by a small secretariat and the services of UKDEL in Brussels.[14] These arrangements were intended to overcome some of the coordination problems that had arisen between the negotiating team in Brussels and Whitehall in 1961–63

(Treasury 1966: 5; see also Heath 1998: 219–20). They also invested an emphasis in the machinery, which has been maintained, giving primacy to the Whitehall location of the UK European policy process over and above that stretching out to and into Brussels.

Unrelated to European policy, there were also alterations at this time in the distribution of functions between Whitehall departments. Nevertheless, they affected the exact line-up of the key departments concerned with European issues. For example, in August 1966 the Commonwealth Office absorbed the Colonial Office and the amalgamated department was in its turn absorbed by the Foreign Office to form the new Foreign and Commonwealth Office (FCO) (Pollitt 1984: 20). In addition there were some evident impacts of Europe on departmental arrangements. Notable was the development of expertise and specialist sections within the relevant key departments both to monitor what was happening in the EEC and later to prepare for entry. The FO's European Economic Organisations Department, established in 1960,[15] was re-named the European Integration Department in May 1968 when John Robinson became its head (Young 1998: 199). An EEC section was established within the External Relations Group within MAFF in the 1960s.[16] Trade, later the Department of Trade and Industry (DTI), and Customs and Excise also developed specialist sections. These were the early prototypes of the departmental machinery for handling European business (see below, Chapter 6). The key departments had also already begun to develop special divisions to help coordinate EEC matters within their own organisations. Other departments, not so central to European matters, tended to use their external relations sections to keep a watching brief (Stack 1983: 124; Wallace and Wallace 1973: 251, 258). In these ways, the impact of European integration was felt by the UK even as a non-member.

Following parliament's endorsement of the Wilson government's decision to apply, the coordination machinery and negotiating team were fully determined by June 1967, and the principles on which the organisation of the negotiations were to be based had been decided by September. However, negotiations had not even begun when, in November, De Gaulle once more vetoed Britain's application. It was not withdrawn, but remained on the table and was re-activated following De Gaulle's resignation as French President in April 1969.

The second application saw a number of changes but they were detailed, incremental adjustments within the framework that had gelled in the period 1961–63. Coordination of policy was shifted from the Treasury to the Cabinet Office, but this was chiefly a function of changes in Whitehall that were unrelated to European policy. The newly created FCO's position became clearer, with the Foreign Secretary chairing the ministerial committee, EUR(M), and its internal organisation being revised. In sum, these were incremental adjustments along the pathway set earlier.

Renewed negotiations (1969–71)

In December 1969 the EC proposed that negotiations should begin,
though they did not actually commence until mid-1970. Within Whitehall
the coordinating machinery established in 1967 had remained in operation
during the period of suspension, though at a less frenetic level of activity,
in order to review the situation, carry out preparatory work and prepare
texts.[17] Between October 1967 and December 1969, for example, EUR(O)
committee met about once a month and considered 71 papers.[18] Thus the
machinery remained in place based on the 1961 prototype; all that was
required was to activate the team and to begin the negotiations.

The first step was taken in October 1969 when George Thomson was
appointed ministerial head of the negotiating team, with the title of
Chancellor of the Duchy of Lancaster, a seat in cabinet and a position in
the Foreign Office. In April 1970, in line with the procedure agreed in 1967,
the negotiating delegation at official level was appointed under Con
O'Neill.[19] Its key members at Deputy Secretary level were John Robinson,
Head of the European Integration Department in the FCO, Raymond Bell
from the Treasury (who like Robinson had been involved in the 1961–63
negotiations), Freddy Kearns from MAFF and Roy Denman from the BoT
(Denman 1996: 230). Patrick Shovelton from the Ministry of Technology
was also involved on a narrower range of issues centring on coal and steel.[20]
Prior to the commencement of negotiations, following the general election
of June 1970, the Labour government under Harold Wilson was replaced
by a more pro-European Conservative administration under Edward Heath.
The ministerial leadership of the negotiating team and the post of Chancellor
of the Duchy of Lancaster, was given initially to Anthony Barber and a
month later, after Barber's appointment as Chancellor of the Exchequer,
to Geoffrey Rippon. Detailed negotiations began in Brussels in late July.

Of course the change in government led to changes in the designations,
ministerial membership, and the complexion of the key European cabinet
committees,[21] but the basic structure of the process remained the same.
The Ministerial Group on the Approach to Europe was re-designated
AE Committee in June 1970 – still chaired by the Foreign Secretary, now
Sir Alec Douglas-Home. The official group at Deputy Secretary level, the
EUR(O) Committee was re-titled AE(O) and continued to be chaired by
(Sir) William Nield. Most of the detailed preparation of negotiations, however, was drawn together through a new committee, the Working Group
on Europe (WGE). It was chaired by Peter Thornton a Deputy Secretary in
the Cabinet Office European Unit (COEU), who occupied 'a central position
in the work of policy coordination' as he also acted as secretary to the
ministerial committee and attended most of the ministerial negotiations
held in Brussels and Luxembourg (O'Neill 2000: 47). The WGE brought
together key officials from the relevant departments and members of

the negotiating team. It spawned, as the need arose, the occasional sub-committee to deal with highly specialised business; these were either serviced by COEU or the relevant lead department. There was, for example, a sub-committee on the financial and monetary aspects of the negotiations chaired by Sir Frank Figgures from the Treasury (O'Neill 2000: 47). The permanent secretaries under the chair of the Cabinet Secretary would be brought in on occasions, but the line in the formal hierarchy of committees was through WGE to AE(O) then to AE and, if necessary, Cabinet. It was at this point in the development of the machinery, with the marginalising of the permanent secretaries, that the policy shaping process of two tiers of official working committees (necessary to deal with the greater level of detail required for actual negotiations and, later, membership), as survived into the 1990s, finally emerged.

The negotiations themselves had two strands: the negotiations proper and the diplomatic wooing of President Pompidou.[22] The negotiations proper were direct with the Council presidency (see Kitzinger 1973: 81–2), rather than with representatives of the six existing member states as had been the case in 1961–63. The EEC member state delegations held their coordination meetings in advance of the negotiating sessions. As determined in 1967, the negotiation team was based in London and only moved over to Brussels for negotiating sessions. The team briefed themselves in London discussing a particular matter with the relevant officials in a particular department then they negotiated in Brussels and if need be telephoned or telegraphed back. The FCO passed information between Whitehall, Brussels and the capitals of the Six (Wallace and Wallace 1973: 253). An important link in the process of acquiring and transmitting information and providing support for the negotiating team when in Brussels was UKDEL, which had grown to a complement of 29 administrative grade staff (Wallace 1973: 91; Stack 1983: 126). Key amongst them was a group of first secretaries – notably Kenneth Christofas, deputy head (and for a while acting head) of UKDEL for most of the negotiation period, David Hannay, Julian Anderson and Mark Marshall. Coordination of negotiating positions within Whitehall was in the hands of the COEU under Nield and Thornton (O'Neill 2000: 45–6), and managed through the system of official committees already mentioned. Progress on the negotiations was regularly reported to cabinet (Kitzinger 1973: 87). COEU officials also took charge of preparations for accession, beginning the drafting of what was to become the government's formal statement on entry (Cabinet Office 1971) and the preparation of the legislation that would be required to be presented to the UK parliament. This latter task began in 1970 under Sir Charles Sopwith, who was appointed as a Deputy Secretary in the COEU and chaired an official committee of legal experts drawn from across Whitehall.

No matter how well organised and conducted were the formal negotiations, there could be little chance of success if the French president exercised a further veto. Thus the wooing of President Pompidou was critical to the success of the whole exercise. Few at the time felt that, despite De Gaulle's demise, French support was assured and the balance of opinion was that a veto was still likely (Greenwood 1996: 152–3). So, while negotiations continued in Brussels, the British ambassador in Paris, Christopher Soames, and officials from No. 10 concentrated on the Elysée and its occupant, Georges Pompidou. This process of bilateral diplomacy began in March 1971 and was aimed at paving the way for a fruitful summit between Heath and Pompidou. Arrangements for the meeting were made through a series of contacts between Robert Armstrong, Heath's Principal Private Secretary, Ambassador Soames and Michel Jobert, Secretary General of the Elysée. Notably this critical initiative centred on the Prime Minister's office and, while the leaders of the negotiating team knew about it, few others in either the FCO or elsewhere were informed. The outcome of these contacts was a two-day summit between the two leaders, held on 20–21 May, at which Pompidou's reservations about UK entry were set aside (for details of the preparations for, and content of, the talks, see Kitzinger 1973: 113–25; Heath 1998: 363–77).[23]

The negotiations were important in further institutionalising the UK approach to handling Europe. The machinery used in the negotiations directly followed the pattern laid down in 1967 and evolved out of that used in the 1961–63 negotiations. The shift of responsibilities for Whitehall co-ordination to the Cabinet Office had become well established, as was the position of the FCO alongside but in a secondary position. These were changes that had little to do with European integration but derived from changes within Whitehall. Another change was that the whole negotiating exercise was much better coordinated at both ends than had been the case in 1961–63 and the approach to handling and determining business was more Whitehall-based and focused. This reflected lessons drawn from the conduct of the earlier negotiations. The change involved the establishment, in the structure and operation of the machinery, of the principle that Whitehall was the home base: a major conditioning factor affecting the development of the UK position. The negotiating team was there, it settled its position in a Whitehall context and *then* went over to pursue that line in Brussels. There was a change also in the refinement of the machinery with the emergence of a committee to handle an area of policy-making becoming increasingly detailed in substance. Also, the scope of involvement and coordination across Whitehall was more extensive than in the earlier negotiations, largely because the European Communities had extended their own areas of competence and activity. The level of understanding in Whitehall about the EC, its structures and operations was also greater than before. Finally, the pre-history of de Gaulle's vetoes of prior applications made evident that the bilateral relationship with France was of as much importance as the official negotiations themselves with regard to the chances of accession. This was an early indication of how bilateralism is intrinsic to Europeanisation.

Adaptation for entry (June 1971–73)

Once the Heath/Pompidou Summit had cleared the way, the final negotiating sessions took place in Luxembourg between 21 and 23 June 1971 (Denman 1996: 237). They were followed in July by the publication of Britain's terms of entry (Cabinet Office 1971). On 28 October 1971, the House of Commons decided in principle in favour of joining the EC on the terms agreed by a majority of 112 votes. Opinion was split between and within the parties, with the Labour opposition officially voting against alongside 39 rebel Conservatives and 68 Labour MPs defying the party whip and voting in favour (Heath 1998: 380). Prime Minister Edward Heath signed the Treaty of Accession on 22 January 1972 (Maitland 1996: 179). Britain's membership of the EC took effect as of 1 January 1973. This 18-month 'transitional' period provided an opportunity to assess the post-accession form of Whitehall's approach to handling EC matters. Here, therefore, was a critical moment for reviewing how British central government would handle the reception and projection aspects of EU membership.

Preparing for full membership involved three main tasks: detailed preparation and passage of legislation through parliament; turning the agreements reached in the negotiations into the Accession Treaty; and establishment of the machinery to handle relations with the EC. The preparation of legislation, already in hand under the auspices of the COEU, was given added impetus in early 1971 as British entry became more certain. The Solicitor General, Geoffrey Howe, was moved to the Cabinet Office to oversee the drafting of the bill under Geoffrey Rippon who, having completed negotiations for entry, had been moved in September 1971 to the Cabinet Office (from the FCO) to oversee the accession arrangements. The detailed drawing together of the drafting of the bill was in the hands of Howe and senior parliamentary counsel, Sir John Fiennes, who drew on the preparatory work of the legal committee chaired by Sopwith. This committee had envisaged a lengthy bill, but Howe and Fiennes and the officials organising the drafting cut this back to only twelve clauses and four schedules (Howe 1994: 67–8). The bill was kept compact for both drafting and tactical reasons. A short bill was less likely to attract amendment and delaying tactics, for:

> if there had to be a guillotine you only had to have 12 slots, 12 clause stand-by debates and it exposed less surface for the divisions that were undoubtedly there in both parties.[24]

According to Heath a brief bill, being clear in its purpose and implications, 'had the virtue of concentrating parliamentary debate around the really important issues' (Heath 1998: 383). Certainly the bill was hotly contested, though it survived intact going through 105 parliamentary divisions without amendment despite some very small majorities of as few as four or five votes. This experience helped to further underline the divisive nature of the issue, more prosaically, the extent to which membership of the Communities would require substantial legal advice and expertise at the very centre of UK policy formulation, and the extent to which the tactical handling of Parliament had to be a central consideration in the development of European policy. The need to keep an eye on parliamentary and party opinion has been a constant theme of the handling of UK/EU policy ever since.

Drafting the Accession Treaty in detail took place from September 1971 and was centred on UKDEL and a drafting group headed by Ian Sinclair, FCO legal adviser, and David Hannay from the FCO (O'Neill 2000: 43). The task was to turn the agreements reached in the negotiations into treaty language. The group liased closely with Whitehall and the European Commission and Council. The decision was taken that drafts of each of the articles would be widely circulated in Whitehall to a list of about 65 named contact points including all the ministries. This process was operated direct from UKDEL and effectively widened out the development of European policy across Whitehall and ensured that all departments had at least some sense of what membership of the EC implied. It was the first real widening of the network for European policy in Whitehall from the rather small and tightly knit group of personnel in departments that had been most involved in the negotiations. The implications of British entry came as a shock to some. One official who was at the time in UKDEL recalled a letter from one of the more peripheral ministries in European matters.

> They had spotted something that did concern them and they literally wrote – 'I am sorry but this is not acceptable, that is not how we do it here'. They had to be informed that the negotiations had been concluded and all we were doing was translating those agreements into Treaty language: in other words 'shut up!' If they had not caught up with this new development then it was time that they did.[25]

The establishment of the machinery for handling UK–EC relations was determined, at least in outline, by early 1972. Inter-ministerial discussions were held throughout 1971. Deliberate attention was given to where key responsibilities should be located. The critical issues were whether EC matters should be treated as foreign or as domestic policy; whether responsibility should be concentrated in the FCO, be based on a non-departmental minister in the Cabinet Office or be concentrated in a single agency such as a Ministry for Europe; how much clout should be given to those made responsible for general coordination; and how the UK's Permanent Representation to the Communities should be organised and staffed. That a coordinating mechanism, a committee or agency, was needed was never in doubt, but whether or not it should be under a Foreign Office or a Home Civil Service chair was a matter of concern. Initially opinion within the FCO was divided on this question but after some discussion there was full agreement that the FCO ought not to make claim to the area for at least two reasons. First, because the FCO was not seen by others in Whitehall as impartial: being variously described as having 'an axe to grind', a 'departmental interest' and as 'being soft on foreigners'. It was felt that to put the FCO, or even an FCO official, at the centre of European policy-making would tend to put the department into permanent opposition with all the other Whitehall departments. Secondly, it was recognised that EC issues were not simply matters of foreign policy but were, to a greater extent, domestic matters. In sum, such a move would not be good for Europe in Whitehall and not be good for the FCO. In the words of one who was a minister at the time:

> You risked marginalizing Europe if it was pushed simply into Foreign Office hands. You even risked marginalizing the Foreign Office itself.[26]

Or, according to a senior official:

> it clearly wouldn't have worked with the FO in the lead. The others just didn't trust them . . . The Home departments always suspect the FO of wishing to give way too soon. It couldn't have been the Treasury either because they never want to give away ever . . . so if you wanted a successful negotiation it was necessary to have a central point between the two.[27]

In order to clarify how best to proceed, a thorough assessment of practice in existing member states was undertaken. This examined how they organised their internal government machines to handle EC issues and how they organised their representation to the EC. So far as domestic arrangements were concerned the British were most impressed with the French case and the use of a powerful inter-ministerial coordinating structure linked to the Prime Minister, the Secrétariat General du Comité Interministériel (SGCI) (see Chapter 9). Attention was given to whether, as in France, the coordinating machinery should be highly interventionist, but in the end it was decided that the UK approach should be more pragmatic and less autocratic. The review concluded that established British practice was superior to that of other countries including France. Once the FCO had settled its position internally, the key departments – notably the Cabinet Office, the FCO and the Treasury – seem to have reached an understanding quite easily and there were no significant departmental turf wars.

The notion of a Ministry for Europe was discussed, but was not considered a serious option (Wallace and Wallace 1973: 254). It would have weakened the FCO, hence there was no support from that corner, but also a European ministry would easily be marginalised unless it was given extensive powers over other departments' business – a prospect few were likely to support.

> it would set up conflicts with the departments if there was a Ministry for Europe with the sort of staff that would be required to do that. The only way of doing it was to have . . . the departments responsible for business – Trade or Agriculture or whatever – producing the drafts and having to agree them with the Foreign Office, the Cabinet Office and Permanent Representation before they went to Ministers.[28]

Agreement on all these matters was assisted by a strong steer at an early stage by Prime Minister Heath. He made his views known in a memo in the summer of 1971. He held that there should not be a Ministry for Europe and that departments should think and act European, and set up machinery to achieve this. The Cabinet Office should be responsible for coordinating the overall effort. By early 1972 this approach had been fully accepted and established. In particular, it had been agreed and endorsed by cabinet committee that the Foreign Secretary would be the UK government's representative on the Council of Ministers and would chair a ministerial committee on EC matters which would report to cabinet. The coordination and preparation of policy discussions were to be the responsibility of the COEU through its official committee network. It would have direct access to the Prime Minister, and he to it, though formally it was to relate to the Foreign Secretary as chair of the ministerial committee. The FCO was to maintain responsibility for communications between Whitehall and Brussels and was given responsibility for taking the lead on certain institutional matters relating to the EC; for participation in the newly established (1970), but discrete, foreign policy cooperation machinery linking member states; and for keeping a continuing watching brief on Europe generally.

There was an interim period, until the completion of the passage of the European Communities Bill through Parliament, before these arrangements came fully into place. From February to July 1972 the Chancellor of the Duchy of Lancaster fulfilled most of the Foreign Secretary's functions with regard to the Communities, including attending interim meetings in Brussels and chairing the ministerial committee on Europe, except on major policy issues. Thereafter the system reverted to the prototype outlined in early 1972 so that effectively it was in July that the agreed approach to handling Europe in Whitehall came on stream. Notably it built on what had already emerged piecemeal and in keeping with Whitehall ways over the years since 1961. There were some changes after July but none was significant in the long run. Most noteworthy of these was the appointment in November 1972 of John Davies as 'Minister for Europe'. He took over from Geoffrey Rippon as Chancellor of the Duchy, and was based in the Cabinet Office, but the special title did not indicate an enhancement of powers or an attempt to create a Ministry for Europe.[29]

It was also agreed that the FCO would be responsible for the overall operation of the Office of the UK Permanent Representation (UKREP) to the EC in Brussels and that the position of Permanent Representative should be filled by a Foreign Office diplomat. UKREP was the successor to UKDEL, transformed into its new guise by the end of 1972 with a complement of 36 administrative grade staff. The new UKREP was different from the old UKDEL. It was more of a mini-Whitehall and more high-powered. Its officials would be involved in on-the-spot negotiations in the EC. By contrast, UKDEL's staff were young, most were in their early thirties, and they had the job of 'sweeping up' after the heavyweights, i.e. ministers and top officials, had been and gone. Now that the UK faced entry and the handling of EC business on a day-to-day basis it became clear that what was needed on hand in Brussels was senior representation from the departments, especially the key ones. Hence in the transitional period more senior people were brought in. Heath had also insisted that UKREP should be staffed both by diplomats and officials from Whitehall home departments on the grounds that this would be an 'effective way of propagating a European outlook within departmental culture' (Heath 1998: 394). The practice was established at this point that the Deputy Permanent Representative would be drawn from a Home department, that there would be a senior official from MAFF, with the diplomatic designation 'minister', and counsellors from the DTI to cover trade, from the Treasury to cover financial and economic matters, and from the FCO to deal with the political side.

The transitional period also saw changes in the relevant departments as they prepared for entry. In October 1971 a second European Integration Department was established in the Foreign Office. This took on many of the more detailed tasks of the first European Integration Department and also incorporated the European Communities Information Unit which had been set-up early in 1970 to provide information concerning the negotiations. John Robinson was promoted as head of both departments (O'Neill 2000: 42–3). This structure of two European Communities departments under the command of one director was maintained thereafter. Also MAFF established its Departmental Committee on Europe (DCE) in 1970[30] and it began the task of establishing the Intervention Board for Agricultural Produce which was tasked with administering the UK payments to farmers under the Common Agricultural Policy (CAP). This was created with a staff of 422 and, according to Stack (1983: 131), made MAFF 'the only department to have set up a new offshoot' as a result of entry. The Treasury through its Finance Western Europe and Commercial policy divisions began to establish understandings about the new budget requirements and created a machinery for forecasting net contributions to the EC budget.[31] Beyond this inner core, in the other affected departments the general arrangement was sustained whereby the external relations divisions became the 'point of coordination within each department . . . rather than for separate European Divisions to be created' (Wallace 1973: 92).

Continuity and change: an assessment

We turn now to appraising the patterns of continuity and change in organising for Europe during the period up to 1973. When did critical junctures occur? When did continuity prevail? Was Europeanisation the principal driver of the institutional arrangements that emerged, or was adaptation influenced as much by unrelated domestic reforms? In order to examine these questions we utilise the five dimensions for assessing change that were identified in Chapter 2. In considering the evidence we also utilise the distinction between the reception and projection responses to Europeanisation. Our overall evaluation is threefold. First, we find that the specific machinery for handling European policy was shaped in almost all of its essential features at the time of the first accession negotiations. Secondly, however, the constitutional implications of joining the EC in 1973 were significant and the consequences for the machinery were important, since it had to be deployed differently once the UK had acceded. Thirdly, these constitutional implications were played down by the Heath government owing to the finely balanced politics of passing the European Communities Bill. We treat each of these three findings in turn.

We have argued that the outline of the mechanisms of organising for Europe within Whitehall gelled at the time of the first application, 1961–63. To be sure, there was no *system* change, since the constitution and the basic principles of the state's organisation remained unchanged at this stage. However, some of the basic *organisations* did change. Oversight of policy coordination was assigned to a home ministry, at this stage the Treasury, and with accountability via cabinet to the prime minister. This set the UK apart from those states which have coordinated policy from within their foreign ministry (see Kassim 2005: 296). The Foreign Office was in charge of the negotiations and diplomacy but only after preparations had been undertaken elsewhere. At the level of *process* the accession negotiations were prepared within a three-tier cabinet-based committee structure: an arrangement that lasted until the late 1990s, at which point a new style of management and the advent of email and video-conferencing contributed to the development of a less formalised system. The need for special organisational arrangements on the legal front was also well recognised at this early stage. In terms of changes in *regulations* there was little by way of formal rules or guidelines. However, the Treasury was vested with the strategic capacity on the issue by providing the supporting secretariat for the cabinet committee. The main *cultural* change derived from the decision to apply for membership, and the recognition amongst the negotiating team and its coordinating committees that this was the policy goal. Apart from that, business was conducted according to the existing practices of Whitehall. From this evidence we conclude that the period 1961–63 represented a critical juncture in organising for Europe.

The second application witnessed only minor change, mainly in *organisations*. The Cabinet Office European Unit took over the functions previously performed by the Treasury and the Foreign Secretary took over the chairing of the ministerial committee. Otherwise the changes simply represented refinements of what had gone before, re-badging of committees and so on. The emergence of the COEU was itself prompted by changes in the practices of Whitehall rather than arising from European prompting. We regard none of the changes from the period 1966–69 as going beyond incremental development along the pathway established in 1961–63. What happens at this stage is attributable to sources of change other than Europeanisation.

The period of negotiation (from 1969 to 1971) also followed this pathway, again with detailed changes, such as the appointment of Geoffrey Rippon, as Chancellor of the Duchy of Lancaster, to lead the negotiations. Committees had again been re-labelled, but simply in accordance with the practices of Whitehall. UKDEL's role was further refined. The most striking change was the need to integrate the French embassy into negotiations because of the importance of establishing agreement between Heath and Pompidou. Although the need to reach agreement with France was of paramount importance and of special significance in light of the pre-history of de Gaulle's vetoes, this effort to integrate bilateral diplomacy with European diplomacy did not find any significant, continuing impact on the organisation of EU policy-making after accession. More recently, however, it has come to be recognised as a key aspect of EC/EU diplomacy. Under the Blair government bilateral diplomacy and EU diplomacy were merged through re-structuring the FCO's internal organisation (see Chapter 5).

The period of accession (1971–73) and accession itself brought about changes, and in this context a more nuanced explanation is required. We also include in Box 4.1 the (slightly contrasting) observations of one of the negotiators, whose diplomatic career included European postings at all levels.[32] From our vantage point we consider first of all the impact of accession on the specific European policy machinery and then consider the much wider context within which that is located. The amount of change that accession brought about in the machinery itself was quite limited. The main change in *organisation* was to the machinery for projecting British policy in Brussels. UKDEL's role during accession negotiations had been very much a supporting one. Upon accession the role of its successor, UKREP, became much greater. As one senior diplomat tasked with the transition remarked: 'We needed a different structure'.[33] Its own organisation had to be re-shaped, and it became a mini-Whitehall in its own right even if, like UKDEL, it remained part of the FCO's management structure. This

---

Box 4.1 The impact of accession from a practitioner perspective

'I think there was an enormous sea change on the day we joined the Community. I think that up until that moment . . . the negotiations were a top priority of the British government of the day . . . They were directed by the Prime Minister personally with very strong involvement of a number of the key ministers in the key departments. But it was run as a very tightly knit, quite secretive operation, in the sense that a lot of work was done which was not shared more widely in Whitehall and, of course, we were not involved in the day-to-day negotiation of Community business . . . The fact was that the negotiating accession operation was a finite, extremely high pressure, high-powered politically, endeavour. Which was quite different from life in the European Community which started on 1 January 1973. The switch from the one to the other was not entirely easy because at that point you had to simply involve every single government department whose area of policy was being discussed in the European Union and to start to coordinate them. But the pace became much slower: it became the pace of European Community decision-making and it was not directed to a single finite purpose, getting Britain in the European Community. So there was, I think, a very big change actually.'

Source: Interview, senior diplomat and former head of UKREP, 28 November 1996.

---

development reflected the fundamental change in its function. As illustration, its top three officials – the Permanent Representative, the Deputy, and the agricultural counsellor – were policy negotiators with key roles in, respectively, COREPER II, COREPER I and the Special Committee on Agriculture. In functional terms it had become a key complement, rather than a subordinate, to the Cabinet Office machinery.

In terms of *regulations*, accession also brought some change. Rules, guidelines and operating practices had to be put into place for dealing with the reality of negotiation within the EC: both across government and within departments. Cabinet Office Guidance Notes and procedures for keeping parliament informed of EC developments were two types of example and very much in keeping with Whitehall practice. In terms of *process* an important new mechanism for preparing the UK's diplomacy in the EC was set up upon accession. This was a weekly meeting held in the COEU and bringing together the core ministries along with any others affected by impending negotiations. It was decided to have the Permanent Representative attend this meeting. What is now called the Friday meeting[34] came into operation as a key process in UK European diplomacy. Except that initially it took place on a Wednesday, with Sir Michael Palliser, the first

Ambassador and Permanent Representative to the EC, returning to London for the day.[35] This involvement of the Permanent Representative in the Whitehall coordinating machinery was also reflected in his appointment as an ex officio member of the cabinet committee. What we see here is that the Permanent Representative was drawn directly into a process bearing the hallmarks of Whitehall's traditional cabinet-based coordination system. This level of integration was distinctive amongst the member states, and it is a unique feature amongst British ambassadors.

Finally, we turn to *cultural* changes. Prime Minister Heath sought to set the tone through his injunction that all ministries should think and act European. In reality there was no sudden change in culture arising from this injunction. It took time for the new realities to sink in, for experience to accumulate, for training to take effect. In addition, the continuing party-political divisions in the early years made it difficult for officials and diplomats to embrace the EC without jeopardising the party-political neutrality that is integral to the British civil service tradition.

If the changes to the machinery were surprisingly limited in nature, the implications for *system* change were more significant. First, as a member state the UK upon accession lost control over parts of its policy agenda; policy lead was now located in the European institutions. As noted in Chapter 3, the scope of this policy agenda has expanded considerably over subsequent decades, although the UK government's agreement has been necessary at each step along the way. Nevertheless, the act of accession was crucial to the consequences for the UK of that evolution at European level. Secondly, the whole machinery had to re-orient itself to a different set of functions. It was one thing to negotiate accession as an outsider but another to conduct diplomacy as a member state. Hence *system* change was brought about by the penetration of the British policy process upon accession. This penetration derived not only from the treaties and the policy actions of the EC institutions. In addition, important principles had been established within the EC legal system, for instance, the supremacy and direct effect of EC law (Weiler 1991). There were important consequences for sovereignty, which has held an important normative status in the discourse of UK governance. As William Wallace has argued, there is a twofold usage of sovereignty in the UK: external and internal (Wallace 1986). The external dimension is associated with the UK as a world power, with a long tradition of territorial integrity, notably through two world wars. Accession to the EC challenged the traditional nation-state basis for the conduct of UK foreign relations as well as economic management. This challenge was not immediately evident due to the aftermath of the 'empty chair' crisis of 1965, which had been resolved by an informal agreement to take decisions unanimously. As we know with the benefit of hindsight, there was a move away from the unanimity norms of the 1966 Luxembourg Compromise in the late 1980s (see Teasdale 1993). UK parliamentary sovereignty, a separate, domestic norm of governance that can be traced to the English Civil War of the seventeenth century, was also affected significantly. The EC's legal doctrines breached the long-standing principle that no parliament could bind its successors (Steiner 1992: 127–30). In principle, UK legislation could be struck down by the European Court and this duly came about in the subsequent period (see Page 2004). This principle, and other implications for the UK's legal system (or, more accurately, systems), did not impact solely upon central government and therefore go beyond the scope of this book. However, it significantly empowered central government in relation to parliament because the former is a participant in European decision-making at the Brussels level, while the latter is not.

Accession was therefore an important break in the Europeanisation of UK central government, even if not for the machinery of dealing with the EC. Indeed, a key development arising from accession was that it broadened the impact of the EC to a wider group of officials than had been involved thus far. Further, in principle it opened up the whole of central government to potential impact from European integration; the extent of the impact was to be determined subsequently in line with decisions of the member governments.[36] However, the perception of the impact of accession was rather mixed at the time. Within the confines of academia there was little work on how governments were affected by European integration and their organisational responses (see Wallace 1973 for a comparative study; Wallace and Wallace 1973 for the UK response). Uwe Kitzinger's account of the UK accession negotiations and the subsequent debate in the country – *Diplomacy and Persuasion* (1973) – displays the importance of the machinery of government to the diplomacy but it did not feature as a theme in the heated debates associated with the ratification process. The impact on central government – other than in discussions about sovereignty – did not feature. And the Heath government sought to downplay the significance of the sovereignty issue. In short, at this decisive stage the Europeanisation of British central government was almost completely out of view. Nevertheless, accession was a critical juncture. It marked a transformation of the overall framework of the UK system of government and in the purpose to which the relevant parts of the machinery of government were now focused: on the dilemmas and pressures of membership rather than the exigencies of entry. However, the machinery itself was wholly in keeping with traditional Whitehall practices so that change in this area, in contrast with change in the framework of governance, was not transformative but incremental and adaptive.

Conclusion: the reception of the Communities in Whitehall

This chapter has revealed that the first systematic response of British central government to European integration emerged at the time of the first, unsuccessful, application for membership during the period 1961–63. This stage, we argue, was the first critical juncture in 'organising for Europe'. The broad outline of the system remained in place in 1973 with accession. Whilst accession changed the functions of the machinery, the extent of institutional innovation was quite small: principally the creation of a weekly meeting to prepare upcoming negotiations. Much of the structure remains recognisable through to the present.

The broad outline of the Whitehall approach to handling EC/EU business can be summarised in institutional terms. The organisational components of the system centred on COEU, the Foreign Office's two European Integration Departments (one external, one concentrating on internal policy) and the office of the UK Permanent Representative in Brussels. Of these the COEU was the most central to the whole system and it was from the very start, unlike other elements in the Cabinet Office, pro-active. It provided advice, convened meetings to discuss issues, was expected to ensure that departments gave full consideration to matters and that government presented a united and coherent position in its dealings with Brussels. The other most involved departments – notably MAFF, DTI and Customs and Excise – had already developed machinery and mechanisms for dealing with EC policy prior to and in the course of the negotiations. The other critical department, the Treasury, had also made some preparations, though to a lesser extent than the others. The key positions at official level had already emerged, forming what was later to be referred to as the troika consisting of the heads of the COEU and the FCO's European Integration Department and the UK's Permanent Representative in Brussels. At ministerial level an important position was held by the Foreign Secretary as chair of the main European Committee, though the exact status of the Cabinet Minister for Europe, as it turned out a temporary creation, was not at this point sorted out. Other ministers and most notably the Prime Minister were also in key positions. These offices and positions formed the nodal points of the network dealing with EU matters: other departments were drawn into this as necessary. This central core was well established at this early point and the whole approach enshrined the established Whitehall practices of balancing light central coordination with a large measure of departmental initiative.

Processes for handling business had also been established – notably the network of cabinet committees, both ministerial and official and in particular the two-tiered system of official committees at Deputy Secretary and lower levels. The contact points for the latter two committees formed the basis of the information distribution system in Whitehall while the material coming from Brussels was channelled through to the FCO from UKREP and then distributed on the relevant nets to the contact persons in Whitehall departments. In effect, even at this early stage, there were two distribution points for material emerging from Brussels: the CO and the

FCO. The need for accommodating legal advice and input had already been acknowledged and the understanding that this needed to be drawn to a central point in the Cabinet Office and through its committees. The procedure had also become well established, especially through the negotiations, that the specialist policy divisions in the relevant department dealt with policy details. Formally speaking, strategic leadership was located in the cabinet or, more precisely, its European committee and in the positions of Foreign Secretary, members of that committee and the Prime Minister, though it remained to be seen if and how such leadership would be exercised. At the official level the small number of key people involved suggested a key role in advising on strategy for the troika and top departmental officials, though again whether and how such power potential might be exploited remained to be seen.

Less development had taken place so far as rules and guidelines were concerned. Here established Whitehall practices applied. Thus the servicing of the European committee net followed traditional practice in the preparation of documents, their distribution and the writing up of minutes, etc. (see Burch and Holliday 1996: 70–7). Other rules relating to confidentiality and secrecy also applied. European business was simply fitted into an already well established corpus of accepted ways of doing things. In general, rules and guidelines specific to the handling of European business had yet to emerge and were to do so in typical Whitehall fashion in line with the development of activities and in relation to particular cases. However, some rules had already been laid down including those covering FCO and home departments' responsibilities for the staffing of key positions. The FCO led on institutional issues while on other issues relevant departments had the lead. In negotiations, on matters of policy detail, the responsible department's line section would lead. The COEU would provide light oversight from the centre and UKREP would supply support for negotiations at EC level. And the COEU, FCO and UKREP, if not already involved, would be kept informed. These guidelines reflected the sentiments expressed in Heath's memo laying down that membership of the EC potentially affected all departments and instructing them to 'think and act European'.

As might be expected developments at the cultural level were the least evident in 1973. The approach to dealing with EC business had to be placed within, and was significantly shaped by, existing Whitehall norms and values about how business should be handled. Two key principles in Whitehall administrative culture were and have proved central to the development of central government's approach to handling EC policy. Both are derived from the convention of collective responsibility: one of the two bed-rock conventions underlying the administrative culture of central government in the UK (see Burch and Holliday 1996: 49–56; Cabinet Office 1997: 6–7). First, the principle of sharing information across and between departments which is a central value of British administration (and one that makes it quite distinct from administration in many other member states). All civil servants are schooled in the practice that material that comes before them that has relevance to any other division in their own department or any other department or agency in central government should usually be copied on. This distribution is determined on the basis of the second principle which can be summed up in the phrase 'the need to know'. This is quite distinct from whether somebody ought to know, for it refers to whether another branch or agency has an interest in the matter. This traditional and established administrative culture of sharing out information if it is necessary to do so is especially pertinent so far as the conduct of European policy is concerned. It is complemented by a further principle derived from the second key convention of British central administration: the individual responsibility of ministers for their departments. This ensures that (1) it is usually the case that only one department or agency will have the lead in Whitehall on a particular area of policy and (2) this lead is clearly distinguished at an early stage in policy development. As we will see these well established principles of Whitehall administrative culture have proved absolutely critical in ensuring a successful expansion and operation of the machinery for handling European matters in Whitehall. In 1973 the creation of an administrative culture regarding Europe per se was hampered by the fact that knowledge of the EC was limited to a small number of officials. Clearly one of the immediate requirements on entry would be to create a larger pool of specialists both to provide the UK contribution to EC institutions and to fulfil the demand that was likely to arise for extra specialist staff in Whitehall. An official estimate during the final round of negotiations in 1971 was that around 500 additional staff would be required in Whitehall prior to entry and a further 1,000 spread over several years thereafter (Wallace and Wallace 1973: 256).

The Europeanisation process began in earnest from 1973, and affected a wider network of civil servants than simply those involved in the *coordination* of UK European policy-making. We argue that the pattern of Europeanisation at this stage had two characteristics. First, due to the contested political climate – soon to become more heated when a Labour government was elected in 1974 with a commitment to re-negotiating membership terms – the posture of British diplomacy in the EC was defensive. Re-negotiating terms of entry, and later seeking reforms to the budget and the CAP, all contributed to this defensive posture. In the absence of launching major initiatives in the EC at this stage, and with the divisive political context, the Europeanisation response in central government was predominantly on the side of *reception* rather than on that of *projection*. Secondly, and consistent with this response, the pattern of Europeanisation was to absorb it as much as possible into the traditional patterns of Whitehall. Thus, in the terminology of Börzel and Risse (2003), *absorption* rather than accommodation or transformation was the order of the day.

In the next three chapters we explore the evolution of central government's response from 1973 in a disaggregated manner, examining first of all adaptation in inter-ministerial networks and in the central departments holding over-arching responsibilities. We then consider more specific functional departments. In doing so, we bring the empirical account up to the end of the Blair governments and establish the key changes over that 34-year period.

Notes

1   This situation finds parallels in other states which acceded to the EU after its foundation. For a comparison, albeit under quite different circumstances, see Klaus Goetz's examination of the impact of the EU upon the ten new member states prior to their accession in 2004 (Goetz 2005).

2   The lower level official committee can be traced back to January 1957 when it was established as the Sub-committee on Closer Economic Association with Europe. In March 1960 it became the European Economic Questions (Official) Committee until, from October 1961 to March 1963, it was transformed into the Common Market Negotiations (Official) Committee (CMN(O)). Throughout its various manifestations this committee was chaired by Arnold France. The upper-level official committee first appeared in December 1958 as the European Economic Questions Official Steering Group which was chaired by Sir Roger Makins (Treasury) until January 1960 and Sir Frank Lee (Treasury) thereafter. In March 1960 this became the Economic Steering (Europe) Committee and from October 1961 to March 1963 the Common Market Negotiations (Steering) CMN(SC) Committee. These committees were chaired by Lee until October 1962. At the ministerial level the Committee on European Economic Association (EQ) was established in October 1959 under the chairmanship of the Prime Minister and from September 1961 to February 1963 this was transformed into the smaller Common Market Negotiations Committee initially chaired by the Prime Minister and thence by the Home Secretary. These ministerial committees had been preceded by a ministerial Committee on the Free Trade Area from March 1957 to October 1959. The critical point is that the committee structure was dealing with the relevant item of policy and was adapted to the EEC question and, later, negotiations as policy changed. Cab 134/1511–17/1520–1544/1546–1547, PRO.

3   Though responsibility for the EEC was also shared with the FO's Western Organisations Department.

4   In the Macmillan government the Home Secretary chaired a number of cabinet committees, and this happened to be one of them.

5   Interview, former member of UKDEL and UKREP, 22 January 1997.

6   The key role of these individuals and especially John Robinson was mentioned by all those interviewed who had a detailed knowledge of Britain's long process of joining the EC. Robinson was First Secretary at UKDEL from 1962 to 1967, Head of the European Integration Department in the FO from 1968 to 1970, and deputy leader of the official negotiating team for UK entry to the Communities From 1970 to 1971. His significant and somewhat

under-appreciated role has been given belated recognition in Hugo Young's, *The Blessed Plot*, 1998.

7 This committee held 147 meetings and considered more than 548 papers during the October 1961 to March 1963 period of its existence, see CAB 134/1520–1544, PRO.

8 The White Paper was not published owing to the failure of the negotiations. Nine White Papers were published on other aspects of the negotiations, see Treasury (1966: 74).

9 Briefing from Cabinet Secretary, Sir Burke Trend, to Prime Minster Harold Wilson, 6 May 1966, PREM 13/905/E(66) 2 and 3, PRO; Memo from Cabinet Secretary to PM, 14 November 1996, PREM 13/1649, PRO.

10 Negotiations with the European Communities, Memo from the Prime Minister, Cabinet Memoranda, 23 May 1967, CAB129/130–C(67)82, PRO.

11 Memo from PM to Foreign Secretary, George Brown, 11 November 1966, PREM 13/898, PRO; and handwritten comment by Prime Minister on memo from William Nield to Michael Palliser, Prime Minister's Office, 26 September 1967, PREM 13/1491, PRO.

12 O'Neill was Deputy Under Secretary in the FO in charge of economic affairs. He had a detailed knowledge of the Communities from his stint as head of UKDEL in Brussels from 1963 to 1965.

13 Cabinet Memoranda, 'Negotiations with the European Communities', memo from the Prime minister, 23 May 1967, CAB 129/130–C(67)82, PRO.

14 Correspondence between Prime Minister and Foreign Secretary, 4 May 1967, PREM 13/1491, PRO; memo from William Nield to Michael Palliser, Prime Minister's Private Secretary (Foreign Affairs), 26 September 1967, PREM 13/1491, PRO.

15 Interview, retired senior director of the FCO, 12 December 1996.

16 Interview, former Head, European Secretariat, 25 September 1997.

17 Including considering the drafts of a White Paper published in early 1970 which assessed the costs and benefits of membership.

18 Cab 134, index, 2822–2825, PRO.

19 Con O'Neill had to be brought back into the FCO in order to head the team. He had resigned from the Department in 1968 – see Young (1998: 198, 224).

20 The Ministry of Technology and the Department of Trade were both absorbed into the new Department of Trade and Industry created in October 1970.

21 For details on the designation of cabinet committees and how these change with a change in Government, see Burch and Holliday (1996: 41–4).

22 We are not concerned here with the issues at stake in the negotiations. For an account of them, see Kitzinger (1973).

23 The key documents from the PRO covering the bilateral diplomacy between Heath's and Pompidou's staff in 1971 are fully displayed on the Margaret Thatcher Foundation website at www.margaretthatcher.org/archive/heath-eec.asp.

24 Interview, former Deputy Head of the European Secretariat, 16 April 1997.

25 Interview, former official in UKDEL and UKREP, 19 March 1997.

26 Interview, Minister in the Heath government, 21 April 1997.

27 Interview, former Head of the European Secretariat, 26 September 1997.

28 Interview, former Head of UKREP, 28 November 1996.

29 Nield left the Cabinet Office to become Permanent Secretary of the new Northern Ireland Office on 17 March 1972. He was succeeded as second permanent secretary in the Cabinet Office and head of COEU by John Hunt who held the post until 1973. At that point he became Cabinet Secretary and was replaced by Patrick Nairne who held the post until 1975.

30 Interview, former Head of the European Secretariat, 25 September 1997.

31 Interview, former senior Treasury and Cabinet Office official, 21 November 1996.

32 Interview, senior diplomat and former head of UKREP, 28 November 1996.

33 Interview, senior UKDEL/UKREP diplomat, 11 December 1996.

34 In Whitehall parlance it is also given the name of the Permanent Representative and the Head of the COES in office at the particular time. Thus, in mid-2006 it was termed the 'Grant/Darroch meeting', as John Grant was the Permanent Representative and Kim Darroch was the Head of the European Secretariat.

35 The first Permanent Representative, Sir Michael Palliser, preferred to have this briefing meeting ahead of the Thursday session of COREPER. Interview with senior UKDEL/UKREP diplomat, 11 December 1996.

36 It should be borne in mind that the impact of the EU did not confine itself to policy but also to procedural issues impacting on the conduct of government, such as later public procurement rules, health and safety requirements, social policy regulation. The regulation of working time, for example, has major implications for the running of the National Health Service.

5

The management of EU business in Whitehall: the hub

The Europeanisation of Whitehall over the period since accession has continued apace. It has built on the institutional framework fully established in 1973. Key trends have been expansion, fragmentation, refinement and these have been coupled with two contrasting trends: centralisation and decentralisation. Expansion has involved a significant increase in the number of participants and departments involved. Fragmentation has taken place as the growth of business has resulted in relatively separate groupings emerging: each dealing with particular areas of business. Refinement has been evident as practices and processes for handling business have become fully established. Centralisation has seen a closer involvement of the core executive on key issues. Decentralisation has taken place on specific issues as departments, territorial ministries and, more recently, devolved administrations have become more involved in the handling of EU policy (on devolution see Bulmer *et al.* 2002; Burch *et al.* 2005; Bulmer *et al.* 2006).

This and the following two chapters sketch out the contemporary features of Whitehall's way of organising for Europe and also how this has emerged. We trace the pattern of Europeanisation since accession in 1973. Chapters 6 and 7 look at the inner and outer cores of the EU policy-making process in Whitehall by concentrating on what happens in departments where the greatest degree of alteration in engagement, activity and administrative capacity has taken place. This chapter concentrates on the three key organisations and the actors connected to them that are responsible for coordinating the handling of EU business above and across departments. These form the hub of the EU policy-making system. Initially, an outline is provided of the contemporary structure and operation of this hub, followed in the second half of the chapter by consideration of the main structural and operational changes to it that have taken place since accession in 1973.

In the UK case it is important to understand that coordination at the hub of government on European matters takes a pro-active form. It is much more than just drawing together proposals emanating from Brussels and ironing out disagreements between departments. Yet a further distinctive feature of the UK approach is that it is not the product of a substantial concentration of staff and mechanisms of detailed oversight and overt control at the core of government. Rather, as noted in Chapter 4, coordination is achieved through the application of traditional tenets of Whitehall culture which emphasise the sharing of information within the system. The significance of central-core actors lies in the fact that they are *expected* to pull together EU policy and positions.

Of course, it is a general steering capacity that is exercised at the hub, as in fact much of the handling of all types of EU business in detail is done in the departments. Requirements for this system to work effectively are that high-salience policy issues which need to engage actors at the hub are fairly evident and that departmental actors do keep others 'in the picture' so that they can judge if and when to intervene. It is when either of these requirements breaks down that the system is in trouble. This lightly endowed machinery for central intervention is often seen as one of the strengths of the UK approach, yet its reliance on departmental information flows is one of its areas of greatest potential weakness. A key issue is whether the growth of business and departmental involvement across the whole of central government has stretched the hub's ability to fulfill all of its tasks and to be adequately aware of what is taking place elsewhere.

The best way to try to understand how EU business is managed across Whitehall is to visualise it as a network with the Cabinet Office European Secretariat (COES) and No. 10 – the Prime Minister's Office – at its heart (see Figure 5.1).[1] The members of this network are engaged in managing the handling of EU business. It is more properly described as a task rather than a policy network in that its members are concerned not simply with policy questions but with managing the whole range of activities affecting Whitehall's reception of EU initiatives, processing of European matters and projection of responses and initiatives back into the EU.[2] It includes not only facilitating the final determination of strategic, high level or contentious EU related policy content, but also facilitating information flows, providing guidance and advice, dealing with matters concerning system-wide staffing and personnel questions (such as placement and training), overseeing the final determination of key negotiating positions, ensuring that legal questions are adequately dealt with, liaising with Parliament over the scrutiny of EU business, dealing with the more contentious EU aspects of the activities of devolved administrations, and assisting in the presentation to the media and the public of the government's broad position on EU matters.

The scope of this network at official level can be defined by the COES's distribution web; in 1997 this consisted of about 130 names including UK embassies in member states. Today it is slightly larger partly because of the increase in member states from 15 to 27.[3] The network also includes the Prime Minister, most cabinet ministers and many junior ministers, though the exact number drawn in depends on the nature and significance of the

Figure 5.1 The European Policy 'hub' in Whitehall (2006)

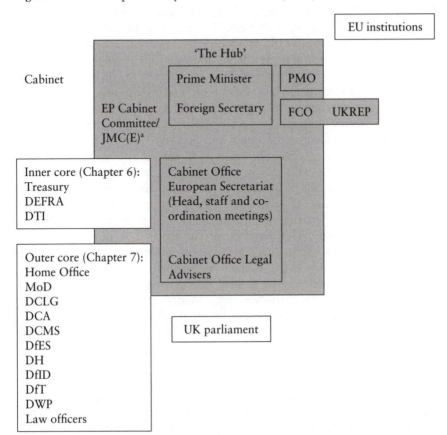

Key: DCA: Department of Constitutional Affairs; DCLG: Department of Communities and Local Government; DCMS: Department of Culture, Media and Sport; DEFRA: Department for Environment Food and Rural Affairs; DfES: Department for Education and Skills; DfID: Department for International Development; DfT: Department for Transport; DH: Department of Health; DTI: Department of Trade and Industry; DWP: Department for Work and Pensions; FCO: Foreign and Commonwealth Office; JMC(E): Joint Ministerial Committee (Europe); MoD: Ministry of Defence; PMO: Prime Minister's Office; UKREP: United Kingdom Permanent Representation to the European Union.

Note: [a] JMC(E) was utilised instead of cabinet committee EP during the later years of the Blair premiership as a way of keeping the devolved authorities in Wales and Scotland engaged in policy-making. EP is the formal venue for ministerial coordination within the hub and is answerable to cabinet and the Prime Minister, whereas ministers from the devolveds are not part of UK government.

issue being handled. This is a characteristic feature of the network; it spreads both more widely and more particularly depending on the activity involved and the policy issue being dealt with. As a generalisation it is over-arching issues as well as unresolved, or incorrectly resolved, and/or potentially contentious issues arising from a lower level that are managed by those at the hub of the network. In effect there are three types of issues that are usually handled outside the hub. First, more particular issues which engage a number of departments are often managed largely through subsidiary networks covering a specific aspect of policy such as Justice and Home Affairs (JHA) and Common Foreign and Security Policy (CFSP) (on these see Chapters 6 and 7). Second, issues that require the involvement and coordination of those with specific expertise from across departments such as lawyers or personnel managers are often managed through subsidiary networks of the relevant specialists. Third, the most specific issues are managed within a department or between two or more departments and need only engage the wider network intermittently if at all. The core and subsidiary networks operate on a principle of minimising activity whereby people participate only if the business is pertinent to them. Thus the EU policy-making network can be defined in a general sense according to its membership but at any particular time according to the business being handled. It is relatively enclosed but highly flexible in its operation.

The structure and operation of the network

The structure of the EU network
The structure of the network can be delineated by the key offices and players which are at the centre of EU policy-making in Whitehall and the formal powers attached to them. They are the COES and No. 10, the FCO's EU Directorate, and the office of the UK Permanent Representation in Brussels (UKREP): collectively termed 'the triad'. They link into a number of other central organisations which together make up the organisational core of the Whitehall system for handling UK–EU relations.

Cabinet Office European Secretariat (COES) and No. 10   In 2006 COES had a staff of 33 (including support staff), though its senior staff numbered 14. It was headed by the Prime Minister's adviser on the EU who was assisted in the management of the secretariat by three senior officials, ten desk officers and two senior administrative staff. The desk officers hold a watching brief for particular aspects of EU policy and they liaise with the associated Whitehall departments (see Figure 5.2). As with all units in the Cabinet Office, staff are on secondment for two to three years from departments.

The functions of the secretariat are outlined in Box 5.1 and can be broken down into nine key tasks. In addition to the head of COES, who from 2000 to 2007 was given by Tony Blair the designation of Prime Minister's

Figure 5.2 COES organisation

EU Adviser to the Prime Minister and Head of the European Secretariat

Deputy Head of European Secretariat

Head of Division   Head of Division

5 desk officers   5 desk officers

Chief Legal Adviser

Head of Legal Advice   Head of Litigation

Support staff

Source: Cabinet Office, European Secretariat.

Adviser on Europe and placed in No. 10, the links between COES and the Prime Minister's Office are close. There are connections into the Private Office of the PM through the secretary dealing with overseas business. There are also connections into the PM's Policy Unit and with other members of the Office such as the Chief of Staff and the Foreign Affairs adviser. In general links between the two offices are close and in this regard, as in some other policy areas, informally No. 10 and parts of the Cabinet Office function almost as an executive office in support of the PM (Burch and Holliday 1999). We calculate that in 2007 in the PM's Office there were two staff engaged full-time and 4 or 5 senior staff who are frequently drawn in, either individually or collectively, to the handling of European business.

On the legal side of EU work COES is given support by the Cabinet Office Legal Advisers (COLA) with a staff of 14: 8 lawyers and 6 support staff. These are formally part of the European Division of the Treasury Solicitor's office (TSol) and have, since 1999, been answerable to the Attorney General's office, but for all intents and purposes they are part of COES. They need to be included in any realistic assessment of the resources available in the Cabinet Office for handling European business. COLA advises COES on the legal aspects of European business and coordinates the drawing together of legal advice and opinions concerning EU matters across all departments. It receives requests for advice from either COES or other departments. Alternatively, its members identify those matters requiring legal opinion from examining the papers sent to it by COES. It is in receipt of nearly all COES papers and sees it as part of its job to inform lawyers in other departments when matters arise that might be of concern

---

Box 5.1 Functions of the Cabinet Office European Secretariat

- *Oversight and conciliation*: detecting and resolving problems at an early stage before disagreements arise and adjudicating.
- *Supporting*: the PM and No. 10 on EU matters.
- *Advisory*: to departments either informally or more formally in Guidance Notes, to the Foreign Secretary in the form of steering brief as chair of the key ministerial cabinet committee EP, and to other parts of Whitehall.
- *Servicing the machine*: on unresolved or high policy issues, clearly isolating the key matters for resolution through officials meetings or ministerial discussion or correspondence; providing neutral chair, compiling agenda, circulating papers, and drafting and circulating conclusions for ministerial and official meetings and/or ministerial correspondence.
- *Strategic thinking*: directing work on formulating the UK's policy towards the development of the European Union and its institutions over the medium term.
- *Implementation*: coordination and oversight of the carrying out of EU obligations by departments and agencies.
- *Devolved administrations' input*: oversight of relations with devolved administrations on European policy questions and responsibility for the operation of the relevant Concordat.
- *Scrutiny*: coordinating the government's requirements for parliamentary scrutiny.
- *Lobbying European negotiations*: through contacts with other governments and prime ministers and or executive offices in other member states, MEPs and interested groups and individuals in Britain.

Sources: Cabinet Office (Departmental Report 2005): 37; and internal documents.

---

to them. COLA works closely with the European Litigation Section which is also part of the European Division of the TSol. This section handles the majority of government litigation before the European Courts. This combination of legal advice and litigation responsibilities in a single division is distinctive to the UK amongst EU member states where the two functions are generally separated. As a consequence the UK is an active participant in ECJ proceedings – even when it is not a party to the case under consideration – and the European Division's distinctive central location in the network enables it to articulate UK interests in cases of significance to British European policy (Treasury Solicitors 2005).[4]

Also placed at the centre in the Cabinet Office is responsibility for shaping the UK recruitment of staff to EU institutions. This function was located in the EU Staffing Branch (EUSB) which was part of a larger grouping responsible for graduate recruitment into the civil service generally. Following a review the functions of the EUSB were absorbed in 2007 into the Civil Service Capability Group in the Cabinet Office. These functions include responsibility for the European Fast Stream of the UK civil service, for raising awareness of career opportunities in the EU institutions, and for providing advice and assistance for applicants, especially to the Commission at A Grade. Also, in liaison with the EU Staffing Unit in UKREP, it covers all secondments and staff inter-changes with the Commission, other European institutions as well as permanent recruitment to the Commission other than at the very top grade. An important focus of attention is the recruitment competitions of the European institutions. The European Fast Stream (EFS) has been designed to ensure a steady trickle of good British graduates into the EU institutions. At its inception the scheme recruited around thirty young graduates each year into the UK civil service but in recent years the numbers fell off to less than a quarter of the original intake. These fast streamers are assigned to a government department and given training in and experience of European business. They then enter those EU recruitment competitions for which they are eligible. All have the option of remaining in the British civil service should they not be recruited by an EU institution. In 2007 the EFS scheme was temporarily unavailable for graduates entering the Civil Service partly because the big enlargement of the EU in 2004/7 required that the recruitment of personnel should be from the newest member states only. Consequently there have been very few posts in the EU coming forward for general recruitment across all member states. All such placements when they do arise are through competition along with applicants from the wider public outside the civil service. What the Cabinet Office through its EFS scheme aims to ensure is that the UK is best able to fulfil its quota and that good applicants with a sound knowledge of UK administration and interests are appointed (Civil Service Fast Stream 2005).[5]

It is worth noting that neither the COES nor anyone else at the hub of the network has responsibility for the training of European specialists across Whitehall; this is a matter that is left to departments. Courses are either provided in house or are bought in through the government's staff training facility, the National School of Government,[6] or through other providers. The staffing and recruitment function is not as closely integrated with COES as is the legal function through COLA, but nevertheless is a part of the central operation. All three elements, and not just COES and No. 10, make up the Cabinet Office's organisational capability for handling European matters.

The EU Directorate (EUD) of the Foreign and Commonwealth Office (FCO)
The EUD constitutes the second element in the Triad. In 2006 this Directorate was divided into three sub-directorates: internal (EU-I) which deals with matters internal to the EU; external (EU-X) covering most EU

overseas questions including enlargement, Common Foreign and Security Policy (CFSP), the Political and Security Committee (COPS); and Eastern Adriatic Directorate (EAD) covering Turkey, Cyprus, Greece and former Yugoslavia. EU Directorate is also responsible for bilateral relations with other member states and with new member states' near neighbours – such as Belarus and Ukraine. Effectively the directorate now covers 40 countries and is responsible for the UK embassies in these countries. The Directorate has about 160 staff in London and in 2005 had an operating budget of £120 million[7] equivalent to about 6 per cent of the overall annual spend of the FCO.[8]

The main functions and organisation of EU Directorate are outlined in Boxes 5.2 and 5.3. So far as linking into EU activities across Whitehall is concerned, EU-I desk officers keep a watching brief on the EU related activities of some domestic departments and deal with institutional issues, on which the FCO has the lead, as well as offering guidance to the Foreign Secretary as chair of the cabinet committee on European Policy (EP). The presentation of European policy is the responsibility of the Public Diplomacy section which is also located in EU-I, though this activity is also spread across the other sections. The Security Policy Group (SECPOL), which is separate from the EU Directorate, has responsibility for EU security and defence policy issues. In addition to these sections UK embassies in

---

Box 5.2 Functions of FCO EU Directorate

The main functions of EU Directorate are:

- to serve as the main formal channel for instructing UKREP and other UK embassies in EU member states;
- to serve as the formal channel for contacts with other member state governments;
- to disseminate information on EU matters drawn from UK embassies in EU member states;
- to argue a particular foreign affairs view;
- to take the lead on formulating policy on Common Foreign and Security Policy (CFSP) and major aspects of EU institutional policy such as treaty reform;
- to encourage bilateral links between UK personnel and counterparts in other member states;
- to give attention to the presentation of UK European policy and its dissemination;
- to provide an input to policy on a wide range of EU business;
- to advise the Foreign Secretary as chair of the cabinet's European Policy (EP) Committee.

Source: Interviews.

Box 5.3 Organisation of FCO's EU Directorate (July 2006)

Director General Europe

European Union, Internal (EU-I), Deputy Director
Responsibilities:
The internal economic and institutional policies of the European Union
including:
- treaty reform and the constitution – institutional questions;
- the economic agenda;
- justice and home affairs and migration;
- Gibraltar and the West Mediterranean;
- bilateral relations with Ireland, Germany, Austria, Czech Republic, Poland, Slovakia, Hungary and Slovenia.[a]

European Union, External (EU-X), Deputy Director
Responsibilities:
- UK input into EU policy on enlargement;
- EU external policy – UK input to EU policy towards third countries, including foreign policy, EC development policy, and bilateral trade relationships and disputes;
- UK input to CFSP including Political and Security Committee (PSC) and General Affairs and External Relations Council (GAERC);
- shared UK input into EU policies on counter-proliferation, counter-terrorism and crisis management;
- bilateral relations with Nordic, Baltic and EFTA states, BeNeLux countries, Belarus, Bulgaria, Croatia, Cyprus, France, Greece, Moldova, Romania, Turkey and Ukraine.[a]

European Union, Eastern Adriatic (EAD)
Responsibilities:
- political and bilateral relations with Turkey, Cyprus, Greece, Italy, Holy See, Malta, Spain, Portugal and Andorra;[a]
- UK policy on the future of Cyprus;
- internal administration of Gibraltar;
- policy towards the countries of Former Yugoslavia plus Albania.

Separate from the EU Directorate

Security Policy Group (SECPOL)
Responsibilities include: EU security and defence policy issues.

Note: [a] Exact location of bilaterals is subject to change.
Source: FCO website, www.fco.gov.uk, July 2006; interview, FCO,
1 March 2005. See also Dickie (2004: 242).

member states play an important role in providing intelligence not only to EU Directorate and the FCO but also to other Whitehall departments.

UK Permanent Representation in Brussels (UKREP)   UKREP makes up the third element in the triad. It is constructed on the lines of a mini-Whitehall, it has a staff complement of around 170 of whom about 120 are officials engaged in policy work.[9] As an overseas delegation it comes within the responsibility and funding envelope of the FCO. About a third of the staff are from the FCO and the remainder are on secondment to the diplomatic service from other Whitehall departments. It is divided into nine sections, each under a Counsellor. UKREP is headed by the Permanent Representative, who relates to the business of COREPER 2, and the Deputy Permanent Representative who relates to the business of COREPER 1 (see Chapter 3). The third key figure in the organisation is the UK's representative to the EU's Political and Security Committee. The functions of UKREP are to act as the UK's representation in Brussels and the formal channel of communication with the Commission. As part of this task it provides advisers, spokespersons or negotiators who participate in the Council, COREPER and other intergovernmental committees (outlined in Chapter 3) which prepare business for the Council of Ministers. Depending on the policy area, the UKREP desk officers either assist UK based civil servants coming over to Brussels to participate in working groups or occasionally they attend as the UK representatives. UKREP officials also liaise informally with other member states' delegations and with personnel from the Parliament and Council on current business; and they gather and transmit information back to Whitehall on current and forthcoming business in the EU. They make an important policy input, at least at the level of tactics, on the basis of their close knowledge of negotiations and others' positions (Humphreys 1996: 34–7; Kassim 2001: 58–9). The EU Offices of the Scottish Executive, the Welsh Assembly Government and the Northern Ireland Executive are part of the 'UKREP family'. Officials from these bodies, although they represent administrations that are separate from the UK government, are able to attend and participate in many of the meetings in UKREP (Bulmer *et al.* 2002: 141–7).

These three core offices outlined above make up the triad; they are at the heart of the handling of European policy. However, if we are to have a comprehensive picture of the hub of the Whitehall EU policy network the Treasury also needs to be mentioned. Its activities are dealt with in detail in Chapter 6, but the Treasury plays a significant part in the oversight and coordination of policy because of its responsibility for expenditure management and control across the whole of government. This reflects the power structure in Whitehall and the central importance therein of expenditure politics rather than any particular features of the EU policy area. From these four sets of offices linkages and contacts on EU issues span out into all the departments of Whitehall, many of the agencies attached to them, and the devolved administrations in Scotland, Wales and Northern Ireland.

Key positions and powers vested in them The key positions at the core of the Whitehall EU policy-making network at the official level are sometimes referred to as the troika or the trio which consists of the Prime Minister's Adviser on the EU and Head of COES, the UK's Permanent Representative, and the Head of the FCO's EU Directorate. At ministerial level the key positions are Prime Minister, Foreign Secretary, and the Secretaries of State for Environment, Food and Rural Affairs, Trade and Industry as well as the Chancellor of the Exchequer. Other senior cabinet ministers may be drawn in depending upon their political significance or if the business being handled relates to the work of their department. A potentially influential figure at the junior ministerial level is the Minister of State (Europe) in the FCO, though a lot depends on the incumbent. In fact personality is an important factor at this level as is the power structure within a particular government and its ministerial team.

At the official level, the Head of COES also liaises with the executives of counterpart governments in the EU usually in consort with FCO officials and members of the PM's staff, and chairs some of the senior officials' meetings dealing with Europe. Other senior officials in COES can also be important, though again much depends on personality and the policy issue in question. This especially applies to the deputies who often chair most of the key Whitehall meetings, while the other senior officials usually manage the desk officers on a day to day basis as well as chairing those meetings that the second in command cannot manage to cover. Sub-section heads in EUD in the FCO are well placed to make a significant contribution to the handling of European business. Also if legal matters are being examined then the head and deputy head of Cabinet Office Legal Advisers (COLA) can expect to be brought into the picture. In effect there is an inner core of about two dozen senior officials from the core institutions plus Europeanised departments – notably DEFRA and DTI (see Chapter 6). These tend to be at the centre of discussions on high policy and are often drawn into those groups that conduct longer-term or strategic thinking on EU matters. To these must be added the PM and the core ministers as mentioned above, one or two special advisers, and one or two others that are drawn in because of departmental responsibility on particular items of business. In sum there is a core of about forty key positions which expands or contracts in accordance with the nature of the business in hand.

Formal powers at this level are limited, ambiguously defined, and are usually expected to be exercised in agreement with others. The Foreign Secretary by dint of chairing the main cabinet committee on Europe, is able to lead on some European matters. In addition he has direct responsibility for those EU matters that fall directly within the re-mit of the FCO such as EU institutional questions. The Prime Minister is responsible for over-all European policy subject, in theory, to cabinet approval. The top COES officials, especially if working in concert with the FCO, can over-rule a department, and the FCO in agreement with COES can refuse to send instructions to negotiators. But these aspects of direct authority are best seen as back stops; the threat is there but it is seldom exercised. Indeed, it is not so much the formal powers that count but the established under-standings about which positions matter and why. An element in determining this way of operating is the standard Whitehall hierarchy, but power and authority are also derived from accepted practice and the skill with which individuals exploit the resources vested in the position to which they are appointed. Despite its lack of formal powers, COES has a significant impact on the process of European policy-making because it is at the centre of the flow of information above departmental level, is known to speak with the authority of the Prime Minister, and has information and can facilitate contacts which others find valuable.[10] The authority vested in top FCO EU positions is slightly different. They are able to take the lead on certain FCO responsibilities; they advise the Foreign Secretary and the Minister of State (Europe) in the FCO; they are experts on how to approach Brussels institutions and member state governments; they have information and access to its key sources; and they are established players in the European network in Whitehall and out into Brussels and with mem-ber state governments. Unlike COES they are not seen as neutral but as having a departmental point of view to pursue. They are most effective when they are in alliance with COES, which is usually the case, and much depends on FCO officials' reputation for tactical and policy awareness, knowledge of the internal workings of the EU machine and for having contacts which can be made available to others.

The Operation of the EU network 2006

Meetings and fora   The key offices and the positions within them that make up the hub of the network are linked together through a series of meetings. These range from the most informal to the most formalised of groupings in the form of a number of ministerial and official cabinet committees (see Box 5.4). European Policy (EP) is the main ministerial standing committee dealing with Europe (see Box 5.5). It is chaired by the Foreign Secretary and it is tasked with determining 'the United Kingdom's policies on European Union issues' and 'overseeing the United Kingdom's relations with other member states and principal partners of the European Union.' Nowadays it meets about once a month but much business is settled through ministerial correspondence between the chair and the other members of the committee.[11] It includes most of the cabinet with ministers from every depart-ment affected by EU policy. Since late 2003 some of its business has been

---

Box 5.4 Coordinating European policy (2006)
Political level
Cabinet/PM

- EUS (European Union Strategy Cabinet Committee, chaired by PM): comprised of main UK ministers, including those concerned with the constitution and the euro. It meets rarely (approx. annually) *'to oversee the Government's European strategy'*.
- EP (European Policy Cabinet Committee, chaired by Foreign Secretary): comprised of ministers from all Departments affected by EU policy. It meets regularly (monthly +) but more often in the guise of JMCE (see below): *'to determine the UK's policy on EU issues'*.
- JMCE (Joint Ministerial Committee on Europe, chaired by the Foreign Secretary): comprised of the membership of EP plus the Scottish First/ Deputy First Minister and Welsh First Secretary and Welsh Assembly Business Manager. Has met regularly over the period since 2003 as an alternative forum to EP: *'to consider the UK Government's position on European Union issues which impinge on devolved responsibilities; to consider the implementation of EU law in the different parts of the United Kingdom; to keep the arrangements for liaison between the UK Government and the three devolved administrations on EU issues under review; and to consider disputes between the administrations on EU issues'*.

Official level

- Senior officials' informal Forward Strategy group
  Occasional meetings of UK government officials to consider medium-term issues and strategy. Chaired by PM's European Policy Adviser, who is also Head, Cabinet Office European Secretariat.
- Friday 'Grant/Darroch' meetings (Permanent Representative and affected departments)
  Examines tactics on short-/medium-term issues arising in the EU. Held in Cabinet Office. Officials from the devolveds are invited. (Note: John Grant was the Permanent Representative; Kim Darroch was the PM's European Policy Adviser and Head, COES.)
- Officials' meetings at working level
  Detailed coordination of policy on specific issues.

Take two different forms:

1 Chaired from the Cabinet Office European Secretariat:
  - system-wide meetings to discuss horizontal issues, e.g. Working Time Directive or Constitutional Treaty;
  - more localised policy issues or problem-solving meetings;
  - meetings on legal issues, convened by the Cabinet Office Legal Adviser.
2 Subsidiary networks
  - regular meetings, e.g. on CFSP/ESDP bringing together MoD, FCO and DfID;
  - ad hoc meetings, e.g. between Home Office and Department of Constitutional Affairs on Justice and Home Affairs matters.

Source: Own data.

Box 5.5 Ministerial Committee on European Policy, composition (2006)

- Secretary of State for Foreign and Commonwealth Affairs (Chair)
- Deputy Prime Minister and First Secretary of State
- Chancellor of the Exchequer
- Leader of the House of Commons and Lord Privy Seal
- Secretary of State for Trade and Industry
- Secretary of State for the Home Department
- Secretary of State for Health
- Secretary of State for Culture, Media and Sport
- Minister for the Cabinet Office and for Social Exclusion (and Chancellor of the Duchy of Lancaster)
- Secretary of State for Northern Ireland, and Secretary of State for Wales
- Leader of the House of Lords and Lord President of the Council
- Secretary of State for Constitutional Affairs and Lord Chancellor
- Secretary of State for International Development
- Secretary of State for Education and Skills
- Secretary of State for Communities and Local Government, and Minister for Women
- Secretary of State for Work and Pensions
- Secretary of State for Environment, Food and Rural Affairs
- Secretary of State for Defence
- Secretary of State for Transport and Secretary of State for Scotland
- Minister without Portfolio
- Chief Whip (Parliamentary Secretary to the Treasury)
- Attorney General
- Minister of State (Europe), Foreign and Commonwealth Office.

The United Kingdom's Permanent Representative to the European Union is also invited to attend.

Terms of Reference

'To determine the United Kingdom's policies on European Union issues, and to oversee the United Kingdom's relations with other member states and principal partners of the European Union.'

Source: Cabinet Office.

---

transacted through the Joint Ministerial Committee on Europe (JMC(E)) which has the same membership as EP plus senior ministers from the devolved administrations in Scotland and Wales. From time to time EP may spawn sub-committees as, for example, in 2000 when a ministerial group on European Trade Issues was established. The PM is not a member of EP but, of course, receives the minutes and will be memoed by the Foreign Secretary, and thus can intervene if he wishes to do so. As chair of EP committee the Foreign Secretary has to be departmentally neutral, hence the FCO Minister of State (Europe) attends EP as the FCO's representative. There was also, under Blair, an EU Strategy Committee (EUS) which was chaired by the PM and tasked with overseeing 'the Government's European strategy and the presentation of the Government's European policy'. It met occasionally to look at the big issues such as policy on the Euro and treaty reforms. It may have been an attempt to pull monetary policy out of the Treasury. If so, it did not work. Unusually it was jointly serviced by the European and Economic and Domestic Secretariats in the Cabinet Office.[12] It also became accepted practice under Major that European business is an item for report on the agenda for each regular weekly cabinet meeting (Burch and Holliday 1996: 58). This provided an opportunity to exchange information rather than discuss the details of policy.

Apart from the ministerial committees and the web of contacts surrounding them there is also a structure of official committees and meetings which handle EU business and which are serviced by and chaired by members of COES. Under the Blair premiership the approach tended to be quite flexible and there was a move from designated standing committees to more ad hoc meetings, set up to deal only with a particular item and drawing together only affected departments. They are seen as 'a better method of getting decisions when the need is urgent'.[13] All of these meetings have a COES desk officer serving as secretary. Papers for ministerial discussion and decision in EP or JMC(E) often go through a COES-chaired official committee beforehand. Attendance at all these committees depends on the issue. The Treasury, as always, attends most meetings as do representatives of the FCO and members of COLA.

In addition to these official meetings, there is often an informal group of senior officials which meets peripatetically to discuss longer-term issues which have arisen or are about to arise on the EU agenda and to consider what needs to be done in preparation for handling them. This group brings together the key senior officials in Whitehall engaged in European business. Under the Blair administration the group was called the Forward Strategy Group. It discussed issues such as future financing of the EU and matters arising from the EU constitutional debate.[14] It has also become established practice that an official group will be formed in the run-up to each UK presidency to consider the likely items that will be on the EU agenda and what the UK approach to handling them should be.

As noted in Chapter 4, one of the most distinct pieces of Whitehall machinery for handling EU matters is the meeting held at about 10 a.m. each Friday in the Cabinet Office. It is really a joint meeting between the head of COES, who chairs, and the Permanent Representative and is attended by teams from the COES, FCO, Treasury and the lead departments for the business being considered, the latter usually attend only for the discussion of their item. The meeting is nowadays run with a video-conferencing facility so not all the participants need to attend in person. Indeed the Permanent Representative sometimes participates through this link.[15] The Friday meeting has always been known in 'Whitehall speak' by the names of its two main protagonists; in 2006 Grant/Darroch. Its task is to consider issues coming up in Councils or elsewhere during the coming week and to settle matters of negotiation strategy, tactics, and, if necessary, further preparation of an issue before proceeding with it. The discussion of strategy and tactics tends to be practical, 'business like and focused', concentrating on what the UK's bottom line and fallback positions should be. It usually deals with two to five main items of business and the agenda is largely set by UKREP and COES. It is not an official cabinet committee and as a consequence representatives from the devolved administrations can attend. It tends to operate in an informal and flexible way; items can be put on the agenda by its organisers at a moment's notice. It does not consider elaborate formal papers, but it does produce a summary of its conclusions which are circulated by the end of the day to all departments and UKREP.

The Friday meeting has become a central part of the process for handling EU matters. One former head of COES described it as 'vital' to the British approach, helping to create a 'coordinated position', ensuring that 'you know where you are going' and 'making people decide'.[16] It also brings the Permanent Representative back into the centre of the government machine on a regular basis. The meeting has consequences for the unity of the UK line and approach in Brussels. One former Permanent Representative described the Friday meeting as 'a kind of steering body',[17] while a former Head of COES described it as 'unlike anything else in Whitehall' as it involves the principal participants mastering, very quickly, a series of briefs and giving advice to departments about how they might wish to change their approach in order to ensure that matters are handled successfully.[18]

Taken overall, these meetings form an important part of the operation of the network. They link key players and institutions together. For example, staff from the Legal Counsellor's section in UKREP are invited to every COLA meeting. More important than these formal points of connection through formal meetings are the informal contacts that make up the overwhelming substance of the relationships involved in the handling of European business.

The connections also importantly spread out not only to departments and their EU policy players, both ministerial and official, but also to parliament so far as the provision of information is concerned, though parliament also has important monitoring functions. The links to parliament are centred on one of the COES desk officers who has oversight of central government's relations with the European committees in both houses of parliament. This especially concerns the scrutiny of EU legislative initiatives which is largely a matter for the European Scrutiny Committee of the House of Commons. Copies of all Commission proposals are deposited in parliament as soon as they appear. The detailed liaison with the scrutiny committee is carried out by each relevant department who brief the committee through Explanatory Memoranda which set out the nature and the implications of the changes being sought. The committees currently handle about 1,100 of these documents – both the EU legislative proposals and the attached Explanatory Memoranda – each year (Study of Parliament Group 2005: 8). As well as oversight of the whole process of departmental handling of parliamentary scrutiny, COES is also responsible for general policy regarding parliament and the handling of EU business. (On parliament and EU scrutiny see Giddings and Drewry 2004; House of Commons 2005.)

Factors shaping the operation of the network   How the network works in practice is determined by a number of factors including the types of information that flow through the network and the manner and extent to which they are distributed; norms and understandings about how business should be done that have built up over time; the input of powerful personalities who effectively exploit the opportunities provided by the network; and the political context.

The life-blood for the operation of the network is the information that flows through it. Information about European business is substantial, it comes in a number of formats, and there are established systems for ensuring its distribution. The pattern of distribution provides some indication of the scope, complexity, variety of operation, and boundaries of the European policy-making network. There are three main flows of information into and around Whitehall. One flow is direct from the EU, usually from the Commission and Council, which ranges from 'Com-Docs' or proposed legislation, to minor pieces of information. There is a vast quantity of this material. For example, in 1996 the Welsh Office received nearly 12,000 Commission documents, all of which had to be sifted to see if they had implications for the department. This material is either sent direct or through UKREP or COES. Another flow consists of material generated within Whitehall such as the minutes and papers for ministerial and official committees and meetings, other inter-departmental meetings and papers and comments circulated by individual departments. In the late 1990s, for example, COES distributed over 300 papers in a typical year for inter-departmental discussion.[19] A lot of this material is distributed through the contact lists for the ministerial and official committees. The officials receiving the documentation will, if thought necessary, distribute it further within their own departments.

In addition to the above there is a constant flow of information, usually in the form of formal emails (these have replaced telegrams since the 1990s) to and from UKREP and UK embassies in other member states. These reports cover negotiations in Councils, COREPER, working and management groups, and attitudes of other member state governments. There is also an irregular flow of information, often at departmental level, from counterparts in other member states. This may be in the form of correspondence or documentation or simply through email or personal contact. These are the main types of material that flow through the network, though whether an individual has access to all or some of these depends on their position within it – whether they are at its centre or periphery – and what they are considered to need to know in order to carry out their function.

Traditionally, control over the flow of information was the province of the FCO; they were the key point of reception, distribution and transmission. The FCO's control in this area has weakened in recent years as EU links direct to the relevant sections in departments have become more common, but the EU Directorate still fulfils an essential role in channelling directions to UKREP and receiving and distributing reports from them.[20] The FCO also is the sole conduit for 'instruction' notes. These are sent to UK officials giving details of what the bottom lines are: i.e. the position that has been agreed in Whitehall that they must follow in negotiations. These instruction notes are nowadays seldom sent.[21] But there are also 'guidance' notes, which, in a less directive way, give advice and guidance on what might be done in negotiation. These usually cover matters that remain to be settled, indicate what points should be got over in the meeting and what outcomes the negotiators can agree to, often providing an indication of negotiation tactics and fallback positions.

As well as the nature and flow of business, the operation of the network is shaped by a set of norms and understandings about how things should be done. As noted in Chapter 4, a key characteristic of the UK approach to the handling of European business is that, in keeping with established Whitehall practice, it depends on sharing information across departments. Underlying the operation of this principle are traditional civil service values of reciprocity and trust. This culture of sharing information is absolutely essential to the working of the UK approach and for ensuring that the lightly resourced coordination mechanisms at the centre can do an effective job.

There is also a key set of understandings about the role and remit of COES. Ostensibly it has limited resources in terms of staff and finance but seeks to coordinate effectively on the grounds that others understand the need to cooperate with it. COES is regarded in Whitehall as having its own pro-active 'style' of doing business. Its members are expected to take 'a grip of an issue',[22] where they detect either a need for coordination or where someone else identifies a problem. COES officials claim that they do not have a particular policy line – 'the only requirement we have is that there must be a policy line'.[23] This position is not quite as tenable as it sounds and there is a built-in tension between its traditional secretariat role of serving the cabinet collectively and its more recently enhanced role of serving the PM in particular. There is also a set of understandings about how coordination is achieved by COES and its partners at the core of the network – especially in the FCO. It is exerted through suggestion and through providing advice and information – 'We rarely bludgeon'. However, COES does expect to be kept fully informed and it is a standard requirement in Whitehall that this be done (Cabinet Office 1999a: 14).

Another key organising principle for the handling of EU policy is departmental lead and that, within a department, the relevant specialist sections will have the lead. This departmentalism is an important complement to and facilitator of light-touch coordination from the centre. Some of these underlying norms about how the EU network should operate are reflected in the aims and objectives of COES (see Box 5.6). These have altered in recent years, and especially since 2000, to reflect the greater prime ministerial focus at the hub of the network.

A further major factor determining the operation of the network is the personalities involved and the surrounding political circumstances. A lot depends on what an individual makes of the position they occupy. This applies to both ministers and officials. Blair was particularly interventionist

---

Box 5.6 Objectives of COES (1998 and 2005)

European Secretariat 1998

'to ensure that, for any EU issue, particularly those affecting the interests of more than one department, there is an agreed government policy that is

- timely [prepared in good time];
- clearly identifies and promotes UK interests;
- is consistent with overall Government policy [and is agreed with all parts of government concerned];
- is realistic [and negotiable, taking account of the positions of other parties to the negotiation]; and
- is followed through effectively'.

European Secretariat 2005

'The Secretariat ensures that the Prime Minister's decisions on European policy are implemented, usually via other government departments, and in particular through the UK Representation to the EU.'

'The Secretariat ensures that the UK's position on European issues is consistent and coherent, and that ministers are informed of departments' views. It also ensures that they are given advice in good time, and that their decisions are carried out effectively by everyone in Whitehall and UK representatives abroad.'

Source: Cabinet Office.

in EU policy and drew COES more closely into the ambit of No. 10. This served to increase the status and potential influence of the heads of COES and its other senior officials. By contrast, the enhanced position of the PM and his advisers has tended to slightly weaken the position of key FCO personnel including that of the Foreign Secretary. This more evident No. 10 presence has been a situation that all three of Blair's Foreign Secretaries – Robin Cook, Jack Straw and Margaret Beckett respectively – had to come to terms with. Moreover, the more leading role on EU policy developed by Blair as Prime Minister was facilitated by a Labour Party in office that was much more at ease with Europe than had been the case when Labour was last in power in the 1970s. This shift in emphasis formed an important part of the changing context that facilitated Blair's more constructive approach to Europe.

Change in the hub of the EU network: 1973–2006

While many of the basic features of the operation of the Whitehall EU policy network were well established in broad outline at accession in 1973, there have been important changes in the way things work since then. These include changes in:

- the scope and size of the network;
- the key positions within and organisation of the hub of the network;
- the structure and operation of the policy-making process;
- strategic capacity;
- the flow of business and the technologies of communication;
- training, recruitment and expertise;
- rules, norms and understandings and practices;
- the projection capability of Whitehall into the EU.

Some of these changes have taken place gradually and reflect the shifting patterns and practices of administration in Whitehall and especially in the core executive. Many of these are long-term trends, but they have been further consolidated and accelerated in the period since 1997. So that, as in the structure of the network, so also in its operation the period of the Blair government marked quite a radical shift in the pace of change – if not its direction.

Change in the scope and size of the network
The overwhelming feature of change in the nature of the Whitehall EU policy-making network and its component parts has been one of growth and expansion. In 1973 the departments substantially involved were Trade and Industry, the Foreign Office, MAFF, the Treasury and Customs and Excise plus the European Unit in the Cabinet Office. Nowadays all departments are involved as well as a number of Executive Agencies, such as the Health

and Safety Executive (see Chapters 6 and 7). Also nearly all departments have created some facility to pull together European business across the department, while at the operational level more officials have been drawn into EU business. In sum there has been a substantial expansion in the number of posts across Whitehall dealing wholly or mainly with European business. Emblematic of this development has been the large growth of EU business in the Home Office since the Maastricht Treaty and in the Ministry of Defence from the late 1990s (see Chapter 7). This increase in staff numbers and costs is difficult to quantify, but we calculate it to constitute the largest collection of civil servants in Whitehall operating in any one field of activity. By our calculation it is a larger population than the expenditure network which centres on the Treasury (Heclo and Wildavsky 1974; Thain and Wright 1995). This transformation in the scope of the network and the number of personnel drawn into it is a consequence of the growth in EU competences and it is one of the most evident indications of the considerable impact that the EU has had upon Whitehall. All departments do now 'organise for Europe'.

Changes in key positions within and organisation of the hub of the network
Growth across Whitehall has contributed to changes in the operation of the hub of the network and the number and importance of the key posts within each of its components: the Cabinet Office and No. 10, the FCO and UKREP. Some posts have emerged as more central to policy-making, while others have declined in importance. One of the most significant changes has been the increased importance of the PM following the creation of the European Council in 1975. This has placed the PM, as head of government, at the centre of European policy-making as reflected in the close connection between COES, especially its head, and the PM and his staff. This relationship was further cemented in 2000 under Blair when the head of COES was officially designated as the Prime Minister's EU Policy Adviser with an office in No. 10. It has led to an increase in prime ministerial staff dealing with Europe. Initially this was mainly a matter for the Foreign Affairs Private Secretary in the PM's private office. However, as prime ministerial contacts with counterparts in other member states expanded, then inevitably on these linkages the principal private secretary and, under Blair, the No. 10 Chief of Staff, Jonathan Powell, have been drawn in. Although the Prime Minister's Policy Unit (PMPU) dates back to 1974 (Burch and Holiday, 1996: 29–30; Kavanagh and Seldon 1999), Major was the first PM to appoint a desk officer especially to cover Europe, a post held by a career civil servant – Jonathan Rees. This initiative was continued by Blair until 2004. He appointed a special adviser in the PMPU, Roger Liddle, as EU desk officer with particular responsibility for links with other social democratic parties across the EU. He was not replaced when he departed

in 2004, but the important point about European policy and the PMPU under Labour is that there has been a greater tendency to involve other desk officers in matters of European policy as they affect their areas of interest. Effectively from one member of No. 10 staff engaged significantly on EC business in 1973 the number has grown to the present complement of around six or seven staff who are engaged either substantially or occasionally on EU matters. The PM's staff have also become much more closely linked in to colleagues in COES than was previously the case. These changes in 2000 had the effect of making the UK/EU policy process more centralised and focused on the prime minister. They partly reflect the Blair government's more prime ministerial approach to governing. But they were also part of longer-term trends, both in the UK and most other member states, concerning the better resourcing of the Prime Minister's Office and the growing importance of EC/EU considerations in domestic policy-making (Burch and Holliday 1999; 2004).

Further changes have also taken place within the Cabinet Office part of the hub of the EU policy network. An early move was the abolition in March 1974 of the cabinet post of Minister for Europe with the arrival of the Labour government under Harold Wilson (Pollitt 1984: 200). This post had been situated in the Cabinet Office and was held by a close associate of Edward Heath, John Davies (Stack 1983: 126–7). The abolition of this cabinet post clarified the position of the Head of COES as the main source of advice to the PM on EC/EU matters. (For a full list of heads of COES, see Table 5.1.) The quality of this relationship, however, has depended

Table 5.1 Heads of European Secretariat since 1973

Name	Dates	Department of origin
Patrick Nairne	1973–75	Ministry of Defence
Roy Denman	1975–77	Department of Trade
Michael Franklin	1977–81	MAFF
David Hancock	1982–83	Treasury
David Williamson	1983–87	MAFF
Roger Lavelle	1987–89	Treasury
David Hadley	1989–93	MAFF
Geoffrey Fitchew	1993–94	Treasury
Brian Bender	1994–98	DTI
David Bostock	1998–2000	Treasury[a]
Stephen Wall	2000–4	FCO[a]
Kim Darroch	2004–7	FCO
Jon Cunliffe	2007–	Treasury

Note: [a] Both David Bostock and Stephen Wall were appointed to be Head of the European Secretariat from a posting in UKREP. In this case the department listed is that preceding their UKREP posting.
Source: *Who's Who* UK, various years, and own data.

on the personalities involved and the style of administration pursued by a prime minister. When the relationship works well the Secretariat operates as 'a European office for the PM and his staff', a kind of 'prime minister's department on Europe'.[24]

Staffing levels within the Secretariat have also changed over the period since 1973. Both at the beginning of the period in 1974 when there was a slight cut in the size of what had been the European Unit (then re-designated the European Secretariat) to a complement of nine senior personnel and in 1977 the down-grading of the post of Head of Secretariat from that of Permanent to Deputy Secretary.[25] This level of staffing remained constant throughout the period up until August 2000 when the senior staffing level at COES was increased by five and the new head, Sir Stephen Wall, was appointed at Permanent Secretary level. The changes in 1974 and 1977 did not necessarily mean a diminution in the status of the secretariat or its head. However, the changes in 2000 amounted to a significant enhancement in the resources and status of COES in the handling of UK EU policy. Other changes took place concerning the provision of legal advice to COES through the establishment of COLA. The European legal advice function was moved from Lord Chancellor's Department to COES and the Treasury Solicitor's Department in 1982[26] and litigation responsibilities were moved over from the FCO.[27] Originally in 1973 there was one legal adviser to COES, who did the job part-time (compared to at least 14 nowadays). This provides a further indication of the expansion of EU related issues and of the extent to which they involve significant legal considerations.

Overall, the establishment and maintenance of the European coordination function in the Cabinet Office was a major innovation in central government. It was, until the reforms of the core executive in 1998 (Burch and Holliday 1999; 2004), the only pro-active unit in the Cabinet Secretariat that had maintained a permanent existence over the long term. COES's more pro-active approach to business when compared to the domestic policy secretariats in the Cabinet Office partly reflects the UK view that EU business requires coordination and agreement if it is to be successfully negotiated in Brussels.[28] Viewed in organisational terms, the picture since 1973 has been one of steady growth of COES especially when defined to include COLA, in numbers, positions, functions and authority. Seen in these terms, the extension of staffing and the closer connection into No. 10 in August 2000, while significant, represents the acceleration and consolidation of a long-term trend rather than a wholly new departure.

The changes in the FCO over the period since accession through to 1998 were less substantial. The critical distinction within the EU side of the FCO between external (i.e. the external relations of the EC) and internal (i.e. the internal relations of the EC) European policy departments was, as noted in Chapter 4, established just after entry in 1974 (Stack 1983: 127).[29] There have been, however, changes in the composition and functions of these sections. Some of these reflected changes in the EU's competences and some

of these reflected efforts to make the UK approach to Europe more effective. For example, the creation in 1995 of a Common Foreign and Security
Policy (CFSP) grouping reflected the expansion of EU business in this area,
though it followed on from a pre-existing unit and represents a consolidation of what was there rather than a wholly new initiative. An important
re-organisation took place in 1998 when the Bilateral Department of the
European Union Division in the FCO was created which took over responsibility for all the member state embassies and diplomatic posts from the
West European Department. This was part of the Step Change project (see
below) and it meant that for the first time all things EU were brought within
the same management structure. This basic structure was maintained and
augmented in reorganisations in 2002 and 2004 as the FCO moved over
from a command structure to a more fluid system based on Directorates
organised more around themes or tasks than geographic areas. Under these
changes the Bilateral Department ceased to exist and its activities were
distributed across the relevant units of the EU Directorate (see Box 5.3).
The aim was to create closer integration between the various EU activities
in the FCO. The Step Change project also led to the creation of a public
diplomacy function tasked with ensuring better public awareness of EU
issues.[30] These changes from 1998 onwards indicate the extent to which
FCO staff and indeed budget resources have been more concentrated on
EU matters.[31]

This pattern of growth in resources and extension in scope to cover more
policy areas also reflects the major changes in the nature of UKREP. In the
period since 1973 this has become more like a mini-Whitehall with desk
officers (usually drawn from the parent department) now covering all
Whitehall departments. Numbers of staff have more than trebled from an
initial complement of 36 policy officials in 1973 of whom 16 were from
the diplomatic service (Wallace and Wallace 1973: 255), to around 120
(UKREP 2005). In the course of this pattern of growth UKREP has become
more 'domesticated' – reflecting the growing impact of the EU upon 'home'
departments. Following the creation of the ESDP, UKREP includes a
military representative and a deputy military representative supported by
seven senior military officers (UKREP 2005: 15 and 31). At the same
time there has been change in the hierarchy of posts in UKREP with the
Agriculture Counsellor no longer the third most senior position. That rank-
ing is now occupied by the UK representative to the Political and Security
Committee. A listing of Permanent Representatives and their Deputies is
provided in Table 5.2.

Changes in the policy process
Changes have also taken place in the policy-making process at the heart
of the network. There has been a shift towards greater informality in the
way the process operates. This shift is reflected in the move at official level

Table 5.2 UK Permanent Representatives and Deputies

Permanent Representatives (all from FCO)	Year	Deputy Permanent Representatives (and Home Department)	Year
Sir Michael Palliser	1973–75	Robert Goldsmith (DTI)	1973–77
Sir Donald Maitland	1975–79	Sir William Nicoll (DTI)	1977–82
Sir Michael Butler	1979–85	David Elliott (DTI)	1982–91
Sir David Hannay	1985–90	David Durie (DTI)	1991–95
Sir John Kerr	1990–95	David Bostock (Treasury)	1995–98
Sir Stephen Wall	1995–2000	Bill Stow (DTI)	1998–2003
Sir Nigel Sheinwald	2000–3		
John Grant	2003–7	Anne Lambert (DTI)	2003–7
Kim Darroch	2007–	Andy Lebrecht (DEFRA)	2007–

Source: Westlake and Galloway (2004: 430) and own data.

from standing to ad hoc committees and the greater use of ministerial correspondence. The committee system post-1973 built on the mechanisms put in place since 1961 with official standing committees at junior and senior levels.[32] This system of standing committees was gradually phased out and had been transformed into a largely ad hoc system by 2003, but with both ministerial and official European strategy committees as well as the long established EP Committee meeting periodically. These new arrangements plus the Friday meeting and the JMC(E) constitute the key formal arenas for the contemporary operation of the EU network (see Box 5.4). This shift away from the formal to the informal aspects of the EU policy-making process is in keeping with the general shift to a more informal pattern of decision-making across the whole of Whitehall.

Amongst the components of the policy process a key development has been the gradual institutionalisation of the purpose and importance of the Friday meeting. When it was initiated in 1973 it was held on a Wednesday and tended to meet about once a fortnight. It moved to a regular, weekly, Friday, slot in 1975, so that its meetings followed rather than immediately preceded the Permanent Representatives' meeting in COREPER 2.[33] Initially the decisions made in the Friday meeting were not recorded but from around 1981 a summary of conclusions has been produced and circulated. According to one of the key participants this totally changed the significance of the meeting, it became 'an operational tool' for handling the flow of policy and the tactics and strategy they entailed.[34] Prior to this change the approach had tended to be rather haphazard with arguments and misunderstandings about what had been agreed, but once COES began to circulate the conclusions, in keeping with traditional practice, these, unless challenged, became regarded as definitive and binding.

Overall the Friday meeting has served a key role in the process of projecting back into the EU the UK position. It has also proved to be a useful educative device for those departments least schooled in EC matters and tactics. Indeed items have been selected on the grounds that a department fairly new to the European field with relatively little experience might 'benefit from talking to people'.[35] According to one former Permanent Representative, it gave the home departments who had prepared the initial brief for their ministers to argue at Council 'an opportunity to try this out on the person who had just come back from the front line'.[36] This could sometimes have rather stark effects as on the occasions when: 'people appeared from departments taking completely bizarre lines, they used to be sort of chewed up by a combination of the Permanent Representative and the Cabinet Secretariat and the Foreign Office Under Secretary'.[37]

This process of educating departments has worked both ways, with those less experienced in European matters finding the attendance at the Friday meeting to be a useful way of gaining information and understanding. This educative function is summarised well by one senior official in one of the less Europeanised departments – the (then) Scottish Office:

> We benefited a lot from being at these discussions . . . [They] give a very good 'feel' of what the key issues are, of Britain's position . . . They provide important administrative and political context for [our department's] work. The discussion of tactics and strategy is very interesting, also how to handle the different set of relationships which makes up the Brussels machinery that is so different from the UK.[38]

In recent years, the educative role of the Friday meeting has declined somewhat as more departments, through direct involvement and cumulative practice, have deepened their knowledge and skills in EU matters. But the role of back-stop has remained significant. Under the Major government this was one means of ensuring that departments with Euro-sceptic ministers did not pursue negotiating lines out of step with the overall government position. During the Blair government's presidency of the EU in 2006 the Friday meeting also operated as the oversight committee for planning and organising the presidency.

The policy process at the hub of the network has also become more fragmented as the network has grown and subsidiary networks have emerged in specific and relatively contained policy domains. This development relates in particular to Justice and Home Affairs, centred on the Home Office, and CFSP and defence involving at its core, the FCO the MoD and DfId (see chapter 7). Fragmentation creates clear challenges for the overall system of policy coordination across Whitehall.

Changes in strategic capacity
Important changes have also taken place in the capacity of senior players in the European policy network to undertake strategic thinking on Europe.

Strictly speaking, ministers are expected to be at the heart of this; but in the past there have been problems because of the intra-party contentiousness of EU policy. This was especially the case under the Major government. A significant innovation was the establishment in 1992 of the Medium Term Group (MTG) which drew together the key senior officials so as to allow for some forward thinking about broad developments in the EU before they crystallised on the EU agenda.[39] As well as early thinking about the 1996 IGC, the Group considered issues such as eastern enlargement, future financing of the EU, the introduction of EMU, CAP reform and so forth. The group met almost covertly given the divisions within the ministerial ranks of the Major government over EU issues. Clearly the MTG fulfilled a need for strategic thinking on the UK's place in Europe ahead of the development of policy by EU institutions. Hence the survival of a similar arrangement through to today in the form of the Forward Strategy Group.[40]

Under the Blair government European issues were not really such a significant source of intra-party and inter-ministerial strife. Consequently, the development of an overall European strategy has tended to be handled at both ministerial and official levels. One key characteristic already noted has been the concentration of activity more evidently on the PM and No. 10. The situation, however, was complicated by the significant role played by the then Chancellor of the Exchequer, Gordon Brown, in all aspects of domestic policy – many of which had an EU dimension. This fissure between No. 10 and the Treasury was a characteristic feature of the organisation of the Blair government and reflected understandings reached between these two personalities concerning which of them should go forward as candidate for the leadership of the Labour party in 1994 (see Naughtie 1999; Bower 2004). This fissure complicated attempts to create a unified approach to Europe especially on monetary matters (Scott 2004).

While strategic thinking became more concentrated on No. 10, initially it tended to engage informal meetings with the relevant ministers and officials such as the Foreign Secretary or Secretary of State for Trade and Industry. It was not significantly developed in the cabinet's European Policy (EP) Committee chaired by the Foreign Secretary. Some strategic thinking took place at minister of state level through the FCO's interdepartmental grouping MINECOR which also involved, from 1999, the relevant ministers from the devolved authorities in Scotland, Wales and, intermittently, Northern Ireland. In 2003 this structure began to change. MINECOR ceased to exist and from late 2003 some of its functions were drawn into the Joint Ministerial Committee (Europe) (JMCE) which engaged the devolveds. From about this time strategic thinking at a higher level became more sophisticated on a collective, official and ministerial basis through the development of the European strategy committees at ministerial and official levels previously noted. The attempt to create a more collective approach was only partially successful as the strategic operation and initiative still remained substantially focused on No. 10.[41] Overall, under the Blair government, this forward, strategic thinking engaged ministers more substantially, was less contentious in party political terms, and the whole process was more centred on the PM.

Changes in the flow of business and the techniques of communication
Changes in the policy process and in strategic capacity to think ahead have been complemented by changes in the flow of business and techniques of communication. These have affected the more flexible and informal operation of the EU network. The gradual growth in the scope of the network has necessitated wider information distribution, while at the same time more disparate and varied types of material have flowed through the system. Nowadays much correspondence is direct from the relevant desk officer to the policy division in the home department and fax and email are extensively used as are direct contacts through telephone and meetings. The consequence of these trends has been to make the tasks of information transmission, distribution and reception more complex and the oversight of these tasks more problematic. Information flows are no longer the monopoly of the centre and increasingly departments have created direct links to UKREP and other states and EU institutions. As noted earlier, this has led to a decline in the FCO position as the key control point in the information flow. In general the adoption since the mid to late 1990s of IT by Whitehall, the development of email traffic, and the increasing use of video-conferencing have had profound effects on the way in which the EU Whitehall network operates.

Changes in training, recruitment and expertise
On the personnel side of the network there have been changes in the training of officials dealing with EU matters. New courses and training activities have been provided. However, this still largely depends on the individual and the department. Much reliance has been placed on learning from doing and budget constraints have affected more formal training provision. Throughout, training has been an area where more needs to be done, especially in a general consciousness raising sense across all departments and beyond the cadre of EU specialists. The incentives for training and enhanced EU engagement remain problematic. As some practitioners recognize, one of the major faults of the system is that there is still 'no career mechanism for integrating European experience'.[42]

Changes also took place in the approach to recruiting UK officials to work in EU institutions. By the late 1980s it was recognised that the British were under-represented in all the Community institutions (Cabinet Office 1996: 6). So the European Staffing Unit (ESU) was created and the European Fast Stream was launched in 1990 to recruit and train young graduates for taking up posts in Brussels (Edwards 1992: 71). Prior to this the placing of staff in European institutions had been a matter of concern but recruitment had not been approached in a systematic way. Liaison with the informal network of British permanent officials in the Commission, in some cases former Whitehall officials, was also developed so as to assist the placing of 'Brits' in key positions (Bulmer and Burch 1998: 619).

Changes in rules, norms and understandings
Changes are also evident in the rules, norms and understandings shaping activity in the network. Precedents have been established over time such as the understanding that the chairmanship of EP committee rests with the Foreign Secretary or that the Permanent Representative is drawn from the FCO and their deputy is drawn from one of the more Europeanised home departments. However, precedents are not always followed, as in the appointments of Sir Stephen Wall and his successor Kim Darroch, both with FCO backgrounds, as heads of COES. This post has traditionally been filled by home department appointees to ensure balance with the Permanent Representative, who would be drawn from the FCO (see Tables 5.1 and 5.2). A further indication of a thickening of the institutional framework has been the development of guidance notes both by COES, pertaining to the whole network, and by departments concerning the handling of business in the particular areas in which they are engaged. Cabinet Office Guidance Notes on aspects of European policy-making have built up over time. In 1996 there were 76 of these notes which provided information and also laid down the proper procedure for officials to follow on various aspects of EU policy-making, such as: briefing for Council working group meetings; communications with UKREP; correspondence with the Commission; general guidance on tactics for negotiation in the EU; and how to interpret and apply the QMV rules (Humphreys 1996: 237–9). Following a review in 1999 the number of Guidance Notes was cut back to 25.[43] New operational rules and understandings have also been established in relation to parliamentary scrutiny of EU proposals. Most notably in 1990 the 'scrutiny reserve' was brought into play – whereby government has undertaken 'to try to avoid taking a final decision on proposals' until parliament has expressed a view.[44] In 1998 this was extended to cover Common Foreign and Security Policy and Justice and Home Affairs (Leader of the House of Commons 1998: 3).

Changes in the projection capability of Whitehall into the EU
Overall, what we see in the period since 1973 is a slow incremental, cumulative development of the approach to handling EU business in Whitehall. The accumulation of these changes amounts to a substantial transformation in UK central government. There was, however, following the election in 1997 of the Blair government, a shift to a higher gear as illustrated by the greater focus of EU policy-making on the Prime Minister's office

and the engagement of more staff at the hub of the network. A series of initiatives was designed to improve the effective projection of UK concerns into and within the EU. These were altogether more transformative in intent if not perhaps in policy effect. These initiatives were drawn together under the 'Step Change' project which was launched by the Blair government in 1998 in response to a review of the UK's approach to Europe following on from the UK's presidency.

Step Change involved an attempt to get away from a passive and reactive approach to the EU.[45] It concentrated on isolating the issues on which the UK could take a lead and the strategy and tactics to be employed. A key feature was a much more significant effort to realise the potential for affecting the intergovernmental forces and interests which shape EU policies and initiatives. Consequently the aim was to shape EU agenda setting at an early stage by conditioning the climate of debate surrounding the run-up to key EU decisions through greater contact and liaison with other member states, leading to exchanges of information, alliances on policy initiatives, and long-term coalition building. This networking offensive had two main foci for relationship-building. First, through developing more extensively bilateral relations between UK ministers and officials and their counterparts in other member states. This applied to all member states but especially Germany, France, Italy, Spain and the Netherlands as well as the new member states and particularly Poland as the largest and most significant of these. The second focus of attention was the relationships between ministers and their party contacts on the centre left in Europe. These initiatives were complemented by a project designed to help shape UK public opinion by encouraging more dissemination of information on the EU (Smith and Tsatsas 2002: 27–33; Smith 2005: 709–10).

Of these initiatives, the contacts with member state personnel were regarded as the most important avenue for development. It was in order to assist in this activity that, as noted above, the European Union Division in the FCO took over responsibility for all the UK EU member state embassies and diplomatic posts. The objective of changing public attitudes involved giving a higher profile and larger campaigning role to the position of Minister of State Europe in the FCO and the creation of a Public Diplomacy function in the EU Division of the FCO. Until 2004 the whole bilateral effort was overseen and monitored by the MINECOR committee (noted above), chaired by the FCO Minister of State Europe.

What was the impact of the Step Change project? A number of initiatives were launched by the British government at EU level, notably on economic competitiveness (the Lisbon Strategy) and security and defence (ESDP) both of which became key priorities of the EU itself. In terms of bilateral ministerial visits, an important part of building coalitions in the EU, they were initially skewed towards France and Germany with 70 and 88 ministerial visits respectively in the years 1999–2000. In the following year more was done to exploit contacts with Spain and Belgium (who held the EU presidency). The Step Change's bilateral programme also contained some innovative features, such as adopting established EU patterns of working with an emphasis on networking and coalition building (Foreign and Commonwealth Office 1999: 53; 2000: 86; 2001: 74). Notably the least active core department in terms of ministerial contacts was the Treasury. So the broad picture of the actual exploitation of the opportunities envisaged in the Step Change programme was uneven. The initiative was enshrined as a Public Service Agreement between the FCO and the Treasury requiring 'a step change in the UK's relations with the rest of Europe' by 2002 (HM Treasury 1998: 77). In 2002–3 the initiative was evaluated, and, as interviews in the COES and the FCO in 2005 confirmed, it was by then deemed to have been successful in raising the government's European diplomacy to a new level.

Clearly, Step Change responded to a perception that the government could be more effective in both the substance of European policy and in its 'projection' response to Europeanisation. It was an approach based on a recognition that the UK had not been fully exploiting the openings available to it to shape EU policy at an early, agenda-setting stage. The Europeanising effect here was quite direct and characterised by institutional changes designed to improve the projection side of the UK's approach to Europe. Indeed, the changes went beyond a mere projection response to include systematic use of the EU as a policy-making resource. However, it is notable once again that the greater alignment between the two institutional systems has been achieved within existing structures and trends of UK governance. Step Change has, therefore, brought about a shift in outlook and it has had some impact on outcomes. Its overall effect in placing the UK more comfortably at the centre of debates in the EU has been somewhat lessened by other factors affecting UK-EU relations, notably the UK's close relationship with the Bush administration in the USA and its involvement in the Iraq war.

Overall these are significant changes in the operation of the network culminating in a greater emphasis on the projection of UK policy into Brussels. They reflect a growing institutionalisation of processes and procedures for handling European policy in Whitehall and out to Brussels. The changes are in response to a variety of pressures, derived from both domestic and European sources. But two factors should not be lost sight of. First, the extent to which the political salience of the European issue has continually impacted on the ways EU policies are handled in the UK. Many changes in the nature and operation of the network have been significantly shaped by the prevailing political climate and the boundaries to initiative that this has imposed. Tony Blair's premiership was characterised by a lack of deep divisions within the administration over the EU and by his personal interest in the issue. Secondly, the role of significant actors in making the best of the opportunities available requires to be recognised. Taking the case of the Head of COES as an example, some, such as David Williamson (Head from 1983–87), Brian Bender (1994–98), and Stephen Wall (2000–4) had a marked effect on the development of European policy. They were held in high regard throughout Whitehall, in Brussels and, most importantly, with the Prime Minister and officials at No. 10 (see Table 5.1). The same would apply to Michael Palliser, David Hannay and Michael Butler amongst the early permanent representatives (see Table 5.2) and to John Robinson as a driver of EU awareness in the FCO and beyond. Others were less challenging and effective. The big impact can come at the ministerial level and certain actors have been especially significant in driving forward UK EU policy-making. In particular, three prime ministers stand out as having had a significant effect on the handling and content of European business: Edward Heath, Margaret Thatcher and Tony Blair. Others have been less comfortable, engaged and effective in Europe, notably Harold Wilson and James Callaghan. And one Prime Minister, John Major, was so constrained by party divisions on Europe in the context of a small and dwindling majority in the Commons, that he had little opportunity to pursue a constructive policy, despite his early aspiration to put Britan at the heart of Europe.

Foreign Secretaries can also matter, especially if they have the trust and support of the PM and No. 10. Labour's first incumbent – Robin Cook (1997–2001) – was not seen as part of Blair's inner group. His policy focus was more on the wider international agenda and aspects of EU external policy and he was seen initially as a Euro-sceptic, certainly by those in No. 10. This meant that the PM tended to rely less on Cook and the FCO for advice on the EU. And this was one of the reasons why Blair sought to have a more congenial source of advice by drawing the COES more closely into the ambit of No. 10. Cook's successor as Foreign Secretary, Jack Straw (2001–6), tended to be more focussed on the details of EU internal policy and he made a significant contribution to European policy. He certainly had more of the ear of No. 10 than his predecessor and he attempted to restore the effective usage of the EP committee chairmanship and later the JMC(E), as a means of restoring some of his and the FCO's hold over the development of EU policy.[46] During her brief tenure as Foreign Secretary, Margaret Beckett (2006–7) tended to be over-shadowed by Blair himself. She did, however, bring to her post a great deal of experience of negotiating in the EU in the tricky area of CAP reform which she had successfully pursued in her previous position as head of DEFRA.

Conclusion

Over the period since 1973 at the hub of the Whitehall European network change has been substantial in terms of the volume and specialisation of business and the level of resource – money and personnel – devoted to it. The network has become more complex and more elaborate, but it has not changed its fundamental character. In broad terms what exists today is recognisably an extension and elaboration of what was largely in place in 1973. However, the growth in activity is so substantial and so wide ranging across Whitehall that, while the overall framework may be similar, at a detailed level the nature and scale of the contemporary operation is quite distinct. This development provides an example of incremental transformative change whereby a series of small, incremental changes over time have amounted to a significant shift in the character of an institution. This transformation is a consequence of the growth in EU competences and activities and it is one of the most evident indications of the considerable impact that Europe has had upon Whitehall. It also means that the significance of this European dimension has to be at the centre of any discussions about how Whitehall now operates. There is, however, from 1997 an acceleration of trends and a significant shift in the approach to policy handling from reception to a greater emphasis on projection.

Overall, significant change is evident. UK membership of the EU has brought about a quiet revolution in what Whitehall does, though not so much in the way it does it. Some of the changes are a direct response to membership; others reflect domestic pressures or secondary Europeanisation effects. Change is steady and cumulative, though the reforms in machinery and process from 1997 onwards do constitute an acceleration of preceding trends and the Step Change project marked a significant shift in intention in the UK approach to handling EU policy. These post-1997 changes certainly moved the disposition of the network to a greater focus on the Prime Minister's Office at its hub and to a greater attention to projecting and pursuing UK interests in the EU. Whether this will survive the Blair premiership remains a moot point. To the extent that these centralising reforms are a logical consolidation of existing trends, it seems likely that they will be maintained. This is a matter to which we return in Chapter 8.

Notes

1 The COEU was re-designated as a secretariat in 1974.
2 On task networks at the core of Whitehall, including the EU network, see Burch and Holliday (1996: 81–106); on policy networks see Marsh and Rhodes (1992).
3 There is a core distribution covering senior posts, which is what is referred to here. There is also a wider distribution net on EU matters of about 350 names which involves the distribution of information concerning the EU.
4 Interview, retired senior legal adviser, 4 December 1996; interview, Treasury Solicitor's Office, 18 November 1996.

5 Interview, Cabinet Office, 18. November 1996; interview, Centre for Management and Policy Studies, 28 February 2005; interview, Cabinet Office, 27 July 2007.

6 Previously the Civil Service College, then the Centre for Management and Policy Studies and, since mid-2005, the National School of Government.

7 Interview, Foreign and Commonwealth Office, 1 March 2005.

8 Foreign and Commonwealth Office 2005, Chart H, p. 224.

9 This was the staff complement in August 2005. Seventeen of the overall total were in the management section – which includes security and reception; also there were 35 other support staff – mainly PAs and coordinators; 9 officers were specifically working on the UK presidency. Hence the overall staffing number could be expected to have dropped by at least 9 after the UK presidency ended in January 2006 (UKREP 2005). See www.UKREP.be.

10 Interview, Cabinet Office, 2 July 1996; internal documents.

11 Interview, Cabinet Office, 26 February 2005.

12 Though this committee was not used as much as originally envisaged (meeting about twice a year), its potential importance lay in the fact that it was chaired by the Prime Minister. It met when there was need for the highest level engagement. Interview Cabinet Office, 26 February 2005; interview Foreign and Commonwealth Office, 1 March 2005.

13 Cabinet Office, internal documents.

14 Interview, retired Cabinet Office official, 14 March 2006.

15 Interview, Cabinet Office, 26 February 2005.

16 Interview, retired Cabinet Office official, 18 March 1997.

17 Interview, retired FCO official, 28 November 1996.

18 Interview, retired Cabinet Office official, 17 April 1997.

19 Interview, Cabinet Office, 2 July 1996.

20 Cabinet Office, internal documents.

21 Interview, retired Cabinet Office official, 14 March 2006.

22 Cabinet Office, internal documents.

23 Interview, Cabinet Office, 2 July 1996.

24 Interview, Cabinet Office, 2 July 1996.

25 Interview, retired Cabinet Office official, 9 April 1997; interview, retired Cabinet Office official, 15 January 1997.

26 Interview, retired senior legal adviser, 4 December 1996.

27 Interview, Treasury Solicitor's Department, 18 November 1996.

28 On Cabinet Office secretariats see Burch and Holliday (1996: 34); Smith (1999: 164).

29 One section dealt with the external relations of the EU and the other with its internal relations.

30 For details of the Step Change programme see Bulmer and Burch (2005; 2006).

31 Interview, Foreign and Commonwealth Office, 1 March 2005.

32 By the mid-1990s these had settled down into EQO* (pronounced 'EQO star'), which was chaired by the Head of COES, usually involved senior officials and dealt with big issues such as future financing, and EQO, which was chaired by one of the senior officials in COES and drew in more junior officials and dealt with most policy issues of significance that affected a number of departments. Connected to these were three more specialist committees: EQO(P) dealt

with issues affecting UK staffing of EC institutions, including the problem of under-representation; EQO(E) dealt with EU enlargement negotiations; and EQO(L) which was the formal means of coordinating legal matters relevant to Europe across Whitehall. For details see Bulmer and Burch (1998).

33 Interview, retired FCO official, 11 December 2006; interview, retired Cabinet Office Official, 15 January 1997.

34 Interview, retired FCO official, 28 November 1996.

35 Interview, MAFF, 6 December 1996.

36 Interview, retired FCO official, 22 January 1997.

37 Interview, retired FCO official, 28 November 1996.

38 Interview, Scottish Office, 23 January 1997.

39 The MTG was formed on the completion of the Maastricht negotiations when it was felt that ministers would benefit from informal advice from senior officials on the prospects for the next IGC. Another reason for establishing the MTG was that the deeply divisive nature of EU issues amongst ministers and within the Conservative party meant that the strategic drive that, constitutionally speaking, was to be expected from ministers was not generally available. The MTG met very informally and initially involved about half a dozen named senior officials who were asked to participate not just as departmental representatives but as persons with considerable experience and knowledge of the EU. It was convened by COES, chaired by its head and drew together grade 2 and 3 officials from the core European Departments: the FCO, DTI, MAFF, Treasury, No. 10 (usually the relevant desk officer from the Policy Unit) and UKREP, with the FCO tending to have the largest representation. It did not consider strategic questions relating to Europe in the abstract and was convened only when a clear problem arose on the EU agenda. The MTG met prior to the formulation of a detailed paper in order to provide a preliminary consideration of the dimensions and content of an issue and the options available for handling it. Any proposals produced by the group would then go through the formal official machinery, before being presented to ministers.

40 Interview, Cabinet Office, 26 February 2005.

41 The ministerial strategy committee, EUS, for instance, only met very infrequently (*c.* annually). It was created in June 2003 partly in response to the need to prepare for an eventual decision and possible actions on UK membership of the Euro. Its original remit was 'to oversee the Government's European strategy, including preparations for UK entry into the single currency, progress on the inter-governmental Conference on the future of Europe and the presentation of the Government's European policy'.

42 Interview, Centre for Management and Policy Studies, 28 February 2005.

43 Interview, Cabinet Office official, 25 February 2000.

44 Cabinet Office, internal documents.

45 For more detail on the Step Change project see Bulmer and Burch (2002; 2005; 2006; Smith and Tsatsas 2002).

46 Interview, FCO, 1 March 2005; interviews, retired cabinet office officials, 28 February 2005 and 14 March 2006.

6

The European Union and 'inner core' departments

Introduction

This chapter explores the way in which the EU has impinged upon the inner core of departments most engaged in EU policy-making in UK central government.[1] In seeking a comprehensive approach, we have prioritised certain parts of the Whitehall European policy-making network. Leaving aside the 'hub' of the network, already covered in Chapter 5, these categories are:

- An inner core of ministries with extensive involvement in the EU: DEFRA, the Treasury and the DTI.
- Other London-based ministries, which have varying degrees of involvement in EU business. These range from the Home Office, which has been significantly affected by the EU since the Maastricht Treaty, through the Ministry of Defence, whose involvement is more recent, to more peripheral ministries such as the Department for Culture Media and Sport (DCMS).
- The 'territorial' ministries prior to devolution and subsequent arrangements in Scotland, Wales and Northern Ireland thereafter.

The inner core is covered in this chapter; the other categories are covered in Chapter 7, which follows a similar format.

In covering each department we focus on a number of key issues: the development of its involvement with EU policy; the principal EU policies which currently bear upon its work; important ministerial contributions to the department's Europeanisation; its 'mission' within the EU; its key players – ministers and officials – and the internal organisation of EU business; and how it interacts with the 'hub', as identified in Chapter 5, and directly with the EU institutions themselves.

In Chapter 3 we saw that Europeanisation led to a widening of the EU's impact upon public policy, but also to an intensification of that impact in policy areas prioritised by the EU at certain points, such as the internal market from 1986 to 1992 or monetary policy following the Maastricht

Treaty. We should therefore expect the number of departments drawn in to European business to grow over the period since 1973, whilst some will become more intensively involved due to the growing density of European policy in the area concerned. However, as our understanding of Europeanisation in Chapter 2 suggested, Whitehall's response has not been one of automatic optimal adjustment to challenges emanating from Brussels. We are therefore accumulating in this chapter empirical data so as to identify the mediating factors that condition the effects of Europeanisation within government.

Department for Environment, Food and Rural Affairs (DEFRA)

We explore DEFRA's separate origins in dealing with, first, agriculture, food and fisheries and, second, environmental policy before looking at how they were pulled together in the restructuring after the Blair's government's re-election in 2001. The Ministry of Agriculture (MAG), as it was then called, first dealt with European policy in the 1950s within its External Relations Group, which was responsible for trade matters. It was from there that MAG (and then MAFF) monitored agricultural developments in the negotiations leading to the EEC, participated in the negotiations led by Heath during 1961–63, and then reverted to monitoring developments during the 1960s, when a large portion of the CAP's regulatory structure was set up. Already before accession an EEC Group had been established within MAFF. Sir Michael Franklin, an early member of the UK's European cadre, was Under-Secretary in the period prior to accession. At this time it was already clear that it was not sensible to confine European business to a particular part of the ministry because of the breadth of impact. Consequently, a working group called DCE – the Departmental Committee on Europe – was set up by Franklin at the start of the 1970s to assist with agricultural accession negotiations. DCE continues to the present, albeit with an adjusted role.

Accession brought a major transformation in the UK's agricultural policy, from a deficiency-payments system to a high-price, protectionist CAP regime (Colman 1992). Policy adaptation lasted until the end of a transition period (January 1978). From a rather later starting point the Common Fisheries Policy, the first measures of which were introduced in 1970, developed into a significant area of European policy (Lequesne 2000). The third major impact upon MAFF derived from EU food policy. This policy gained momentum in the late 1980s with the single market initiative. Other EU policies, such as on the environment (habitats, conservation etc.), also impinged upon MAFF even before it was re-structured into DEFRA. Sir Michael Franklin, then MAFF's Permanent Secretary, observed in 1988: 'there are few corners of the department which are not influenced to a greater or lesser extent by what goes on in Brussels . . . In Whitehall terms it has moved the Ministry from the periphery to the centre' (Franklin 1988: 55). If that comment was an early indication of the breadth of impact, the depth of Europeanisation was revealed by the food safety scares, notably bovine spongiform encephalopathy (BSE) in the 1990s and foot and mouth disease in 2001 and 2007. Both these outbreaks had to be resolved within an EU framework in order to permit the resumption of trade in beef and livestock respectively. Thus, agriculture and fisheries had arguably become the most Europeanised policy areas. In 1996 agriculture was reported to represent some 40 per cent of proposals emanating from Brussels, although the figure had earlier been 80–90 per cent. As a senior official told us in 1996, 'virtually everyone in the Department deals with Brussels'. Moreover, John Gummer, the Secretary of State (1989–93) was wont to say '80 per cent of my budget is controlled from Brussels'.[2]

Under Labour two key domestic developments have occurred, with some discernible adjustment to the department's handling of EU business. The first key impact was devolution. On 1 July 1999 policy responsibilities for agriculture, food and forestry were transferred to the devolved authorities in Scotland and Wales but with European policy remaining reserved to the UK government (see Bulmer *et al.* 2002).[3] As a consequence, a more formalised set of arrangements was established to coordinate this policy area, given its overwhelmingly Europeanised character (see Bulmer *et al.* 2002, especially pp. 107–26). The second development was the creation in 2001 of DEFRA. The new department absorbed MAFF but the latter's responsibilities for food policy had been passed to the Food Standards Agency, set up in 2000, and made accountable to the Department of Health. A separate development at EU level has been further reform of the CAP, including some re-nationalisation of policy. To the extent that gradual re-nationalisation takes place at EU level, responsibility within the UK shifts from central government to the devolved authorities, reflecting the terms of the devolution settlement. De-Europeanisation – a rare phenomenon – therefore facilitates devolution of policy in the UK. Also worthy of note has been the attempt to move from a focus on agricultural product markets to greater emphasis on rural communities and sustainability; hence the use of rural affairs in DEFRA's title.

The extensive regulation of agriculture has meant considerable ministerial involvement through attendance of Council meetings. For instance, in 1996 there were 13 meetings of the Council of Agriculture Ministers but also five sessions of the Fisheries Council. The two Council formations are now combined and meetings held approximately on a monthly basis (see Table 3.4). The Special Committee on Agriculture is the key preparatory body for the Council (excluding fisheries). For much of the period of membership the UK's representative on the SCA occupied an important role in UKREP's establishment: historically the 'number 3' position.[4] Agriculture has declined in the UKREP pecking order subsequently and CAP reform is scaling back the regulatory importance of the SCA. Even so, the agriculture and fisheries team in UKREP comprises no fewer than eight officials.[5] The 'traffic' of specialist officials from the directorates of MAFF/DEFRA to various EU committees at the pre-proposal, decision-making and policy-management stages has been extensive.

Coordination of EU-related policy within DEFRA and MAFF has evolved over the years. However, one basic principle has remained unchanged, namely that EU business has been mainstreamed across the department. A central unit in MAFF – in 1996 an EU Division but later an EU and International Group – was responsible for overarching functions. These included: policy coordination; 'horizontal' issues, such as CAP reform; issues where other Whitehall departments hold the lead, such as treaty revision; liaison with Parliament; and, from 1999, devolution. The challenge for DEFRA was the integration of the two separate EU coordination systems that it inherited and which serve two different Councils: Agriculture and Fisheries, and Environment. In early 2005 this integrated coordination task was undertaken by a European Union and International Coordination Division, responsible to both the agricultural and environmental directorates-general of DEFRA. It was a team of around a dozen officials and carried out similar coordination functions, albeit with noticeable variation for each of the Council formations.[6] Further streamlining reforms to the coordinating system were introduced after the 2005 UK presidency.

The *agricultural* policy coordination system within DEFRA continues to be based on DCE. It prepares meetings of the Council or the SCA. With the advent of new technology video-conferencing takes place to permit participation from Brussels because it is important that UKREP and Whitehall-based agricultural officials agree negotiating positions. Depending on the EU agenda the relevant policy line-divisions will be represented and a negotiating position finalised. Prior to devolution 'territorial ministries' could attend on matters of great salience to them. Since then the devolved authorities have tended to participate through their offices in Brussels, using the UKREP video link. A 'DCE Notice System' disseminated guidelines on procedures relating to European policy-making.[7] The coordination of European policy in the fisheries and food domains has been distinct in both MAFF and DEFRA because the EU procedures are distinct. Thus, a junior MAFF/DEFRA minister normally leads the UK delegation rather than the Secretary of State.

MAFF was a key player at ministerial and official levels of Cabinet co-ordination. Senior figures, such as the Deputy Secretaries and Permanent Secretary, were likely to have extensive experience of the EU.[8] Although the Europeanisation of the Department of the Environment was well behind that of MAFF, the indications are that DEFRA as a whole has extensive experience of the Cabinet Office network on European policy and the Brussels network.[9]

Policy issues with a consequence for other Whitehall Departments are handled either on an ad hoc basis or more formally through the COES machinery. Long-standing debates about reform of the CAP have been handled through COES machinery because of, most notably, the interest of the Treasury, the FCO (e.g. because of linkages with enlargement) and even the prime minister where the issue reaches the European Council's agenda, as it sometimes has. The CAP retained significant insulation within the EU institutions from other policy areas until the late 1980s at least. However, the policy's cost and consequent political salience in the 1970s and 1980s via the UK's high budgetary contributions ensured that the CAP and MAFF were less insulated within Whitehall than in some other states.

Although MAFF was responsible for the conduct of UK agricultural and fisheries policy in Brussels, the territorial departments (Welsh, Scottish and Northern Irish Offices) had administrative autonomy within the confines of UK-wide government policy. Part of the rationale for this de-centralisation lay in the different character of agriculture across the UK (see Bulmer *et al.* 2002, 107). However, administrative autonomy took on a new, political character from 1999 with the introduction of devolution, including for agriculture and fisheries.[10] Thus a Scottish official took the following nuanced view of the role of the then UK secretary of state, Nick Brown, in the post-devolution era: 'As long as he is on this side of the channel he is the minister for England; as soon as he crosses the Channel he is the minister for the UK.'[11]

Over the period since membership there had been a fairly consistent set of MAFF norms concerning European policy expressed in an internal document quoted at interview: 'implementing our obligations efficiently and seeking a more rational CAP while avoiding discrimination against UK businesses'.[12] MAFF therefore had the two-pronged objective of trying to make the CAP work for the UK (and especially England) while trying to reform it from within because the protectionist and expensive nature of the policy ran against British preferences.

The contribution of individual ministers within MAFF to Europeanisation has, in our judgement, been less than in the case of the DoE (see below). To be sure, different policy styles have been exhibited by individuals. John Gummer (Minister of Agriculture 1989–93) was clearly much more at ease with his European colleagues than his successor, Douglas Hogg (1995–97), who had to contend with most of the diplomacy associated with the BSE crisis. Margaret Beckett, the Secretary of State (SoS) in DEFRA (2001–6) was cited as an effective negotiator by observers in Whitehall. The Labour anti-marketeer John Silkin (Minister of Agriculture 1976–79) was distrusted by colleagues such as the Chief Secretary to the Treasury, Joel Barnett, for making concessions to partners in the Council that went beyond what had been agreed in the Cabinet Committee (Barnett 1982: 158–9; see Gregory 1983: 149). Our perception is that in this policy area the 'juggernaut' of the CAP, a policy in full swing when the UK acceded, has hampered individual ministers' impact. Their inter-personal and negotiating skills may have made differences here and there but major issues such as reform have been in the hands of successive prime ministers.

The Department of the Environment (DoE) is an interesting case study of Europeanisation that has been examined in detail by Andrew Jordan (2002; 2003). The DoE was set up in 1970 by the Conservative Prime Minister, Edward Heath. Its title was something of a misnomer, since it was created out of three ministries with responsibilities for: public buildings and works; housing and local government; and transport. To them was added the Central Unit for Environmental Pollution, previously located in the Cabinet Office (Jordan 2002: 27). What we now think of as environmental policy was a very small part of the DoE's tasks. In addition, there was also virtually no European environmental *acquis communautaire* for the DoE to adopt upon accession. Another aspect of EU policy subsequently fell to the DoE, namely the administration *in England* of the EU structural funds.[13]

During the 1970s the British approach to European environmental policy was overwhelmingly one of resistance. It is captured well in comments made to Andrew Jordan by a former UKREP official (2002: 34):

> Our job in Brussels was to kill proposals before they took root, to neuter those that did come up for active discussion and to find ways of reducing the practical effect of those that did get agreed. But like Canute, in the end it was an impossible job because we were always rowing against the political tide in Europe.

During the period 1979–88 European policy on the environment was 'at its most active and innovative' (Jordan 2002: 35). By this time, policy on key areas such as environmental impact assessment in connection with land use planning, the quality of drinking water and bathing water had been adopted at the European level without positive engagement by the DoE. As these directives came to the implementation phase and the UK govern-ment found problems or simply resisted, it fell to a British environment commissioner, the former Labour MP Stanley Clinton-Davis, to sanction infringement proceedings against the Conservative government for non-compliance (Jordan 2002: 37). Further, when EU legislation and infringe-ment proceedings started to impact adversely upon policies held more dearly by the Thatcher government, such as water and energy privatisation, the DoE's policy neglect could continue no longer. Indeed, Mrs Thatcher intervened to order an interdepartmental review of environmental policy that forced the Secretary of State, Nicholas Ridley (1986–89) to take a stronger involvement in the work of the Environmental Protection Group (Jordan 2002: 38). The consequence was an end to the persistent 'reception' of policy from Brussels. Instead the Environmental Protection Group (EPG) was empowered both within the DoE and in Whitehall, and could start making a more positive approach in the EU by seeking 'projection' of British policy preferences to the EU level.

Some of the explanation for the accumulated lack of engagement by the DoE with European environmental policy was attributable to the ministerial level. The DoE experienced quite a high turnover of secretaries of state – three in 1983 alone, for instance – and few of these were interested in environmental policy or its European dimension. Other issues, such as urban regeneration or local government finance, preoccupied ministers like Michael Heseltine (1979–83, also 1990–92) and Kenneth Baker (1983–86) (Jordan 2002: 29). Jordan attributes the DoE's Europeanisation to the period 1988–2000 (Jordan 2002: 40–2). The turnaround in its approach was accelerated by two engaged Conservative ministers, both Europhiles: Chris Patten (1989–90) and John Gummer (1993–97). Patten's junior minister, David Trippier captured the new approach in the following terms (quoted in Jordan 2002: 40):

> it is vital that we play a leading role in the formulation of new legislation. To do this we have to be engaged. We have to be in constant dialogue with [Commission] and other member states. We have to be constructive and proactive in our approach. We cannot be influential if all we do is barrack from the sidelines. *We have to learn to think European.*

Resources were strengthened by increasing the size of EPG and by creating a specific division for European environmental policy. But the political interest declined somewhat under the succeeding ministers (Michael Heseltine and the Euro-sceptic Michael Howard). John Gummer, who had come from MAFF, where EU business was mainstreamed, decided that further momentum was needed. This decision was reportedly attributable to his first attendance of the Council of Environment Ministers, 'which was a bit of a shambles . . . He had a sense in which the officials were not worldly wise to all of this. Gummer said "right I want things to happen, get us more focused on Europe. It is 80 per cent of our environmental protection business, its happening out there [Brussels] not here, so go away and do it"'.[14] In consequence, he launched a European professionalism initiative in order to secure a change of culture. The initiative comprised a more systematic effort to place DoE officials in UKREP or on a detachment to the Commission; improved training and awareness-raising within the ministry; and the publication of a guide to environmental negotiation in the EU, written by a DoE official, who had just served a two-year term in UKREP (Humphreys 1996). By the end of the second Major government the DoE was running a much more engaged EU policy operation from its Environment Protection Strategy and Europe Division (EPSED). Its response had moved from 'reception' to 'projection'.

The first Blair government caused some organisational upheaval, as environmental policy was located in the large but unwieldy Department of the Environment, Transport and the Regions under Deputy Prime Minister, John Prescott. Environmental policy was coordinated on one side of the department, while transport was coordinated elsewhere along with oversight of horizontal issues such as liaison with Westminster or EU treaty reform.[15] Nevertheless, Prescott and his ministers were active in pursuing European environmental policy, including during the UK presidency of the EU in 1998 (Young 2000: 163–4). The subsequent merger of environmental responsibilities with MAFF's work into DEFRA further underpinned the Europeanisation of UK environmental policy-making.

DEFRA is one of the key players in European policy. It is a department where the importance of European experience is recognised across the board. Our interviews indicate that it is the one Whitehall home department where a European 'tour of duty' is not seen as a threat to career plans but, rather, a means of advancement. EU policy is integrated across the board. EU training is extensive, with significant in-house provision. The 2007 Departmental Report named CAP reform as part of DEFRA's Public Service Agreement (PSA) targets (PSA 5), while the department is in the lead with the government's objective of becoming an EU leader in sustainable procurement by 2009.[16] The EU dimension is strongly integrated into the other PSA objectives, which serve as performance indicators to justify public expenditure. In sum, we consider DEFRA to be a highly Europeanised department: arguably *the* most Europeanised one of them all.

The Treasury: defensive Europeanisation?

The Europeanisation of the Treasury has, we shall argue, been uneven and incomplete in nature and hampered by the persistently defensive postures adopted on the substance of European policy (for an alternative account see Pickering 2002). In one sense this seems odd, for it was a Treasury Permanent Secretary, Sir Frank Lee, who played a central role in shifting the terms of debate, culminating in Harold Macmillan's application for EEC membership in 1961. During negotiations and after accession, the Treasury has provided key personnel to UKREP and several heads of the COES (see Table 5.1). However, the Treasury has had a strong and long-standing Atlanticist orientation towards global institutions. To the extent that this has declined over the period since 1973, the Treasury has still had to conduct a defensive policy towards the EU. It has had to contend with the adverse consequences of the EU budget, whereby the UK's net contributions could only be placed on a more equitable basis by the creation of a rebate (or abatement, to use official terminology). The UK's currency cooperation with other member states has been brief and traumatic, and the opt-out from the single currency continues. Resistance to EU efforts to introduce tax harmonisation has been bipartisan in nature and opposition to QMV on this issue remains one of the UK's so-called red-line institutional issues under the Labour government. The overall impact of these circumstances has been, in our opinion, a hindrance to the Treasury being able to project a constructive policy in the EU. From the late-1980s it advocated, in conjunction with the Bank of England, a single market in financial services. Under Gordon Brown's chancellorship there were efforts to encourage further economic liberalisation, exchange of good practice in employment policy and initiatives in e-commerce. Significantly, all these areas of constructive Treasury European policy have avoided classic supranational methods of integration. They have either embraced negative integration (the dismantling of trade barriers) or, more recently, the Open Method of Coordination (OMC). In other words, the more supranational, hierarchical mode of EU governance seems to bring grief to the Treasury, whereas it has been more at ease with horizontal patterns that rely on the economic or political market-place to determine optimal policy.[17]

Despite the Treasury's rather lukewarm attitude towards integration, what seems to have happened is that its work has become so enmeshed in EU business that a small cadre of officials with EU experience has come through, and some shift in outlook is underway. In the words of a former insider, 'The European Union is now a pervasive part of the Treasury's culture' (Pickering 2002). This quotation strikes us as resembling a student exam question after which follows the word 'discuss'! As we shall argue, awareness of the EU is now doubtless much greater but the impact on Treasury culture is a rather different matter.

The impact of EU policy on the Treasury is extensive but has grown significantly since accession. By the 1990s finance ministers were meeting almost as frequently as foreign ministers, reflecting this development. The *EU budget* impacts on UK public expenditure and gives the Treasury an interest in the substance of all of the EU's spending programmes. In consequence, the Treasury has a stake in any policy area with spending implications: the CAP, structural funds, research policy and so on. The Treasury leads the government in the annual EU budgetary negotiations but medium-term financial reviews of the EU budget are regarded as matters to be negotiated by foreign ministers and heads of government (the European Council). Within Whitehall the Treasury is a major player in shaping this policy. The Treasury has set important procedures across government in order to control the impact of EU expenditure (see below). The main external response was the attempt to secure (and subsequently to retain) a rebate system on contributions, which was achieved by Margaret Thatcher at the Fontainebleau European Council in 1984.

EU *policy on taxation and customs duties* also has a domestic impact on public expenditure, for which the Treasury is responsible. European *monetary policy* – from the Snake in the 1970s, through the Exchange Rate Mechanism (ERM) to the single currency – has had a major impact on the Treasury's responsibilities. Monetary cooperation was underway even before UK accession. Sterling was for a brief period a participant in the currency arrangements known as the Snake in 1972, prior to accession. The main subsequent impacts upon the Treasury have come with negotiations on setting up the European Monetary System in the late-1970s (Ludlow 1982) and then with the IGC on EMU ahead of the Maastricht Treaty (Dyson and Featherstone 1999: 582–99). With long periods of non-participation in the ERM and the Euro, European monetary policy has not had qualitatively the same Europeanisation-impact as full involvement would have entailed.[18] The Treasury ceded some of its monetary policy powers to the Bank of England when the latter was granted independence by the Labour government in 1997, thus re-distributing the impact somewhat.

In the area of *macro-economic coordination* the EU makes reports on member states' performance, although its supranational powers are limited in this area, except for Euro-zone states. The Treasury is again responsible in domestic terms. The *Lisbon Strategy on economic reform* in Europe, launched in March 2000, set the objective for the EU of becoming over the next decade 'the most competitive and dynamic knowledge-based economy in the world' (European Council 2000). It brings the Treasury into a process of benchmarking with other member states on a range of micro-economic issues, as well as the preparation of an annual report to the Commission on the National Reform Programme on growth and employment.[19] The Lisbon Strategy's antecedents lie in initiatives undertaken on employment in the aftermath of the 1997 Amsterdam Treaty. The Labour government has been an advocate of this policy and has sought to export some of its ideas to other member states. The Europeanisation-effect is less intrusive: in part because the Labour government played an important part in shaping the policy. The more voluntaristic nature of the OMC policy process means that it is peer pressure rather than legislation that drives the EU's impact upon this aspect of the Treasury's work. Finally, several *internal market* activities impact on Treasury responsibilities: for example, liberalisation of the financial services sector and public procurement rules.

The organisational impact of the EU on the Treasury has been complex and not especially transparent. A separate division for the EC was created in 1972, once accession was clear.[20] Geoffrey Edwards reported 'that a European Community Group (of Divisions) emerged as part of the Treasury's Overseas Finance in 1982' (1992: 81), although one of our interviewees dated this development to the mid-1970s.[21] In the late 1990s, with the Treasury in the vanguard of management reforms and de-layering, Craig Pickering captured the basic Treasury set-up thus:

> European work in the Treasury is handled by a combination of gathering
> what is regarded as core EU work together as a specialism, in a central
> 'European' unit, and by farming out European issues which require know-
> ledge of other policies to other parts of the Treasury. (2002: 587)

However, two senior Treasury interviewees indicated that this division of
labour was reinforced by a development unrelated to the EU: the 1994
Fundamental Expenditure Review (FER).[22] Described in 2004 by Gus
O'Donnell, the then Permanent Secretary, as 'a pivotal moment in the
Treasury's recent history', it prompted reforms that focused resources on
the department's key objectives (O'Donnell 2004). Increased dispersal of
EU business across the department ensued, reducing what was seen as
core EU work.[23]

In 2005 there were two EU units, both located in the Directorate for
Macroeconomic Policy and International Finance and sub-divided into teams,
making up the so-called 'core'.[24] Pickering (2002: 588) states that 'no more
than 30' officials were involved in core European work. By summer 2007
directorates had been re-organised and one unit – simply entitled 'Europe'
– was located in the International and Finance Directorate. Its four teams
have responsibility for: coordination and strategy; EU finances (covering
the EU budget and the associated periodic 'financial perspectives' reforms);
European economic reform (a new team established in the second Labour
government); and European economics (which includes monitoring other
member states' economies – part of the Lisbon Strategy). The coordination
and strategy team is responsible for briefing ministers ahead of Council
meetings, in particular ECOFIN.[25] The second unit from 2005 has disap-
peared, and this is perhaps not surprising since it was concerned with EMU
Policy and Euro Preparations.

The Treasury's work goes beyond these EU policy areas; responsibility
for the others is farmed out to elsewhere in the department. Amongst the
areas affected are financial services, broad economic policy issues and taxation, which are located in other policy directorates. Then there are those
parts of the Treasury with an active watch over domestic public spending.
The work of the EU Finances (EUF) Team is closely inter-connected with
that of the spending teams in the Public Services and Growth Directorate.
These are responsible for monitoring individual ministries in connection with
domestic public expenditure. They are brought in when corresponding
EU spending programmes are at issue, with EUF providing central coordination. The Treasury's interest in other departments' EU policy is not
confined to budgetary aspects but extends into the substance of policy.
Thus, officials working on science and industry policy in its Enterprise and
Growth Unit have dealt with Treasury input into policy on EU structural
funds, such as their periodic review, or the Framework Programmes in
science and technology (see also Pickering 2002: 588). In both these cases

policy-lead was elsewhere – in the DTI – but the Treasury input was influential because of its grounding in a wish to restrain expenditure growth and secure cost-effective policy. This motivation arises because the UK, as a net contributor to the EU budget, will be contributing disproportionately to particular EU spending programmes. In this way the distribution of policy across the Treasury draws a much larger group of officials into the EU network, affecting a majority of policy teams.[26] Some other EU business that falls to Treasury ministers, notably on taxation, is handled outside the Treasury, for instance by HM Revenue and Customs (formed in 2005 from the Inland Revenue and Customs and Excise) or the Financial Services Authority.

What about the impact on the Treasury's relatively large ministerial team?[27] The Chancellor of the Exchequer has overall policy responsibility. Other ministers in the Treasury deal with EU business as a function of their domestic responsibilities. The Chancellor does not attend what used to be the Budget Council or deal with that issue when it is on the ECOFIN agenda; that is usually dealt with by the Economic Secretary. Arguably the most unorthodox Treasury minister under Labour was Lord Simon, the former chairman of BP, who held the joint Treasury–DTI post of Minister for Competitiveness in Europe. Entering government from BP was unorthodox; the joint position with the DTI was unusual; and his multi-lingual skills were unprecedented for a British minister. He was able to 'network' across the EU in a manner that was quite unprecedented for a UK minister. During the 1998 presidency, for instance, at an informal ECOFIN held in York Lord Simon

> was a good foil for the Chancellor because he is good at the things the Chancellor finds more difficult . . . socialising and that sort of thing . . . You could put him next to [German Finance Minister] Waigel and they could talk in German, able to make small talk as well as heavy talk.[28]

However, Lord Simon was only in post for two years (1997–99).

The Treasury's interaction with the broader Whitehall network of EU policy-makers is extensive. The Treasury will routinely participate in any policy discussions where there are EU budgetary implications, such as the 'Friday meeting' (see Chapter 5). The Chancellor is a central figure in both government generally and EU policy. This derives not only from the status of the office and the extensive impact of EU business, but also from the fact that the Treasury has a Whitehall-wide remit because of its ability to intervene in public spending matters of individual ministries. In addition, successive Chancellors have sought to retain European monetary policy as a reserved domain. This situation held under the Major premiership (with Norman Lamont and Kenneth Clarke as Chancellors) and, earlier, when Nigel Lawson shadowed the Deutsche Mark despite PM Margaret Thatcher's reservations. She, it is worth remembering, took advice on

European monetary policy from Sir Alan Walters, a critic of the ERM, and a very public fall-out occurred, resulting in Lawson's resignation as well as that of Walters. (George 1994: 226–7). Under Blair's premiership executive authority was split between the PM and his staff, on the one hand, and the Chancellor of the Exchequer and the Treasury, on the other. The split between Blair and Brown was seen as a fault line under the former's premiership (Naughtie 2001; Scott 2004), and had consequences for the economic aspects of European policy.

A particular instance of the Treasury being seen as conducting a discrete European policy occurred in June 2003 when the Chancellor reported on the five economic tests he had set in November 1997 for judging whether to recommend joining the Euro. The Treasury carried out a very thorough report, accompanied by 18 EMU studies.[29] However, the PM was pretty much presented with a *fait accompli* on the matter (Scott 2004: 224–5). As one interviewee put it, 'Part of the problem was that the Prime Minister couldn't get the advice direct from the Treasury and [the COES] were inhibited in giving him the advice because [it] didn't have access to the sources'.[30] Discussion in the Cabinet came afterwards and served to give a collective appearance to a decision on which the Chancellor's role had been decisive (Scott 2004: 225).

As a result of this degree of autonomy, the personality of the Chancellor can impact on the conduct of European policy. The importance of some episodes of integration has heightened this situation. The negotiations in the IGC on EMU were a particular episode of importance that coincided with Norman Lamont's tenure as Chancellor. Dyson and Featherstone consider his role in those negotiations in some detail (1999: 597–9). 'Lamont was, by general consent, a poor negotiator: ill at ease in large set-piece negotiations and lacking the skills to gain allies . . . in private conversation' (1999: 597). Indeed, as regards attending ECOFIN Councils, Lamont 'used regularly not to go'.[31] However, his negotiating skills and behaviour were even more critical in September 1992, when British participation in the ERM came under pressure. He was widely seen to have abused his position as chair of an informal ECOFIN Council, held in Bath, and an opportunity to have a realignment of currencies was lost (Stephens 1997: 226–62; Dyson and Featherstone 1999: 683). Indeed, questions were even asked as to why Nigel Wicks, the Treasury's Second Permanent Secretary and UK member of the EC Monetary Committee, had failed to restrain Lamont (Stephens 1997: 234). Having enraged the President of the German Bundesbank, Helmut Schlesinger, over the weekend, Lamont and PM John Major were left without a potential ally in tackling the sterling crisis that emerged the following week, culminating in ejection from the ERM on 'Black Wednesday', 16 September 2002.

Kenneth Clarke, Lamont's successor as Chancellor, by contrast, was perfectly at ease in Brussels. As one interviewee put it:

The Treasury mandarins [other than Wicks] used to say to him, 'Why do you go to ECOFIN every month, we could always send your deputy'? . . . Ken Clarke would say to these rather incredulous sort of mandarins 'Because an ECOFIN is the most important thing this week. No I am not going to do some domestic business and miss a key ECOFIN.' He like[d] that circuit and he would impart that message, that this mattered to him, and that did boost the value of Europe in the Department, because you knew that the Chancellor thought it really mattered, what happened at ECOFIN.[32]

Gordon Brown, by contrast, was not seen as particularly at ease in EU meetings. Prior to taking office in May 1997, Brown had originally been regarded as a Euro-phile but as Chancellor he was regarded as following a more critical, even Euro-sceptic, line. He was reported to think a lot about Europe; however, his economic pre-occupations – as 'the most active micro economic Chancellor there has been bar none' – tended to lead him to look at states where lessons could be drawn on competitiveness and productivity. In consequence, 'when he look[ed] for economic and social models for what works, understandably in view of the empirical evidence he [wa]s looking as much across the Atlantic . . . more to that than Europe'.[33] The Chancellor's reliance on Atlanticist special advisers, such as Ed Balls, was also a notable characteristic. There was also a sense of some Treasury officials being insiders, while others felt excluded. Outside the Treasury the Department was seen as having become more secretive on European policy. Thus, there were two consequent features of Gordon Brown's chancellorship. First, the inner group of officials and advisers around Brown did not seem to have had a significant degree of European experience. And, second, the Treasury was seen as not part of the otherwise much more joined-up approach to EU policy.

Four features characterise the Treasury's broad response to Europeanisation. First, it has been defensive. Second, European policy has been a second-order objective in the department's key priorities. In this sense the Fundamental Expenditure Review (FER) of 1994 may be seen as entrenching a prioritisation of policy goals such as on public spending, monetary policy and so on, while European policy assumed lesser significance, almost ghetto-ised organisationally despite the widespread impact of Europeanisation. The symptoms of this situation are relatively straightforward to identify. The two EU groups in the Directorate for Macroeconomic Policy and International Finance have a difficult task in trying to integrate all the European dimensions of the Treasury's work. This method of organisation runs a risk – especially for a department which is not especially Europeanised – that 'a lot of people who are rather inexpert about how the EU works tend to end up doing EU negotiations and not doing them very well'.[34] The Europe team cannot offer tactical advice on the highly technical policy concerns of the entire Department: from energy liberalisation, through pensions reform to state aids. In DEFRA, as we have seen, the integration of EU business across the department succeeds because a facility for European business is regarded as important to the careers of its officials. However, the Treasury context is different.

> The Treasury is full of people who don't know a vast amount about Europe and don't think a lot about it. It is regarded in lots of ways that the Brussels-based culture is a pretty alien culture where they . . . talk a different language in every sense and it has not been central to a Treasury career.[35]

There have been efforts to improve the level of EU training. In-house training now requires the acquisition of European skills alongside those in micro- and macro-economics, but the impact of this across the Department will take some time to work through.[36]

A third characteristic is the way that Treasury rules on EU spending programmes have had the effect of superimposing domestic public spending goals on European policy objectives, with pervasive, government-wide impact (see below). Spending departments are in effect obliged to sign up to the Treasury's defensive European policy. Similarly, in monetary policy, European activity was for a long time regarded as an irritant. This is reflected in the words of a Treasury official in 1996:

> EMU . . . in my view has not been a great Treasury success because we have been consistently insular. And, when I say Treasury, I include ministers in that because you can't separate ministers from the machinery. We have consistently over the last 10 years under-estimated the political commitment and degree of technical competence of those dealing with it. We have tended to hope that it would go away. This is no longer the position but it is a bit late now.[37]

Fourthly, career paths of officials in the department strike us as confirming ghetto-isation. Officials with a speciality in the EU do not seem to reach the upper echelons of the department – with very few exceptions – and seem to be 'promoted out': e.g. to COES, the Prime Minister's Office, to EU institutions or to other departments in Whitehall, or remain within the Directorate for Macroeconomic Policy and International Finance. At interview we were told of specific senior former Treasury officials who were now out of favour, whilst another in Brussels was felt to have 'gone native'. It is difficult for outsiders like us to know whether these instances are well-founded but, if accurate, they suggest that a European expertise is not helpful to attaining the most senior posts in the Treasury. Finally, even the Treasury's mission seems to ghetto-ise European policy. It is subsumed within one of seven PSA objectives, namely to 'promote UK economic prospects by pursuing increased productivity and efficiency in the EU, international financial stability and increased global prosperity, especially protecting the most vulnerable'.[38]

The Treasury and the EU budget: the Treasury rules OK?

As noted earlier, Treasury rules on European spending have a pervasive impact across Whitehall. Axiomatic to UK public expenditure control from the mid-1970s has been the notion of cash limits (now termed Departmental Expenditure Limits), introduced to assert Treasury control over spending departments following a breakdown of the existing system (see Thain and Wright 1995: 45–7). It was the Treasury's clear view that cash limits should not be breached by virtue of flows of additional funds from the EC to UK spending departments. There are four categories of EU spending where special Treasury rules have applied in order to take account of the 'cash limits' principle. Category 1 relates to agricultural spending. Category 2 concerns the structural funds. Category 3 relates to other (largely internal) EU spending, where EUROPES applied until abandoned in November 2003. Category 4 applies to overseas aid. The basic principle was the same, namely that the Treasury sought to claw back from the relevant department any additional funds that it expected to receive from the European budget.

The predominance of agricultural expenditure as a proportion of the EC budget upon accession has meant that CAP expenditure has largely been taken for granted over the subsequent period. However, were the EU to sanction a significant increase in agricultural expenditure – a highly unlikely prospect, given successive UK governments' efforts to reduce such spending – the Treasury would seek to claw money back from the DEFRA budget. In any event, the government's policy is to further reduce CAP spending, as was demonstrated by PM Blair during the 2005 presidency, where he sought such a commitment from European counterparts in return for negotiations on the British rebate (Whitman 2006: 61–2).

The arrangements for Category 2 spending date back to the negotiations regarding the regional and social funds in the early years of UK membership. The Treasury had to decide whether the EC money should be regarded as additional or not.

> The doctrine from the Treasury's point of view was a very straightforward economic one, which was that the Treasury, as always, was concerned with the controlled total of public expenditure and it was clear that we were going to be a net contributor to the Community budget on a substantial scale and that would, other things being equal, increase the total of public expenditure and be an additional strain on the Government's ability to contain expenditure. And therefore the Treasury regarded it as essential that any gross receipts that we got from Brussels should go to reduce the net contribution and could not be swallowed up by departments.[39]

Procedurally, therefore, the Treasury would reduce the spending ministries' budgets accordingly.[40] However, as European funding was also to be additional at local level, the Treasury would similarly reduce the support going to recipient local authorities via its distribution mechanism for local authority capital spending. This measure ensured that neither the central government department nor local authorities would receive extra funds. Of course, from the perspective of the European Commission this arrangement undermined its objective of trying to add value to pre-existing domestic regional and social policy. It therefore took the matter up with the UK government after DoE complaints about the system had been leaked in the British press. Eventually an agreement was reached in 1992 between the then UK Permanent Representative, Sir John Kerr and Bruce Millan, the (UK) Commissioner with responsibility for the structural funds (see Bache 1998: 105–7). Did this undermine Treasury spending rules? Not a bit: 'We produce figures which show that national level spending is additional but we've changed the distribution system so that it doesn't have this effect.'[41] In fairness, this practice is not unique to the UK, although the specific explanation of its origins and mechanics is distinctive.

EUROPES came about for similar reasons. It was prompted by the growth in the early 1980s of new spending programmes in areas such as research and development. The fundamental Treasury practice was to negotiate a cash ceiling for UK research policy with the DTI. However, any UK receipts from European research programmes would have had the effect of raising the cash ceiling. And the EU was developing new multi-annual programmes at this time, such as the European Strategic Programme of Research and Development in Information Technology (ESPRIT), launched in 1984.

> the Treasury proposition was that there should be a limit to the total spent on research and within that limit the scientists and the DTI and the other Departments concerned had to chose if it was going to be spent on European programmes or was it going to be spent on domestic programmes. Because what had become apparent over the previous period was that there was simply no discipline on the DTI negotiators. They had no incentive to bargain hard to keep the amount of spending down when they went off to Brussels.[42]

Gradually over the period 1983–84 ministerial correspondence developed between the Treasury and, once again, the DTI, albeit with support from allies such as the FCO. An instruction was issued that the matter should be resolved. As the key Treasury official put it: 'I locked the DTI in my room one day and didn't let them out until they had agreed.'[43] And thus was born the European Public Expenditure Survey (EUROPES), whose impact extended across central government to cover *any* department which had a spending programme that was not covered by the other three categories of spending. It was fully incorporated into the annual domestic Public Expenditure Survey (PES) from 1998 (on PES see Thain and Wright 1995).

The basic operational practice with EUROPES is to calculate what percentage of the EU budget is contributed 'net' by the UK. Using this percentage, the Treasury then calculates the sum in relation to individual EU spending programmes. It then deducts the sum concerned from the annual domestic public expenditure settlement of the department to which

---

Box 6.1 Treasury controls over EU spending programmes within UK government

'The main objectives of EUROPES are to contain the cost to UK public expenditure of EC spending; to ensure that any additions to UK public expenditure, resulting from EC spending, are considered alongside other bids in the annual Public Expenditure Survey; and to encourage Government departments to take a closer interest in proposals for EC spending in their areas of policy responsibility, eg in terms of UK priorities and value of money.'

'In addition . . . there are two other inter-related objectives of EUROPES, as important as any explicit savings that may be secured. Imposing financial responsibilities on departments:
   a. encourages them to take a robust line in Brussels' negotiations, helping to contain the UK contribution to the EC budget;
   b. encourages proper assessment of EC spending plans, by comparison with similar activities in their domestic programmes. This supports the two important principles of securing value for money from the Community's budget and ensuring that EC expenditure is consistent with our own priorities, so far as possible.'

Source: HM Treasury 1996: 3–4.

---

the programme is attributed. In this way EUROPES is not even regarded as part of European policy because it is part of the public spending process.

The Treasury was crystal-clear about the purposes of EUROPES (see Box 6.1). However, in our interviews across Whitehall we encountered quite varying knowledge and understanding of the system. Awareness of its impact was undoubtedly at its greatest in the DTI. European coordinators in ministries with EU spending programmes generally displayed a grudging acceptance of EUROPES. However, a former UK Permanent Representative was much more trenchant:

> that is a pernicious system . . . The point about EUROPES is that the Treasury don't even have to lift a finger. It actually saves the Treasury from having to get involved in the policy argument. They just laugh and say: 'Well you can decide, you can spend twice as much [on an EU programme] if you want, then it just comes off your EUROPES, so it's up to you.'[44]

On the other hand, a former Treasury official reported on discussions of EUROPES with finance ministries in other states: 'they all say "God, I wish we had a system like that"'.[45] Only a small number of our interviewees understood how it worked and could see the bias it introduced into UK European policy.[46]

There have been occasional attempts to review the EUROPES system. One attempt was made by Michael Heseltine when President of the Board of Trade in John Major's government.[47] Eventually a review came to the conclusion that the system had outlived its purpose, not least because it had become extremely complex to operate. EUROPES was withdrawn in November 2003.[48]

The final category of spending relates to overseas aid. The overwhelming majority of EU aid is made via the European Development Fund (EDF). The EDF is usually funded for periods of some five years and linked to each phase of the Lomé and then Cotonou Conventions on aid to the African Caribbean and Pacific countries. However, the EDF is not part of the EU budget, and is funded quite distinctly. The UK is not required to pay a fixed share of the EDF, although once it has agreed its share it must adhere to that for the five-year period. The impact of Treasury rules on the Overseas Development Administration (ODA), and subsequently DfID, has been that there is a fixed aid budget, so any contributions to the EDF are at the expense of national development aid. The OECD's Development Cooperation Directorate reviews the effectiveness of different donor schemes and judged UK development aid to be more effective than EDF aid. Hence, given Treasury rules, the incentive in Whitehall was to cut back on EDF spending and use the national programme instead. And that is what happened, for instance, in the eighth EDF (from 2000), where the UK reduced its share of contributions to the EDF from 16.3 per cent to 12.7 per cent.[49]

How did this look from a more disinterested perspective? A former Permanent Representative commented

> I am afraid it used to drive me almost up the wall. The five-year negotiation of the Lomé Convention . . . was absolutely unbelievable because the whole of ODA was mobilised for three years before . . . and through the whole negotiation to fight every inch of the way against any spending in Europe, irrespective of whether it was good or not, because the whole of ODA's future for the next five years was predicated on how much money our share of that was.

For aid that is paid through the EU budget itself, such as food or humanitarian aid and aid under the PHARE programme from the 1990s to new democracies of central and eastern Europe as well as the western Balkans, a separate system known as attribution applies. This is because the Treasury rules discussed above cannot apply in view of the fact that the UK is not a recipient of development aid. The UK's share of abated *gross* contributions to the EU budget is calculated in order to generate the charge to be made against the budget of the Department for International Development (DfID).[50] Here a perverse consequence of Treasury rules was that such aid agreed to at EU level in the 1990s for the prospective accession states of eastern and central Europe tended to displace national development aid that was likely to be destined for the poorest states.[51]

As can be seen quite clearly, the impact of the Treasury's rules for controlling EU spending has been extensive.[52] More generally, the Blair governments' pre-occupations with policy delivery, executed through Public Service Agreements (PSAs), led to a focus on policy outputs, while the EU's role in helping achieve them may be neglected. The FCO and DEFRA are notable in giving some prominence to the EU *per se*. But it is the spending rules that have had the greatest impact, potentially distorting both individual departments' European policy and their spending priorities. The overall effect, in our view, has been to spread the Treasury's defensive posture towards the EU to other parts of Whitehall as well. Treasury spending rules have had the potential to run counter to the government's stated European policy, as led by the PM, the FCO and the COES. In reality, the policy of successive governments has been defensive towards the EU, so no conflict has been apparent. Under Blair, however, greater potential for division emerged because of his pursuit of a constructive European policy (Bulmer and Burch 2005).

The Department of Trade and Industry (DTI)

The Department of Trade and Industry and its predecessor, the Board of Trade (BoT), were affected by the European integration process from the very outset. As noted earlier, it was an official from the BoT, Russell Bretherton, who had participated briefly in negotiations that eventually led to the creation of the EEC. Interest in EEC developments was of a monitoring nature but the department was much more directly and actively involved with the creation and operation of the European Free Trade Association, which was a British initiative.

In light of its trade responsibilities the department was clearly of central importance to any accession negotiations and established itself as a key player in European policy coordination as a result (see Chapter 4). During the accession talks in the early 1970s negotiations on issues such as tariffs and quotas were conducted by the newly established Department of Trade and Industry. Created in 1970, and integrating the Ministry of Technology, this re-organisation was characteristic of a number of such changes over the following decades. The department has a mixed mission – being responsible for market-making as well as market-correcting policies. This mixed role was a factor behind its repeated re-organisation in the 1970s and intermittently thereafter, and even the short-lived idea of re-naming it the Department of Productivity, Energy and Industry (pronounced dopey) in the immediate aftermath of the Blair government's re-election in May 2005. The upheavals of the 1970s are particularly striking; at times the BoT/DTI was split in different ways – notably into Trade, Industry, Prices and Consumer Affairs – and then re-constituted, sometimes with Transport and Energy incorporated.[53] To compound matters, individual secretaries of state have had short tenures. At four years Patricia Hewitt (2001–5) was the longest serving secretary of state. The departures of Conservative SoSs Leon Brittan (1985–86) and Nicholas Ridley (1989–90) both arose from European matters (Edwards 1992: 82). As a result of frequent re-organisation, ministerial turnover and its rather diffuse mission the DTI's significance to EU policy-making can easily be under-estimated by observers from outside of government.

What, then, were the main areas of EU policy impact on the DTI during the Major/Blair eras? Core issues were EU external trade policy and the EU's internal market. Other EU policies impacting centrally upon the DTI were: industrial policy (which can include sectoral policies such as telecommunications); energy policy; science and technology; the competitiveness agenda (which impacts on the DTI and the Treasury as well as bearing on the Cabinet Office's then coordinating role on regulatory reform); important aspects of the structural funds (but not implementation); industrial relations measures; consumer protection; and equal opportunities. The single market programme (1985–92) and the 2000 Lisbon Agenda on competitiveness have at different times given strong saliency to particular DTI responsibilities. In fact, the DTI has had an involvement in more Council formations than any other department: Employment, Social Policy and Consumer Affairs; Competitiveness (Internal Market, Industry and Research); and Transport, Telecommunications and Energy. Additionally, its trade responsibilities – reflected in a senior DTI official serving as representative on the important Article 133 Committee – fall under the External Relations Council (General Affairs and External Relations Council GAERC) (see Figure 3.1; and see Hayes-Renshaw and Wallace 2006: 90–4, on the Article 133 Committee). Hence in December 1996 one of our DTI interviewees was able with justification to assert that 'We are the biggest practitioner of EU business in the whole of Whitehall'.[54]

The range of DTI responsibilities highlights the observation made earlier about the rather incoherent set of policies located in the DTI. Thus, while its internal market and competitiveness policies are clearly about making markets work, science and technology, the structural funds, consumer protection and equal opportunities are concerned with market-correcting policies. Moreover, the latter two may generate the kind of regulations that other parts of the DTI are striving to reduce! Despite the apparent incoherence of mission, since the 1980s the DTI has been in the front-line of most of the UK government's positive economic policies on the EU: advocating the single market from the 1980s, advancing the competitiveness agenda as part of the Lisbon process (and pushing for regulatory reform as part of this process), as well as advocating an open world trade policy on the part of the EU.

A European directorate has been in existence in the department in some form or other since accession in 1973. This directorate has been responsible

for most of the EU 'core business' as well as for all matters of parliamentary scrutiny, training, 'horizontal' issues such as treaty reform, bilateral
relations on EU policy and so on. A few areas tended to fall outside the
directorate's remit, notably the structural funds, industrial relations and
science and technology. The Europe and World Trade Directorate was
the key unit at the end of the Blair era but the arrangements for European
business have been rather fluid. In 1996 it was co-located with trade; in
2000 it was moved to the Enterprise and Innovation Group. The directorate's
mission was:

> to make the UK an effective partner in the EU, and more widely, to develop
> open, dynamic and efficient markets and so contribute to creating a highly
> productive UK economy within a competitive EU and a sustainable world
> trading environment.[55]

In 2000 the (then) European Policy Directorate had some sixty staff,
including the administrative level.[56]

The Office of Science and Technology, and later the Office of Science
and Innovation, was central for dealing with specific EU policies, in particular the Framework Programmes.[57] Externally the Office would support
the science minister in negotiations about the programmes. Internally, it
was placed directly in the firing line of the EUROPES system. It would take
the initial public expenditure 'hit' from the Treasury but would then seek
to attribute its impact to the benefiting Department, since the OST/OSI really
serves as a coordinating body. Ultimately, the EUROPES impact would be
passed on to, for instance, a science function in a Whitehall Department,
such as DEFRA, or to one of the research councils. The position put to us
in the OST in 1996 was thus: 'There is a disincentive to spend any money
... through Europe. But at the same time there is an incentive to try to
spend the money that *is* going to be spent in Europe on things which are
useful'.[58] In other words, EUROPES meant that departments and research
councils in receipt of EU research funding could expect to find cuts in national
programmes over which they had more control.

At ministerial level one of the DTI's ministers of state usually took responsibility for EU policy, generally in line with the department's internal organisation. In the third Blair government Ian Pearson was appointed minister
responsible for European and world trade policy, in a joint post with the
FCO that reflected the latter's involvement in trade matters. Generally, DTI
officials considered ministers as effective when they made the effort to network with counterparts as part of pursuing British policy.[59] The Secretary
of State him/herself tended not to be a key player in EU negotiations, although
by setting the tone in the department an important impact may be felt. Thus,
the domestic publicity campaign by SoS Lord Young (1987–89) to get UK
business to prepare for the single market had a big impact. Even Euro-
sceptics, such as Young's successor, Nicholas Ridley, favoured the opening

of European markets. However, he 'wanted the EEA [European Economic Area] to be negotiated in such a way that it could be a 'bolt-hole' for the UK in the event we wanted to leave the EU – not quite the government's policy – resulting in some problems'.[60]

Throughout the period of membership the DTI has played a full role in the EU policy-coordination bodies. It has provided most of the Deputy Permanent Representatives in UKREP and two heads of the COES. The DTI has consistently produced senior members of the cadre of EU-savvy officials. It has a strong commitment to in-house training on the EU, which is an important component of the DTI's training plan. In policy terms it has a generally positive posture, notably on the single market, the Lisbon Strategy and trade. This posture on economic policy contrasts with the Treasury's defensive stance on EMU and the budget and with the long-standing trench-warfare on the part of MAFF/DEFRA to reform the CAP. With its positive agenda, the DTI had generally been a supporter of QMV in the Council in order to over-rule minority protectionist states. However, the industrial relations responsibilities, inherited in 1995 when the Department of Employment was re-organised, found the DTI on the defensive and opposing QMV in this area.

In summary, the DTI has been a key Department in dealing with the EU. Its stance was more positive than the other 'inner core' departments. However, its mission was much more diverse and scarcely coherent. In addition, the organisation of its European policy functions has been affected as much by changing EU policies as by the intermittent re-organisation of the department. Of these, Prime Minister Gordon Brown's replacement of the DTI with the Department for Business, Enterprise and Regulatory Reform was merely the most recent manifestation.[61]

Conclusion

Our review of the nature and sources of change will be combined for all departments at the end of Chapter 7. In the meantime it is instructive to compare how these three inner-group departments have responded to the EU. There are obvious similarities in organisational response; they and other ministries need to create arrangements to deal with parliamentary scrutiny, treaty reform and such like. However, the respective disposition of each of the three departments has been distinctive.

MAFF was thoroughly Europeanised through necessity from a very early stage because it had to fit in with the prevailing European policies – the CAP and CFP – even though both created difficulties for the UK. For MAFF the critical juncture was accession, since many of its activities were immediately affected by the Communities. The DoE adopted an ostrich-like approach of ignoring European policy impact until it was flouting European law and had to adapt to the exigencies of membership. It then moved quite rapidly, facilitated by ministerial intervention, to a position of positive engagement. The critical junctures came with the efforts of Chris Patten (1989–90) and John Gummer (1993–97) to secure the DoE's positive engagement with the EC. This posture has gradually seen the development of a strong British imprint on EU environment policy. DEFRA combines MAFF's early Europeanisation with the later conversion of the DoE.

The Treasury's disposition is quite different. Its policy towards the EU is defensive. Unlike in DEFRA European policy and expertise have not been mainstreamed. Gordon Brown's priorities and ministerial style over his influential tenure of the chancellorship offered little encouragement for change. The efforts of Tony Blair and the FCO to engineer a step-change in the conduct of the UK's European policy did not have much impact on the Treasury (see Bulmer and Burch 2005). Furthermore, Treasury financial rules have been pervasive and have impacted on all departments engaged in European spending programmes. The Treasury, as in domestic policy, challenges the policy-coordination functions vested in the Cabinet Office and derived from the Prime Minister. A key aspect of the development of the Treasury's organisational disposition to the EU was the translation of domestic spending procedures into the European domain, brought about by the crisis in UK net contributions to the EU budget in the first decade of the 1980s.

Of the three ministries the DTI has been the most successful in developing positive policy initiatives for the EU. However, its responsibility for a number of EU spending programmes risked turning it into a cipher for the Treasury's defensive posture in respect of market-correcting policy. The DTI certainly adapted well to the EU. However, beyond trade, internal market and competitiveness policies the ministry's responsibilities resembled something of a 'rag-bag' that lacked coherence.

In comparative terms, then, we would argue that the MAFF/DoE/DEFRA response to Europeanisation has been one of 'transformation' (see Chapter 3). These Departments underwent fundamental re-organisation and a process of mainstreaming EU business into their activities. The Treasury has made the most limited adaptation, namely 'absorption'. EU business has largely been integrated into the existing arrangements. With the European budget and monetary integration as continuing problematic issues for a succession of UK governments, regardless of their party-political make-up, it is unsurprising that the Treasury has found it difficult to pursue positive engagement with the EU. Finally, the DTI's adaptation may be characterised as one of 'accommodation'. Its diverse range of responsibilities for EU policy has led to significant adaptation but the lack of coherence in its policy brief has not enabled a real transformative change. Nevertheless, the experience of all three departments highlights the way in which the FCO has lost control over traditional external relations (see Smith 1999: 234).

We turn now to much briefer sketches of adaptation elsewhere in central government.

Notes

1   For the early period of membership some information on the early impact of integration upon central government departments is available in Gregory (1983: 130–6).
2   Data and quotes from interview at MAFF, 21 November 1996.
3   Devolution of these policy areas to authorities in Northern Ireland was suspended for most of the period from the official transfer date of 2 December 1999 until spring 2007 owing to disagreements connected to the peace process and decommissioning of weapons. On Tuesday 8 May 2007, following the election of a 4-party executive of 12 ministers, devolved government was again introduced to Northern Ireland.
4   In early 2005 the SCA representative was London-based, mirroring the situation in the early years of membership when David Williamson, later head of the COES and then Secretary-General of the Euroepan Commission, was a 'commuting-member' of the SCA. Interview, DEFRA, 1 March 2005.
5   www.ukrep.be/agri.html, accessed 12 July 2007.
6   Interview, DEFRA, 1 March 2005.
7   Other staff guidance is available; for instance we were shown a 1996 guide to institutions (MAFF 1996).
8   Both Deputy Secretaries in 1996 (Kate Timms and Richard Carden) had been in the Cabinet Office European Secretariat (COES). Timms had been Head of Agriculture in UKREP and the first woman to chair the SCA, namely during the 1992 British presidency (Westlake 1995: 201). The Permanent Secretary as of 2001 (Brian Bender) was a former Head of COES. He then became Permanent Secretary in DEFRA but in 2005 moved back to the DTI, also as Permanent Secretary. The Director General (equivalent to Deputy Secretary) for Food and Farming in early 2007, Andy Lebrecht, is a long-standing member of the European cadre, having served in UKREP in the late 1980s and later headed the EU Division in MAFF. He subsequently became Deputy Permanent Representative in UKREP.
9   The Director General for Environment in 2005, Bill Stow, was a former senior official in the DTI with responsibility for internal market policy and then Deputy Permanent Representative in Brussels (1998–2003). Several heads of the environmental directorate and its divisions have significant track-records in EU business; some are former MAFF officials.
10 For a review of the institutional changes in the agricultural sector, see Bulmer *et al.* 2002, Chapter 5.
11 Interview, Scottish Executive Rural Affairs Department, 29 June 2000. A Liberal Democrat, Ross Finnie, held the agricultural portfolio in Edinburgh at the time, denoting a new 'party politics' associated with coordination.
12 Interview, MAFF, 21 November 1996.
13 The departmental location of this task has been subject to change. In the second Blair government it fell to the Office of the Deputy Prime Minister (ODPM); after the ODPM's abolition in May 2006 it fell to the Department

for Communities and Local Government but in both cases with much of the work decentralised to the Government Offices in the English regions. The 'territorial' departments and then, after devolution, the devolved authorities have been responsible for counterpart activities beyond England. The creation of the government offices in the regions under John Major's premiership meant that some of the England-related work was more decentralised: a development extended with the creation of Regional Development Agencies (RDAs) under Blair. However, both the government offices and the RDAs are accountable to the parent department in Whitehall. Historically the DTI has had responsibility for negotiating policy on behalf of the UK government in matters relating to structural funds.

14 Interview, DoE, 12 December 1996; interview former minister, London, 21 July 1998.

15 Interview, Department of the Environment, Transport and the Regions (DETR), 10 November 2000.

16 For DEFRA PSA targets for 2005–8, see www.defra.gov.uk/corporate/busplan/spending-review/psa2004.htm; for the Sustainable Procurement Action Plan, see www.defra.gov.uk/environment/sustainable/index.htm: both accessed 12 July 2007.

17 On these modes of policy in the context of Europeanisation, see Bulmer and Radaelli (2005).

18 The UK was a member of the ERM from 5 October 1990 to 16 September 1992.

19 The autumn 2006 report is available at: http://ec.europa.eu/growthandjobs/pdf/nrp/UK_nrp_en.pdf, accessed 12 July 2007.

20 Interview, former Treasury official, 6 December 1996.

21 Interview, former Treasury official, 6 December 1996.

22 Interviews, HM Treasury, 21 July 1998 and 10 October 2000.

23 Prior to the reforms prompted by the FER an under-secretary coordinated core EU business, which included the agricultural division. All under-secretary positions were abolished after the FER and the agricultural division was moved to the Spending Directorate.

24 See the organogram at: www.hm-treasury.gov.uk/media/565/0A/organogram_070605.PDF, accessed 14 June 2005.

25 Since a decision in 2002 the ECOFIN Council incorporates the work of the (previously separate) Budget Council.

26 Pickering estimates that 29 of the 59 Treasury teams in 2001 'would encounter EU issues at least occasionally' and two cross-cutting teams had a 'purely EU remit' (2002: 590). By comparison, one of our interviewees quoted in 1996 a rather higher figure of 40 of the then 56 teams, again with two cross-cutting EU teams (EU budget and EU monetary affairs). Interview, Treasury, 21 November 1996.

27 We refer here to the arrangements in the third Blair governement, as presented on-line at: www.hm-treasury.gov.uk/about/ministerial_profiles/minprofile_index.cfm, accessed September 2005. However, this broad organisation is consistent with the period of Major and Blair's premierships. One notable exception concerns the period when Lord Simon was a minister based in both the Treasury and the DTI (see below).

28 Interview, Treasury, 21 July 1998.
29 Full details can be obtained at the Treasury's website: www.hm-treasury. gov.uk.
30 Interview former senior COES official, 28 February 2005. The inability of the PM to receive independent advice from the Treasury was stated to have 'never been the case until this government'.
31 Interview, Brussels, 19 March 1997.
32 Interview, Brussels, 19 March 1997.
33 Unattributable interview, Whitehall, 10 October 2000.
34 Unattributable interview, Whitehall, 10 October 2000.
35 Unattributable interview, Whitehall, 10 October 2000.
36 Interview, Treasury, 21 July 1998.
37 Interview, Treasury, 10 December 1996.
38 The objectives are set out on the Treasury's organogram. See www. hm-treasury.gov.uk/media/565/0A/organogram_070605.PDF, accessed 5 July 2005.
39 Interview, former Treasury official, 6 December 1996.
40 Traditionally the DTI has taken the lead on the European structural funds but the main spending ministries at the outset were the Department of the Environment (regional fund), the Department for Education and Employment (social fund) for England and the 'territorial' offices for Scotland, Wales and Northern Ireland. Within UK government it was Michael Heseltine, as Secretary of State at the DoE, who mounted a major campaign against the original form of these rules (see Bache 1998: 105–7).
41 Confidential interview, HM Treasury, 21 November 1996.
42 Interview, former Treasury official, 6 December 1996.
43 Interview, former Treasury official, 6 December 1996.
44 Interview, FCO, 28 November 1996.
45 Interview, former Treasury official, 6 December 1996.
46 A small number of interviewees wanted us to explain how it worked!
47 Interview, DTI, 2 December 1996.
48 Telephone interview, HM Treasury, 12 July 2007. One of the main problems was that much time and effort were being expended on identifying to which Department (new) expenditure programmes would be attributed under EUROPES. We were given a flavour of this when a diplomat with responsibility for CFSP indicated that the sending of election monitors to Albania led to exchanges as to whether this was to be attributed to the FCO as foreign policy or to the then Overseas Development Administration (ODA) as development policy. Interview, Foreign Office, 10 December 1996.
49 Interview, ODA, 25 November 1996.
50 This contrasts with the calculation of *net* contributions that is used for EUROPES, since the UK is a recipient of funds.
51 Interview, ODA, 25 November 1996.
52 Special arrangements apply where the incidence of EU budgetary commitments impacts on the territorial (and then devolved) authorities because the impact of EUROPES or rules on the structural funds became inter-twined with the so-called 'Block Grant'.

53 A review of the organisational upheaval is provided by the DTI's website: www.dti.gov.uk/about_dti_history.html, accessed September 2005.
54 Interview, DTI, 2 December 1996.
55 Source: www.dti.gov.uk/ewt, accessed 5 September 2005.
56 Documentation provided at interview, DTI, 3 August 2000.
57 In 1996 18 senior staff were engaged in this function. Interview, OST/DTI, 21 November 1996.
58 Interview, OST/DTI, 21 November 1996.
59 In 1996 an interviewee identified Francis Maude, Tim Eggar and Ian Taylor as effective in this respect (despite their views on the EU varying from the Euro-sceptic to Europhile); in 2000 a similar exercise led to the naming of Lord Simon and Helen Liddel. Interviews, DTI, 2 December 1996; 3 August 2000.
60 Interview, DTI, 2 December 1996. The European Economic Area was the arrangement whereby the remaining EFTA states could participate in the European single market without signing up for the full range of EU activities.
61 On taking office in late June 2007 Gordon Brown created the Department for Business, Enterprise and Regulatory Reform, which took on many of the DTI's functions but excluding science and research: see Written Ministerial Statement on Machinery of Government Changes: www.pm.gov.uk/output/Page12181.asp, accessed 12 July 2007.

7

The European Union and the 'outer core'

This chapter is concerned with the EU's impact upon, and the European policy-making patterns of, the outer core of central government. First, we deal with those departments not considered hitherto. In order to provide some diversity we consider two departments which have been affected by the EU relatively recently – the Home Office and the Ministry of Defence (MoD) – alongside other departments where the impact has been of longer standing but of a lesser order of magnitude. The Home Office and the MoD are the 'new kids on the block' of European policy-making in Whitehall. But, as will be seen, they are also at the hub of subsidiary networks established in connection with, respectively, Justice and Home Affairs and the European Security and Defence Policy. Secondly, we consider the role of the territorial/devolved authorities, namely the Scottish, Welsh and Northern Ireland Offices prior to devolution and their successor authorities from 1999. Our treatment of the departments follows that employed in Chapter 6 but in less detail. The account offered in this chapter is of the EU's impact being widespread but the timing of its impact depending on developments at the EU level. At the same time, the impact of Europeanisation has been conditioned by unrelated developments within UK central government, of which devolution is a prominent example.

The Home Office[1]

The Europeanisation of the Home Office (HO) commenced in earnest with the Maastricht Treaty. Prior to that, Europeanisation had been limited. The Council of Europe had sporadic impact; and EC economic policies affected issues such as data protection, frontiers and cross-border crime. A third impact came from Trevi: terrorism, radicalism, extremism, violence, information – the framework created in December 1975 to coordinate counter-terrorism and, later, the fight against drug trafficking and serious international crime (Lavenex and Wallace 2005).

By contrast with these activities, the Maastricht Treaty brought about a qualitative transformation in the HO's work. It introduced formalised EU structures to deal with a large range of activities. By 1996 the following policy areas were affected: immigration and asylum, organised crime, terrorism, drugs, child abuse, racism and xenophobia, police cooperation, criminal policy, extradition, mutual legal assistance, and emergency planning. The impact was felt across a significant number of the department's policy divisions. The HO had to make a significant organisational response to coordinate all these different strands of its EU work. A team of some ten officials was responsible for policy coordination in late 1996.[2] The substance of policy, however, was dealt with by the line divisions. The central impact of the new Justice and Home Affairs (JHA) pillar of activity also gave the HO an important coordinating role. Until the structure was overhauled by the Amsterdam Treaty, JHA activity was coordinated at EU level by the K4 Committee, and the UK representative was from the Home Office.[3]

JHA activity has been one of the most dynamic (and complex) areas of recent EU policy. The 1997 Amsterdam Treaty had an important impact by prioritising the creation of an 'area of freedom, security and justice' (Walker 2004). Previously JHA tasks had been confined to the intergovernmental third pillar, and the Major government had been insistent on this separation: both during the Maastricht negotiations and again in the IGC in 1996–97. However, under the Amsterdam Treaty a phased transfer to the EC pillar commenced in respect of responsibilities for visas, asylum, immigration and other policies relating to the free movement of persons, as well as cross-border judicial cooperation in civil matters. Common measures were to be set up by May 2004 but until this time the Commission would have limited powers and QMV would not apply. Residual matters in the third pillar would comprise police and judicial cooperation in criminal matters. The K4 Committee was replaced by the Article 36 Committee (dealing with residual third-pillar business) and SCIFA (the Strategic Committee on Immigration, Frontiers and Asylum), which dealt with communitarised policy issues (see Table 3.1). A further feature of the Amsterdam Treaty was the incorporation of the Schengen Agreement into the European treaties. This agreement, which had initially brought together France, Germany and the Benelux countries to create a passport-free area, and later expanded in membership and scope, was incorporated into the activities of the EU. The UK was not a signatory because it maintained domestic border controls except for UK–Ireland travel and consequently secured an opt-*out* of its provisions but with the possibility to opt *in* to specific aspects.[4] Since the Amsterdam Treaty, work programmes have become very developed: first with objectives set out at the Tampere European Council in 1999; and then with 'The Hague Programme', agreed in November 2004 and covering the period 2005–10 (Lavenex and Wallace 2005).

Counter-terrorism initiatives have become a particular focus of attention since the 9/11 attacks in New York (2001) and then the Madrid and London bombings in 2004 and 2005 respectively.

As a result of this growing EU activity by 2005 the staff complement for coordination in the Home Office's European and International Unit had grown to 'a headcount of 28' officials.[5] These figures do not capture the full extent of the impact, though, because it is the number of affected officials in the Home Office's directorates that would reveal this most fully. Alas, no data were available at interview but it was revealing that the Immigration and Nationality Directorate, whose work was especially affected by the EU, had set up its own European Policy Department. The growth of JHA business also had a big impact upon the work of UKREP. In early 1997 the coordination of JHA in UKREP was being undertaken in the office of the legal counsellor. By early 1997 a complement of three senior officials, two on secondment from the Home Office, were engaged with JHA work. As we were told in 1997 by an UKREP diplomat:

> The statistics of its growth are quite fantastic in the sense of, from running something like a hundred documents a year, we now have something like fifteen hundred documents a year in the third pillar. We have between twenty-five and thirty groups including the steering groups and the K4 committee.[6]

By 2005 UKREP's JHA section comprised nine officials.[7]

Ministerial involvement in JHA policy has grown in line with this trajectory of development: from one Council meeting in 1993 to six in 2006 (see Tables 3.3 and 3.4). In an apocryphal story a senior Commission official told us:

> Even recently it was reported that one Home Secretary was told that next week he had a meeting in Brussels and he replied that that was a breach of contract. The Home Secretary stayed at home: that was the job description.[8]

Quite different postures were adopted by the Conservative and Labour governments in the period since the Maastricht Treaty. The Major government, with Michael Howard as Home Secretary from May 1993, was combative in trying to limit the impact of JHA cooperation and opposed at all costs to it being integrated into the mainstream of EC activities (communitarisation). 'The minister's policy . . . [was] driven entirely by arguments in the Tory Party', as one UKREP diplomat put it in Brussels.[9] By contrast, the Labour government began to see potential benefits from playing a more positive role in policy. For example, in April 2000 under Jack Straw the UK joined the Schengen agreement on police and justice cooperation. It also took an active role in the lead-up to the Tampere European Council on JHA and made joint proposals with the French and German governments concerning asylum and immigration policy. In the wake of the 9/11 attacks in 2001 the Labour government took a pro-active position in favour of a pan-European arrest warrant. It also sought enhanced EU cooperation following the July 2005 bombings in London. Thus, the response under Labour shifted emphasis from Europeanisation as reception to projection, as successive Home Secretaries sought EU solutions to UK policy concerns.

The UK delegation to the JHA Council meeting in February 2005 comprised the Home Secretary, Charles Clarke, the junior minister with European responsibilities, Caroline Flint, and the Scottish Justice Minister, Cathy Jamieson. Not all of this team could be accommodated in the Council delegation but this permitted the Home Secretary, for example, to hold a bilateral meeting with a counterpart outside the Council session.[10] As elsewhere in government, ministerial aptitude for EU business is as much a function of personality as of anything else. Michael Howard was not pursuing a policy line where aptitude for EU business was at a premium. David Blunkett's visual disability made him a reluctant traveller to Council sessions and European policy was not a particular interest. Charles Clarke, by contrast, combined a Europhile position and interest with political 'feel' and an outgoing, if sometimes outspoken, style to make an effective 'operator' in the EU. Caroline Flint's European responsibilities meant that she would deputise for the Home Secretary if he could not attend a Council. Other members of the ministerial team would have a lot of EU business to deal with but would not normally go to Council sessions.[11]

In its coordinating role the HO had to liaise with other key players on JHA work, namely the FCO, the Cabinet Office, the Department for Constitutional Affairs and HM Revenue and Customs.[12] The FCO and COES were involved because of institutional issues and because of their responsibility for the general conduct of UK–EU relations. It should not be forgotten that access to intelligence from the FCO's embassy network is also important to this policy area like many others. In addition, JHA has become much more outward-looking and is a component part of EU relations with the USA, Russia and many other non-European countries. Revenue and Customs' involvement derives from their operational combat against cross-border crime and fraud. Finally, the LCD/DCA was involved because of its judicial responsibilities. Beyond this group of five departments the territorial departments (and later, the devolved executives) also had a particular interest because of the different judicial and criminal legal systems in Scotland and Northern Ireland, and the specific engagement of the latter with counter-terrorism. The Scottish Executive became particularly concerned at the rapid development of judicial cooperation measures in the aftermath of the 9/11 attacks because sensitivity to the different legal circumstances north of the border was liable to neglect. The HO also has to coordinate with various operational agencies, notably the police.

Given the more intergovernmental nature of JHA – at least until the early 2000s – bilateral relations with partner states were important for senior officials in the HO. We were told in 1996 that there was a 'very substantial' amount of such contact at all levels. Characteristically, the UK government had a closely coordinated policy on JHA and sought to exploit the less coordinated approaches of its counterparts. One senior official in the HO under Howard told us his role was trying to 'wind them up to take a firmer line against their foreign office'.[13] In the spirit of a more utilitarian-constructive European policy on the part of the Labour governments bilateral relations are no less important. For example, Charles Clarke had had three bilateral meetings on the fringes of the February 2005 Council meeting, and senior officials were reported to have made recent visits to Madrid, Paris and Berlin.[14]

It is difficult to identify a Home Office 'mission' with regard to EU policy. Under Michael Howard the long-term political view was that the integration of policy in this area should go no further than what had been agreed to at Maastricht. Under the Blair governments European policy has been used to deliver domestic policy goals as appropriate. Thus the EU has been regarded as an opportunity structure available to enhance performance-delivery. The HO has thus moved from a department with sporadic involvement in the 1980s to extensive involvement. Organisationally and procedurally its work was transformed, and the Maastricht Treaty may be seen as representing a critical juncture in the Home Office's work. However, 'reception' prevailed, since the Conservative government was pursuing a defensive policy. That has changed under the Blair governments. In our judgement, using the growth of business, the impact on the department's organisation and the political response to the EU, the HO has undergone a shift from a reception to a projection response over a ten-year period from 1993: a compressed microcosm of the broader pattern of Whitehall adaptation. Continuing opt-outs, notably on the Schengen border control regime, means that there are areas where the HO remains defensive.

Ministry of Defence

The Europeanisation of the Ministry of Defence (MoD) has been even more truncated, since the main impact has occurred in the period since 1998. Previously the EU's impact was partly indirect and partly something of a curiosity. The indirect impact increased as the EU began to develop a competence for security policy, notably through the CFSP provisions in the Maastricht Treaty. A complicating factor at European level was the existence of a separate organisation, the Western European Union (WEU), which could be seen as the forum for joint action by the European 'pillar' of NATO activity. On issues where defence policy was affected indirectly in this way by the EU, it was clearly necessary to have a policy input from the MoD. However, the policy-lead was held by the FCO on these matters. The curiosity element was that mainstream EC business also impacted on the MoD and was handled by the European Union Cell, which had been established in 1995 within the Environmental Policy Directorate.[15] The location of this cell was attributable to the MoD being one of the biggest landowners in the UK, and therefore significantly affected by legislation. Another curiosity was that civilian personnel working on German military bases were subject to the Maastricht Treaty's Social Chapter, from which the UK had opted out under the Major government. In addition, the MoD had experienced extensive legal action for damages from servicewomen who had been dismissed on the grounds of pregnancy due to breach of EU equal opportunities legislation. Thus the MoD had European business to contend with under the Major government, and the EU Cell provided advice on all areas of European policy for the Euro-sceptic Defence Secretary, Michael Portillo.[16]

By 2005, however, prompted by the creation of the European Security and Defence Policy (ESDP), EU business had come to represent a significant strand of MoD defence policy.[17] Efforts in the lead-up to the Amsterdam Treaty to create an EU-level defence responsibility foundered, not least because of the UK government's insistence on the primacy of NATO. Thus, EU actions under the CFSP could go no further than peace-keeping operations, and the EU's impact on the MoD was quite limited. However, policy changes especially in the UK led to the December 1998 Anglo-French St Malo Declaration calling for a broad-ranging EU military capacity. A year later at the Helsinki European Council governments agreed on ESDP headline goals, including the ability to deploy a Rapid Reaction Force. At the 2000 Nice European Council the member governments agreed on treaty changes to provide for the creation of a Political and Security Committee, a European Union Military Committee and an EU Military Staff (see Figure 3.1). In July 2004 a European Defence Agency was established in Brussels. These developments represented seismic changes to the architecture of defence policy in the EU, which can now offer a full range of foreign-policy actions from economic support/sanctions through to a military response. The ESDP's impact was made clear by a senior official in the MoD, who reported in February 2005 that 'we currently have more soldiers on EU operations than we do on NATO operations'.[18]

The EU Military Committee meets on a weekly basis to offer advice to the Political and Security Committee (COPS), which is where the substantive preparation of the Council takes place. Meantime CIVCOM (the Committee on Civilian Aspects of Crisis Management) deals with civilian protection matters. Intergovernmental meetings in ESDP do not necessarily follow regular Council practice.[19] ESDP thus has its own institutional 'logic': much of it practice imported from NATO or the now superseded Western European Union (WEU).[20] At a more detailed level national representatives are working on specific projects designed to increase the EU's collective defence capability, for instance in the domain of 'strategic airlift': the provision of large aircraft for transporting troops (and refuelling transport planes) to facilitate deployment. All this activity is designed to ensure that member states collectively have effective capability but none of the hardware belongs to the EU itself. The capabilities agenda is being driven forward by the European Defence Agency, to which Nick Whitney, a former director-general in the MoD with responsibility for NATO and EU policy, was appointed as first Chief Executive.[21]

The MoD's organisation is unusual because there are parallel civilian and military organisations. The MoD's engagement with international organisations – NATO, the EU and, to a much lesser extent, the United Nations (UN) – is organised under a director-general. NATO policy is located in one directorate; EU and UN business in another. Knitting the two activities together is a military group of some six personnel, headed in February 2005 by a naval captain. The military staff are integrated with the civilian team but report up to the Chief of Defence Staff, whereas the 'civilians' report up to the Permanent Secretary as in any other department. The military group's work prioritises either NATO or the EU depending on the planning activities or cycles under way. The EU team under the Director EU/UN amounted in February 2005 to six officials, although augmented by planning for the UK presidency later that year.[22] The integration of EU work with NATO has limited the amount of re-organisation.

Following the pattern elsewhere in Whitehall, the EU team is responsible for coordination within the ministry and horizontal issues, such as institutional reform. It also has a remit for training up staff on EU business, including military personnel at the Defence Academy in Shrivenham or the defence colleges. And it is responsible for liaison with Parliament in conjunction with the FCO. Like the HO, the MoD engages with the Cabinet Office network on horizontal issues, such as treaty reform or the Working Time Directive. If ESDP is a major issue on the EU's agenda, it may feature on the agenda of the Friday meeting. However, otherwise the substance of ESDP is conducted in a much smaller network. Key participants apart from the MoD are the FCO and UKREP. In the former, EU-X (external) deals with the CFSP but a separate directorate is responsible for security policy (Security Policy Group: SECPOL) and is the MoD's main counterpart. Where ministerial coordination is required, the principal players are from these departments, plus the Secretary of State for International Development (for instance, in connection with disaster relief), and potentially also the Prime Minister. Within UKREP, as in the MoD itself, there are two teams. One is an ESDP team – three officials as of 2007 – which is incorporated into UKREP's external relations section – and staffed by MoD 'civilians'.[23] Then there is a military representation team comprising personnel from the armed services who staff the various military committees: eight personnel in 2007.[24] The military personnel in UKREP are closely integrated with the military representation to NATO, also in Brussels.

The ministerial level is obviously important in something as politically sensitive as defence policy. However, it is important to note that Tony

Blair as prime minister was personally involved in the development of the ESDP, since it stemmed from a bilateral summit and was pursued in the European Council (see Bulmer and Burch 2005). The mission to strengthen European defence policy is firmly embedded and has been included in the jointly owned public service delivery targets between the MoD and the FCO with the Treasury. By contrast with the Home Office, therefore, an explicit European-policy commitment is firmly established and must be delivered. Moreover, the UK is in the vanguard of the ESDP's development.

Other Whitehall departments

We now turn to the remaining non-territorial departments in Whitehall. Their engagement with the EU is generally less than those considered hitherto (see also Table 7.1). A general pattern is observable in each case (except where noted otherwise below), namely the existence of a European coordination function, which is also responsible for liaison with parliament. Detailed business is passed to the relevant functional unit. Departmental lawyers will be drawn in when legal advice is needed on policy initiatives

Table 7.1 EU Policy domains and responsibilities amongst the 'outer core' departments[a]

Whitehall department	EU policy area	Lead or support role?
Communities and Local Government	Regional policy and planning	Support (England only)
Constitutional Affairs	Civil justice, judicial cooperation, data protection, human rights	Lead
Culture, Media and Sport	Audiovisual, culture, sport	Lead
Education and Skills	Education and training policies	Lead
Health	Public health, food policy	Lead
International Development	Development policy, humanitarian aspects of CFSP	Lead (development)
Transport	Transport policy	Lead
Work and Pensions	Social security, employment	Lead (social security); employment shared with Treasury

Note: [a] Excludes the Cabinet Office, GORs and the devolved authorities.

or when infringement proceedings are threatened, or as cases before the courts necessitate. All departments may attend Cabinet Office coordination meetings but prefer instead to do so only when they have a pressing policy issue that requires consideration there. The secretary of state of each of the departments considered in this section – including the Attorney General – is a member of the Ministerial Committee on European Policy (EP) in its formation as of August 2005 in Tony Blair's third term of government (see Box 5.5). We deal with the departments alphabetically, since the more logical organisation, namely using the date each department was first affected by European policy, is not possible. In many cases the impact of European policies upon accession or as they subsequently evolved was upon departments which no longer exist due to re-organisation.

The Department for Communities and Local Government (DCLG)
The DCLG was created in May 2006 and took on the responsibilities previously attached to the Office of the Deputy Prime Minister (ODPM). It is essentially an English department in the UK government. The main areas where the EU impacts on its work are in respect of: social exclusion, regeneration and regional planning. Most of these responsibilities can be traced back to the EU's impact on the Department of the Environment that became residual, so to say, when environmental policy proper was integrated into DEFRA. The DoE had originally been responsible for the disbursement in England of European regional development funding but this task was gradually passed to the Government Offices in the Regions (GORs – see below). The role of the ODPM/DCLG has become one of liaison and oversight on European regional policy rather than front-line delivery. Under the ODPM European policy was coordinated by the Corporate Strategy and International Unit, located in a central Corporate Strategy and Resources Group.[25] During the UK presidency of 2005 the ODPM was not designated any responsibility for a Council formation, clearly indicating the department's 'outer core' status.[26] However, John Prescott played a more important personal role as Deputy Prime Minister. For example, he conducted some bilateral meetings ahead of the European Council, deputising for Prime Minister Blair. He hosted an informal Council meeting in Bristol in December 2005 on sustainable communities: one of the department's core responsibilities. Without John Prescott as minister the political importance of the DCLG in European policy has declined. Tellingly, none of the department's 2005–8 PSA targets mentions an EU dimension.[27] In short, the DCLG has European responsibilities but they do not closely map onto an individual EU policy area and, moreover, are only for England.

Department for Constitutional Affairs (DCA)
The DCA was also a relatively new department, dating from 2003, although its responsibilities were absorbed into the Ministry of Justice,

created in May 2007 shortly before Tony Blair stepped down as Prime Minister.[28] The DCA was responsible for representing UK government interests in the EU (and the Council of Europe) on matters of criminal, civil and family justice, data protection, human rights and pursued initiatives in these areas during the 2005 UK presidency of the EU.[29] Although some of these areas of work have intensified as a result of the growth of judicial and police cooperation, the origins of the DCA's European responsibilities go back to an earlier period of EU membership. The Lord Chancellor's Department (LCD) had been the lead-department for matters relating to lawyers' right of establishment in the EU, an issue which developed saliency with the single market. It also oversaw issues of access to justice and was concerned with the judicial cooperation components of JHA activity that commenced with the Maastricht Treaty.[30] In the mid-1990s four lawyers in the LCD's International Division took on these duties as a coordinating unit but also dealing with quite a bit of the substantive policy work. The division was plugged into the lawyers' network centred on the Cabinet Office Legal Advisers, based in the Treasury Solicitor's Department (see Chapter 5). However, JHA policy-*making* was coordinated by the Home Office.

With the launch of the DCA the aim was to create a 'mainstream public service department', whose functions would correspond to those of a justice ministry.[31] As it turned out the DCA served as a transitional arrangement to just such a solution, which incidentally has brought UK practice closer to that elsewhere in the EU. The DCA's EU work was located in its International Relations Branch. The European policy workload of the DCA was increasing, especially after the EU agreed 'The Hague Programme' in 2004, which was designed to enable 'citizens and businesses to exercise their rights in other countries by promoting cooperation between the legal systems of the [27] member states'.[32] The DCA was also formally responsible, because of its constitutional responsibilities, for the concordats which provide guidance on relations with the devolved authorities on, *inter alia*, European policy.[33] European policy represented a small part of the DCA's work, and it would be exaggerating to consider it Europeanised. Nevertheless, the burgeoning of judicial cooperation was having a significant impact. The rules of engagement in this policy still give member governments the main levers of power, in contrast with the growing communitarisation of asylum and immigration responsibilities of the Home Office.

Department for Culture, Media and Sport (DCMS)
Since the 1980s the EU has had a growing impact on the policy responsibilities now associated with the DCMS. Three domains of impact can be identified and they correspond to the ministry's name: culture, media and sport.[34] The EU's impact on audiovisual policy grew considerably as the sector became more internationalised in parallel with the development of

the single market from the 1980s, when the Home Office held responsibility within Whitehall. Culture was brought under the EU's remit in
the Maastricht Treaty of 1993. The evolution of EU involvement in sport
policy has been accretive, for example through the *Bosman* ruling on soccer
transfers that arose from free movement regulation, (see Parrish 2003). In
the area of cultural policy the EU runs programmes on cultural activities
and preserving built heritage and these necessitate departmental oversight.
The Culture and Audiovisual Council meets about once per presidency but
is now absorbed into a wider formation with Education (see Table 3.5).

The Department of National Heritage (DNH), the predecessor of the
DCMS, was first established in 1992 and brought together responsibilities
from other departments, notably the Home Office. It was reported to us
that there had been an explicit decision at a review in autumn 1995 that
there should be no EU coordinating office: a distinctive feature of the department.[35] Hence the three parts of the department tended to coordinate
things within their own domain and then liaise across the (relatively small)
department when necessary.[36] Overall, the impression in early 1997 was
of a relatively undeveloped organisation for EU policy. As of 2005 the basic
organisational principles remained unchanged. Broadcasting, arts and culture, and sport remained in different parts of the DCMS. One paradox
was that the DCMS was at its most coordinated on European policy when
the UK held the presidency; in both 1998 and 2005 it had a temporary
presidency unit.[37]

Department for Education and Skills (DfES)
The DfES's engagement with the EU was quite modest. Amongst the
EU policy issues that it had to tackle were the Erasmus and Socrates
schemes for student mobility and the Bologna Process, which is bringing
closer approximation in patterns of higher education qualifications and practice across EU states. The Leonardo da Vinci Programme for vocational
training impacted on the department's skills agenda. Also affected was
the mutual recognition of teaching qualifications. These policy impacts
developed from the 1980s. During this period the department has at times
existed separately but also as a joint department with employment. Given
the larger impact of the EU on employment policy there is evidence
that the profile of European policy in the department was higher when
integrated with employment.[38] Unusually the DfES's European expertise
was provided during the second and third Blair governments by a Joint
International Unit, shared with the Department for Work and Pensions.
This unit was accountable to the DfES via the latter's Lifelong Learning
and Skills Directorate.[39] Ministerial involvement in the EU occurs when
education and youth issues are considered by the Council once or twice
each year. Although the DfES was not an especially Europeanised department, the joint unit gave it a strong reservoir of expertise carried forward

from the Department of Education and Employment of the first Blair government.

Department of Health (DH)

The Department of Health had European responsibilities from the very outset of UK membership (it was the Department of Health and Social Security until 1988). In particular it was responsible for the E1/11 scheme that enabled EU-wide access to health provision.[40] From the mid-1980s the DH was affected by the burgeoning impact of the single market on such issues as mutual recognition of medical professionals' qualifications and pharmaceuticals regulation. It has also been involved in EU health and safety policy.[41] The EU gained formal responsibility for aspects of public health under the Maastricht Treaty. In the 1990s food safety became a prominent domestic and EU policy issue, and the DH became a key player. The Food Standards Agency, which is accountable to the DH, is one of several such agencies accountable to the DH, and with a European dimension to their work.

In 1996 EU business was located in the DH's International Branch. With quite a large staff of 29 this branch was responsible for monitoring policy developments and participating in EU policy-making.[42] A major bloc of work consisted of administering the E1/11 scheme. The International Branch was tucked away in the DH's Resources and Services Group, which covered IT, personnel and finance rather than policy substance. Far from being Whitehall's finest exemplar of Europeanisation, there was a real sense of resignation about the marginalisation of EU business in the DH at interview. It is worth bearing in mind that, earlier, in March 1996, the Secretary of State, Stephen Dorrell had announced that BSE could be passed to humans through the food chain. This announcement, made at quite short notice because of a possible leak in a tabloid, was to have major implications not only in the UK but also to prompt the beef export ban to the rest of the EU. However, the officials advising the Secretary of State did not make proper consultation of the International Branch, which would have drawn attention to the European ramifications. 'No one had a thought that Europe would be interested.' As our interviewee put it, the issue demonstrated 'how pathetic we are as a Department in thinking Europe'.[43] This episode helped make the DH more aware of the European dimension of its work, but it was a case of locking the stable door after the horse had bolted.

As of 2005 EU business was located in the International Division. The wide-ranging but diffuse effects of the EU were reflected in the extensive programme of DH-sponsored events during the 2005 UK presidency. They included ministerial meetings (in the Council and informally); meetings for heads of agencies and chief professional officers; and for regulators. Four areas of policy were affected by the schedule: health inequalities; patient safety; pharmaceuticals; and food and nutrition.[44] Overall, the DH is not an especially Europeanised Department or a key player in the broader EU network. However, it is open to major legislative or judicial impact from the EU. In the former category the Working Time Directive has been an ongoing concern for the DH because the working hours of junior doctors exceed the EU maximum and therefore need special exemption in order that hospital provision is not adversely affected. Equally, decisions of the ECJ, such as the May 2006 Watts judgement, can be fundamental. It conferred on patients the right to elective treatment in another member state.[45]

Department for International Development (DfID)
DfID is affected by the EU in two principal ways: first, and most immediately, by development policy; and, secondly, by its interests in humanitarian issues that feature in the EU's CFSP. The latter impact developed from the 1990s, whereas the former has existed since accession. A slightly different Europe-related connection is where DfID gives aid to European pre-accession states. Prior to the election of the Blair government in 1997, the Overseas Development Administration (ODA) was responsible for this policy. The ODA's organisation was characterised by a relationship between EU coordinators (in the EU Department with a total staff of ten) and 'geographers', located in units overseeing the disbursement of development aid to particular regions of the world, and which included central and eastern Europe plus Balkan states.[46] The coordinating functions of the EU Department included monitoring issues such as the efficiency and effectiveness of EU aid as compared to the national programme. The geographical departments took responsibility for EC (and national) aid programmes in the specific territory.[47] The organisational principles remain similar in DfID but under Labour it is headed by a Cabinet minister.[48] Key partners of DfID on European policy are the FCO's EU External Department, since humanitarian and aid policy necessarily align with the broader objectives of the CFSP. EU policy plays quite an important role in DfID. However, as noted in Chapter 6, Treasury rules have combined with questions posed about the efficiency of EU aid regimes to provide some disincentives to adopting European policy solutions.

Department for Transport (DfT)
The impact of European integration upon the domestic responsibilities of the Department of Transport (DoT) was latent from the UK's accession, as the Treaty of Rome included provision for a transport policy. However, translating this provision into reality had proven to be slow. Particular impetus came, from the 1980s onwards, with the single market programme. It invigorated those areas where progress had previously been weak, notably in liberalising road haulage, air transport and shipping within the EU. Other issues where the EU has had an impact include the creation of a common

format for driving licences, transport infrastructure issues and the regulation of drivers' hours in the road haulage sector. Policy on transport safety
developed from the 1990s. In many of these matters the DoT has to liaise
with other UK bodies, such as the local authorities or the Civil Aviation
Authority. However, the growth of agency government has been particularly
vigorous in this policy area, so bodies such as the Highways Agency, the
Driver and Vehicle Licensing Agency, the Marine Safety Agency are also
brought in, but with the DoT taking the lead in Council negotiations.

In 1996 the DoT had a European Division with no fewer than four
branches that coordinated policy and was located in the Strategy and Analysis
Directorate alongside other more policy-specific directorates on, for example,
aviation.[49] Interestingly, it had undertaken a survey across the department
to quantify the amount of bilateral relations and contacts with other EU
member governments shortly before our interview. We were told that the
figure was more than 80 per month. One of the ministers, Lord Goschen,
the aviation and shipping minister, had been given the lead on European
issues and usually represented the government in the Council. Ministerial
turnover in the DoT was quite high during the Conservative governments
of 1979–97 but it is worth pausing to examine the impact of Nicholas
Ridley's tenure as Secretary of State (1983–86). Ridley was a Euro-sceptic
minister and a major advocate of privatisation, deregulation and liberalisation. Taking his cues from the latter, he played a key role in setting
in train the ideas that led on to airline liberalisation in the EU.[50] In a
somewhat unorthodox move he summoned senior officials to a Saturday
morning meeting to consider how best to put his policy principles into
practice. From the perspective of international aviation liberalisation, it was
argued that the European context (bilaterally and in the EC) held the best
prospect of progress. Ridley's response was reported to be 'Right, let's get
on with it.'[51] The Secretary of State's input was to empower officials in the
aviation division. And the UK government proved to be highly influential
in a policy area that was turned upside down over the ensuing decade (see
Bulmer *et al.* 2007: Chapter 3). Here we see how a 'minister matters' but
not through having a 'touchy-feely' approach in Brussels in the manner of
Ken Clarke or indeed Tony Blair but simply through mobilising resources
in his department.

In 1996 our interviewees noted that the European division had been
subject to several re-organisations over the period since 1994 alone! This
upheaval took on a grander scale as the whole transport portfolio was
shuttled around after Labour's election in 1997 before ending up in what
is now styled the Department *for* Transport (DfT).[52] By the end of the
Blair premiership EU policy was coordinated in the Environment and
International Division, contained within the Directorate for International
Networks and Environment.[53] Despite all the upheavals the DfT is quite
strongly affected by EU policy, with decisions on all modes of transport

being taken in the two Council sessions chaired by the then Secretary of State, Alistair Darling, during the 2005 UK presidency.[54]

Department for Work and Pensions (DWP)

Created in 2001, the DWP brought together social security and employment responsibilities previously located in different departments. As with the DfT, so the DWP is significantly affected by the EU. Part of the impact, dating back to accession, relates to administrative arrangements concerning social security for migrant workers. EU efforts to combat poverty also impinge on the DWP, although when we interviewed in the department of Social Security (as it then was) in 1996, the Secretary of State, Peter Lilley, was following a policy of trying to repulse this creeping EU competence.[55] The EU's main impact on the employment responsibilities of the DWP dates back to 1989, when the Social Charter was launched and the Department of Employment was responsible. As a senior official in that Department put it: 'within six months of the Social Charter the number of staff dealing with the EC in the [International] Directorate had trebled'.[56] During this period there was extensive policy coordination on employment because of the political sensitivity arising from the Conservative government's opposition to EU social regulation and highlighted by the UK opting out of the Maastricht Treaty's Social Chapter. With the Amsterdam Treaty, however, the Blair government opted *into* the Social Chapter. The Department for Work and Pensions also has overall responsibility for the European Social Fund. More recently, the EU's agenda relating to combating social exclusion became part of the Open Method of Coordination and a more horizontal form of Europeanisation, where member governments compare national approaches and try to identify 'best practice' (see Bulmer and Radaelli 2005). The DWP thus has to submit its Employment Action Plan to the European Commission and is involved widely in the EU's employment strategy. Pensions policy is another DWP responsibility affected by the OMC process.

As can be seen, the DWP has wide-ranging EU commitments.[57] However, these European responsibilities have had to confront a set of upheavals unrelated to the EU. The antecedents of the DWP are the DSS (and before it, the DHSS) and the Department of Employment/Department of Employment and Education. As departmental responsibilities were re-shaped, so EU activities have had to be re-organised. More recently they were located in the Joint International Unit shared with the DfES (see above).[58] This arrangement has provided an element of continuity for the handling of European policy in an otherwise turbulent institutional context, since the unit was inherited from the Department of Education and Employment.

Cabinet Office

The Cabinet Office was covered in Chapter 5, namely the roles of the COES and the EU Staffing Branch. A specific policy function came to play a key role in recent times, namely efforts at 'better regulation'. Following the March 2000 Lisbon European Council commitment to enhancing the EU's competitiveness, and the groundbreaking report of the Mandelkern Group in November 2001, the EU has prioritised improving and simplifying the regulatory environment. The UK government has been at the forefront of these steps. Within central government these efforts to reduce the regulatory burden were located within the Cabinet Office, and since 2005 in its Better Regulation Executive. Better regulation was a key priority for the UK's 2005 presidency programme as part of a coordinated effort with preceding and succeeding presidencies.[59] On becoming Prime Minister, Gordon Brown relocated this function, which has a strongly Europeanised dimension, to the newly created Department for Business, Enterprise and Regulatory Reform.

Government offices in the regions
Government offices had existed in the English regions for many years but had an ad hoc status. They served different departments and lacked a European policy focus. However, under the Major government *integrated* government offices in the regions (GORs) were created, bringing together functions attached to the DTI, DoE, DoT and the Department of Employment. Increasingly the GORs took on a key role in the expenditure in England flowing from the EU structural funds. Under Labour a 1998 reform created Regional Development Agencies, formally accountable to the DTI, which worked with the government offices on the EU funds.[60] Following a major review in 2006, and in light of the scaling back of structural fund aid to the UK following eastern enlargement of the EU, the government offices are to give up much of their responsibility for managing this EU funding.[61] The GORs' European work is principally concerned with policy-delivery and is declining with the re-direction of structural funds to areas of greater development need elsewhere in the EU.

Law officers
The law officers – the Attorney General, the Solicitor General and the Advocate General – also have an engagement with European policy. Essentially they serve as a central source of legal advice or represent the government in litigation and are supported by a small office. In January 1997 there were two lawyers in the office dealing with the EU.[62] Their responsibilities were rather mixed. The Attorney General, as a member of the Cabinet Committee on Europe might seek advice from his officials. Equally, on a major issue a cabinet minister might want advice beyond his or her own department's legal service, especially where matters had a political dimension. Given the cabinet divisions on European policy at the end of the Major government, there was no shortage of politically sensitive EU policy issues, for example the policy of non-cooperation on Europe.

Another example was the ratification of the Maastricht Treaty. Both cases required close involvement on the part of the Attorney General. In the event of any disagreement between ministers on legal aspects of the EU, the Attorney General – with the support of the office – would be required to arbitrate. The Attorney General also has to oversee all litigation against the government on EU-related matters, whether at the ECJ or in the domestic court structure. In very high profile cases before the ECJ the Attorney General or Solicitor General might represent the government rather than leaving this role to legal counsel.[63] Not surprisingly, the EU specialists from the office maintain close links with the legal network focused on the Treasury Solicitor's Department.

Agency government

A major feature of UK public administration over the last decades has been the growth of agency government. This term encompasses a range of long-standing non-ministerial departments as well as a burgeoning number of executive agencies following the 1988 'Next Steps' initiative. Many of these are also affected by the EU. Key examples are the Health and Safety Executive, HM Revenue and Customs, the Environment Agency, regulatory offices such as the Office of Communications or the Office of Fair Trading OFT, as well as more specialised bodies and even devolved ones. All these bodies have had to organise for Europe. Their organisational response is typically in reception mode, as their parent ministry may determine the projection response, especially at ministerial level.

The devolved authorities[64]

The devolved authorities are, of course, not part of UK central government, since they are accountable to elected assemblies in Belfast, Cardiff and Edinburgh. However, this situation has only applied since devolution in the first Blair government and was only reinstated in Northern Ireland in May 2007 after a lengthy suspension dating from October 2002. Prior to devolution in 1999 the Scottish, Welsh and Northern Ireland Offices were parts of central government, although they were not always considered part of the 'Whitehall village'.

Central to understanding the pre- and post-devolution situation is the asymmetry in the UK system.[65] The policy responsibilities of the Welsh, Scottish and Northern Ireland Offices (henceforth 'the territorials') differed markedly and their institutional histories were different.[66] The EU's impact on the territorials varied according to the responsibilities of the individual office. All three were affected by agriculture and fisheries, the structural funds and environmental policy, for example. But the Welsh Office (WO) had not been affected by the CAP upon accession, since it had only assumed responsibility for agriculture domestically in 1977. Special legislation was often necessary in Scotland and Northern Ireland on the domestic implementation of EU policy for legal reasons, notably Scots law. On matters such as education or home affairs the asymmetrical nature of the UK's administrative de-concentration normally required Scottish and Northern Irish engagement but had more limited implications for Wales. In addition, Northern Ireland has had a separate civil service, whereas the British civil service has covered the mainland as a whole and continues to do so post-devolution.

The common feature to all three of the territorials was that none of them had a 'policy lead'. The appropriate UK department held that responsibility. Hence the role of the territorial offices was to try to ensure that they had full information on any implications of EU developments for their responsibilities; to make a timely input to the formulation of UK European policy; and to fulfil EU implementation requirements within their own territory. Central to these functions was the maintenance of good channels of communication with departments in London. Of the three, the Scottish Office (SO) was the most engaged because of its greater range of interests in European policy, its greater resources, and a greater degree of pro-activity, especially after 1991. There were essentially five channels open to the territorials in responding to Europeanisation:

- bilateral relations between officials or ministers with their counterpart department in London, for instance in agriculture through DCE (see Chapter 6);
- participation by officials in Whitehall's inter-ministerial committees including under the auspices of the COES (subject to resource and logistical constraints);
- policy-making participation by the three territorial secretaries of state in the Cabinet Committee on Europe or by ministerial correspondence;
- participation in Council working groups or even the Council itself, subject again to resource constraints, size constraints on Council delegations and to the approval of the UK lead-department; and
- the development of European experience and 'Brussels intelligence' through the encouragement of officials to take a secondment to UKREP or the Commission.

Each of the territorials experienced the growing impact of the EU upon its responsibilities but in a different way from UK departments in London. The case of Scotland offers illustration. Whilst the impact of the EU initially was upon Scotland's agriculture department, it later became more widespread. For instance, the structural funds impacted on the Development Department. This widening impact led the Conservative Secretary of State, Ian Lang, to institute a management reform in 1991 (Scottish Office 1991): a further instance of an engaged minister making a difference. This review resulted in the (to our knowledge) only effort undertaken in government to make a formal assessment of the impact of the EC/EU on a department. It also led to a pro-active policy to encourage SO postings in Brussels (see Smith 2001; 2006). The territorial offices each established internal coordination mechanisms in order to monitor the impact of the EU. For example, in the late 1990s they were located respectively in the SO's Development Department and the WO's Economic Development Group.[67] These coordinating offices were concerned with horizontal issues like EU treaty reform, training and liaison with the Whitehall coordination network: something which created logistical obstacles, although all the Offices had a small staff in London who could attend COES meetings.

These arrangements were generally successful, although there were a number of instances where the territorials were critical of their London counterparts for lack of consultation. For instance, during William Waldegrave's period as Secretary of State for Agriculture (1994–95) CAP reform proposals were developed in consultation with the Treasury but without involvement on the part of the territorials. When this development came to light there was extensive ministerial correspondence: both procedurally about the lack of consultation and also because the proposals were seen as standing little chance of success (Bulmer *et al.* 2002: 111).[68] In 1995 a reporting mechanism was set up on 'territorial discord' within the Cabinet Office's Domestic and Economic Secretariat to try to limit such instances.[69]

The Blair government came to power with a commitment to devolution. In putting this into effect in 1999 the legislation reserved European policy to the UK government. However, because EU policy impacts on devolved competences such as agriculture, the new authorities were to be 'involved as closely as possible' in the formulation of UK European policy (Welsh Office 1997: 22, 3.47; Scottish Office 1997: 14, 4.12). The policy asymmetries were perpetuated under devolution: for example, Scotland received legislative powers in approximately the same domains as those held by the Scottish Office. The critical difference, of course, was the creation of local accountability: in this case to the Scottish Parliament. However, the asymmetry was compounded by the differing institutional arrangements established across the three executive authorities (henceforth the 'devolveds'). In Scotland an executive and parliament were created. The National Assembly for Wales (NAW), by contrast, created no clear executive-legislative division; indeed, the NAW had no legislative powers. This arrangement proved unsatisfactory and in 2007 the notion of a Welsh Assembly Government was formalised as the executive and distinct from the Assembly.[70] In Northern Ireland the particular context of the peace process enabled the establishment of a power-sharing government presiding over the existing government departments in the province to form the Northern Ireland Executive.

How did this constitutional change within the UK impact on the way in which the new authorities organised for the EU? Each executive authority had to rethink its internal coordination for EU business, adjust relations with departments in London and its role in the processes based on the COES. In addition, each has had to reconsider its presence in Brussels, including relations with UKREP. Ministers in the devolveds are no longer part of the UK government and their role in European policy has had to be rethought. In the early period of devolution, especially with arrangements in Northern Ireland suspended, politicisation of European policy was minimised by the presence of Labour-led governments in Cardiff and Edinburgh, albeit a coalition with the Liberal Democrats in the latter. While Labour has remained in power in Westminster, the political constellation of mid-2007 (following the restoration of devolution in Northern Ireland and new elections in Scotland and Wales) is rather different and has brought fresh challenges to EU policy-making in the UK. A minority Scottish National Party government took office in Edinburgh; a Labour–Plaid Cymru coalition took office in Cardiff; and an all-party executive was installed in Belfast under First Minister Ian Paisley and Deputy First Minister Martin McGuinness of the Democratic Unionists and Sinn Féin respectively. The political diversity in the UK's new system of multi-level governance is striking and is likely to impact on EU policy.

The main guiding principle for the UK government was to ensure a smooth transition, based on the translation of the pre-existing arrangements of public administration to the post-devolution period (see Bulmer *et al.* 2002: Chapter 3). The main device for doing so was in the generic Memorandum of Understanding (Cabinet Office 1999b; ODPM 2001; Scott 2001), which was underpinned with more detailed arrangements for cooperation in specific policy areas, such as on the EU (see also Bulmer *et al.* 2002: 194–204). Further underpinning came from a set of Devolution Guidance Notes.[71] The most important institutional innovation in the devolved UK was the creation of the Joint Ministerial Committee (JMC). Like the EU Council it can meet in different formations and brings together ministers from the UK government and the devolveds. It has a formation for handling European policy – JMC(E) – whose membership broadly resembles the Cabinet Committee for European Policy (EP) and adds ministers from the devolveds (see Box 7.1). It has met quite frequently; as Foreign Secretary (2001–6) Jack Straw utilised it practically as a substitute body for EP and to enable the devolveds to be part of the active information-sharing of UK government. However, JMC(E) had originally been conceived of as a problem-solving forum, but had not taken on that role. In the more variegated UK from May 2007 it may have to if, for example, the SNP-led administration in Edinburgh decides to politicise an area such as EU fisheries policy, where it may feel Scotland's interests need stronger articulation in Brussels. Just as ministers in the devolveds are no longer

---

Box 7.1 Membership of the Joint Ministerial Committee on Europe (2006)

Secretary of State for Foreign and Commonwealth Affairs (Chair)
Deputy Prime Minister and First Secretary of State
Chancellor of the Exchequer
Leader of the House of Commons and Lord Privy Seal
Secretary of State for Trade and Industry
Secretary of State for the Home Department
Secretary of State for Health
Secretary of State for Media Culture and Sport
Minister for the Cabinet Office and for Social Exclusion (and Chancellor of the Duchy of Lancaster)
Secretary of State for Northern Ireland and Secretary of State for Wales
Leader of the House of Lords and Lord President of the Council
Secretary of State for Constitutional Affairs and Lord Chancellor
Secretary of State for International Development
Secretary of State for Education and Skills
Secretary of State for Communities and Local Government and Minister for Women
Secretary of State for Work and Pensions
Secretary of State for Environment, Food and Rural Affairs
Secretary of State for Defence
Secretary of State for Transport and Secretary of State for Scotland
Minister without Portfolio and Labour Party Chair
Attorney General
Minister for Europe
First Minister, Scottish Executive
Deputy First Minister and Minister for Justice, Scottish Executive
First Minister, Welsh Assembly Government
Other Ministers of the Scottish Executive and Welsh Assembly Government may be invited to attend as necessary.

No. of meetings of JMC (E) (full years only): 2003: 4; 2004: 11; 2005: 9

Note: Northern Ireland ministers were not attending at this time due to the suspension of the Assembly.
Source: Hansard, 6 Dec 2006, Column 482W, written answer by Geoff Hoon, Minister for Europe.

---

members of the UK cabinet, thus necessitating a new arrangement like JMC(E), so their officials may no longer automatically participate in Cabinet Office committees. However, the declining use of formal meetings, such as EQ(O) – see Chapter 5 – has the advantage for the devolveds that they can participate in informal arenas: the important Friday meeting, for instance.

Table 7.2 The organisation of European business in the devolved executives

Institutional arrangement	Scottish Executive	Welsh Assembly Government	Northern Ireland Executive
Location of European coordination and strategy function	Office of First Minister; junior minister with specific responsibility	Office of First Minister	Office of the First Minister and the Deputy First Minister
Name of coordination unit	Europe, External Affairs and Culture	European and External Affairs Division	European Policy and Coordination Unit
Name of Brussels office	Scottish Executive EU Office	Welsh Assembly Government's Brussels Office	Office of the Northern Ireland Executive in Brussels

Source: websites of the three 'devolveds': www.scotland.gov.uk; www.wales.gov.uk; www.ofmdfmni.gov.uk, all accessed 26 July 2007.

How can the new arrangements be summarised?

- Each of the three devolved governments has created new arrangements for organising European policy and the purposes are broadly similar (see Table 7.2). For example, the focal point in the Scottish Executive (SE) for EU business was at first centrally located, in the Executive Secretariat. It was the central point for liaison with Whitehall and other devolveds, for coordination within the Executive, for engagement with the JMC(E), liaison with the Scottish Parliament, and it oversaw the activities of the office in Brussels (Bulmer *et al.* 2002: 60–1). In July 2007 this European function was located in the Europe, External Affairs and Culture Directorate, in First Minister Alex Salmond's Department. An initiative of the SNP Administration – and distinctive feature to the SE – was to appoint a Minister for Europe, External Affairs and Culture, namely Linda Fabiani.[72] The Scottish Executive published a four-year European Strategy in 2004.[73]
- The JMC(E), the Friday meeting and informal meetings enable participation in inter-ministerial negotiations in the UK government but the devolveds are excluded from meetings that are exclusively within the UK cabinet-based system (see Figure 7.1).
- The devolveds have strengthened their links to Brussels by the creation of representative offices. These enable links with the EU institutions and intelligence-gathering. They are regarded as part of the UKREP 'family' and close relations are maintained. Care has been taken not to pursue

Figure 7.1 The coordination of EU policy, post-devolution

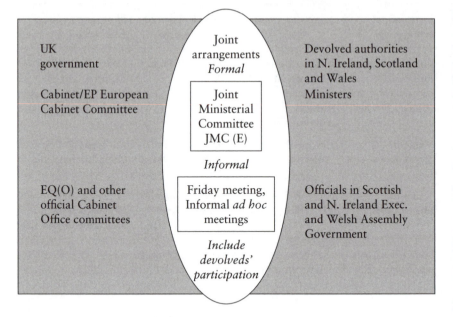

UK government

Cabinet/EP European Cabinet Committee

EQ(O) and other official Cabinet Office committees

Joint arrangements *Formal*

Joint Ministerial Committee JMC (E)

Informal

Friday meeting, Informal *ad hoc* meetings

Include devolveds' participation

Devolved authorities in N. Ireland, Scotland and Wales

Ministers

Officials in Scottish and N. Ireland Exec. and Welsh Assembly Government

Source: Updated and revised from Bulmer *et al.* (2002: 56).

a parallel European diplomacy to that of UKREP except where there is a clear sub-state dimension. The offices have also maintained liaison with 'their' respective Members of the European Parliament.

• The devolveds continue to be able to participate in EU-level official meetings and in the Council of Ministers, subject to agreement with London. This participation is very selective; for example, Scottish participation on fisheries.

Of all the channels for influencing the EU available to the devolveds, the route to Whitehall continues to be the most important. This situation is likely to continue because European policy is a reserved power for the UK government. As a result, the devolveds' involvement is conditional and dependent. Were the devolveds to begin to become overly assertive in the eyes of the UK government, the latter would be able to deny access to information on European policy or potentially restrict access to policy-making (see Bulmer *et al.* 2006). Thus far the pattern of engagement has been pragmatic and based on shared norms that were inherited from the pre-devolution period, with only limited complaints.[74] One consequence of devolution is that some aspects of UK European policy have started to become more internally variegated. For instance, the UK government opted at EU level to permit variation between the devolveds in how they implemented the 2003 CAP reforms because it followed the logic of devolution (Burch and Gomez 2004). Such developments place new demands on coordination at the level of UK central government.

The intersection of EU impacts on central government and devolution represented a fundamental change in the different dimensions of policy-making: in the system, the organisation, the process and its regulation (see Bulmer *et al.* 2002, 158–75). Whilst the shared civil service culture has demonstrated much continuity thus far, it is quite likely that distinctive logics will develop in the devolveds over time. The devolution settlement is being reformed in Wales, is at an earlier stage in Northern Ireland, and is subject to new political dynamics with a minority SNP Executive in Edinburgh. In short, to use the words of former Welsh Secretary of State, Ron Davies, 'devolution is not a single defining event but a process'.[75]

Conclusion

In reviewing the findings of Chapters 6 and 7 we reflect on the critical moments and junctures in European policy-making. Further analysis is presented in the next chapter.

A first important conclusion is simply the sheer breadth of the EU's impact across UK central government. Existing contemporary studies focus on 'the hub' of European policy-making which we considered in Chapter 5 (Bulmer and Burch 1998; 2005; Kassim 2000a; 2001; Allen and Oliver 2006) or are much briefer or selective in outlook (Buller and Smith 1998; Smith 1999). Andrew Jordan's account of the EU's impact on the DoE is the main exception (Jordan 2002; see also 2003), although Forster and Blair (2002) include some policy case studies. Therefore, a first fundamental conclusion to these two chapters is to note the sheer impact of the EU across the whole of central government including executive agencies and the English regions. The impact was also felt on the territorial offices and that now falls to the devolved executive authorities, posing challenges for both them and the UK government in managing their engagement in EU policy.

A second key conclusion is that the impact of the EU has grown significantly over time, as new policy competences have developed at European level, and as these have in turn become more deeply developed and, in many cases, subject to more supranational processes (QMV, engagement of the EP, litigation by the Court). This evolving process presents new challenges for central government, triggered by innovations at EU level. As we saw in Chapter 6, MAFF was Europeanised to a large degree upon accession because the common agricultural and fisheries policies had such a major impact. The DoE neglected European policy and found itself obliged to change position, not least because of infraction proceedings. The Home Office found itself impacted upon by the Maastricht Treaty and the MoD because of the launch of the ESDP.

Thirdly, the Europeanisation-effect needs to be disaggregated in a more fine-grained picture. The simple creation of EU level competences does not automatically cause Europeanisation. A number of scenarios are possible. Under one an EU competence exists but is not used, so the impact on the UK government is latent rather than actual: for example, the case of European transport policy until the single market. Under another, new competences may have been agreed but the governmental response is neglectful (for example, the DoE) or is positively resistant (HO under Michael Howard or the Treasury's response to the EC budget, complete with its resultant public expenditure rules – see Chapter 6). A third scenario entails simply dealing with the impact but in a reactive manner: the response, for example of many of the 'outer core' departments. Finally, there is the pro-active Europeanisation-effect, where the EU is utilised constructively – potentially even to seek to export UK ideas and policy to the EU level. Examples here include the DTI and the single market; the DoT under Ridley and air transport liberalisation; the Prime Minister/MoD and defence policy (leading to the ESDP's creation); the Cabinet Office and 'better regulation'. What seems to be clear is that the third scenario is the default response of UK government. By contrast, resistance to the impact of the EU or the directly opposed position of using it pro-actively as an opportunity structure is a function of an explicit ministerial position. Resistance was particularly associated with Euro-sceptic ministers during the Major governments. Pro-activity has been greater under the Blair governments but there were instances under Thatcher and Major. Europeanisation is therefore in part a function of ministers, and their civil servants are obliged to toe the line (see also Buller and Smith 1998: 183).

The pro-active response also highlights our fifth conclusion, that Europeanisation is not simply a downward flow from EU level: a finding well established in the broader literature (see Bache and Jordan's review 2006b: 20–3). If the party-politics permit and the political will is present, UK governments can place their stamp on the EU. As Anand Menon (2004a) has asserted, 'Britain has . . . become one of the most skilled countries at shaping the EU'. The EU is an opportunity structure available to the UK government for solving policy problems that cannot be tackled in other arenas. Europeanisation is also about recognising this situation: something that has been haphazard and contingent upon party-political divisions until the Blair government's 'Step Change' initiative in 1998 (Bulmer and Burch 2005).

A sixth and final conclusion is that the impact of the EU is also a function of separate domestic dynamics that lie behind the continuing re-organisation of government. One example of this came about as we were completing this study, with Gordon Brown's re-shaping of a number of government departments. Other such changes have happened at the time of cabinet re-shuffles or as part of re-organisations of the machinery of government: for example the growth of agency government or the introduction of devolution. The Europeanisation of central government cannot be understood without taking these developments into account as well (see Chapter 8).

Notes

1   In May 2007 the creation of a new Ministry of Justice led to some of the Home Office's functions, notably on criminal justice and the prisons, being re-located. Our treatment of the Home Office pre-dates this move.

2   Interview, Home Office, 23 November 1996.

3   The committee's designation derived from the article number in the Maastricht Treaty (Lavenex and Wallace 2005: 462).

4   The Schengen Convention had developed in a rather ad hoc way because it lacked developed central institutions. Hence, as Lavenex and Wallace note (2005: 465), when the Amsterdam Treaty was signed there was no definitive text on the body of decisions that had been taken under the Schengen arrangements. In a quirk of the EU system, it fell to the UK presidency in 1998 to identify the Schengen *acquis* and oversee its incorporation into the EU, even though the UK had never been a participant (Ludlow 1998: 577): a task that fell to the UKREP legal counsellor.

5   Interview, Home Office, 25 February 2005.

6   Interview, UKREP, Brussels, 18 March 1997.

7   Information from www.ukrep.be, accessed 31 October 2005.

8   Interview, Secretariat-General, European Commission, 17 March 1997.

9   Interview, UKREP, Brussels, 18 March 1997.

10   Interview, Home Office, 25 February 2005.

11   Interview, Home Office, 25 February 2005.

12   During the Major government and in the early Blair era the partners were the Lord Chancellor's Department and HM Customs and Excise.

13   Interview, Home Office, 23 November 1996.

14   Interview, Home Office, 25 February 2005.

15   Interview, Ministry of Defence, 5 December 1996.

16   Interview, Ministry of Defence, 5 December 1996.

17   On the ESDP's development, see W. Wallace (2005), on which the following section draws.

18   Interview, Ministry of Defence, 28 February 2005. British forces in Iraq were not, of course, part of a NATO operation.

19   Some are held in member states rather than in Brussels or the presidency country. Also some of the committees have a presidency serving for several years rather than six months. For instance, the EUMC was chaired by an Italian, chosen for a term of several years. Interview, Ministry of Defence, 28 February 2005.

20   In that sense the Europeanisation-effect is at its largest for those EU states that have not been in NATO or the WEU.

21   For further details, see the agency's website: www.eda.europa.eu/ accessed 18 July 2007.

22 All data here and in this section arise – unless otherwise noted – from interview, Ministry of Defence, 28 February 2005.

23 Data from: www.ukrep.be, accessed 18 July 2007.

24 Data from: www.ukrep.be, accessed 18 July 2007. Unlike all other UKREP officials, these are MoD, rather than FCO, postings.

25 Interview, ODPM official, 10 March 2005. Also sourced from the ODPM organisational plan: www.odpm.gov.uk/stellent/groups/odpm_about/ documents/page/odpm_about_029314.pdf, accessed March 2005.

26 See 'UK Presidency of the EU: UKREP Guide', sourced from: www.ukrep.be, accessed 31 October 2005.

27 See www.communities.gov.uk/index.asp?id=1503442, accessed 22 July 2007.

28 The Ministry of Justice also took over some responsibilities from the Home Office.

29 Source: www.dca.gov.uk/eupresidency2005/index.htm, accessed 10 November 2005.

30 Information on the LCD is sourced from an interview, Lord Chancellor's Department, 9 December 1996.

31 See 'DCA Manifesto: For a New Department': www.dca.gov.uk/dept/ manifesto.htm, accessed 10 November 2005.

32 See www.dca.gov.uk/eupresidency2005/index.htm, accessed 21 July 2007.

33 Responsibility for the concordats had previously been with the ODPM. On the concordats, see Bulmer *et al.* (2002: 36–9).

34 Interview, Arts Division, Department of National Heritage, 22 April 1997.

35 Interview, Department of National Heritage, 22 April 1997. The justification for this arrangement was that the amount of EU business was small, coordination would necessitate an extra layer of staff, and there had been an adverse public expenditure settlement.

36 This seemed a plausible arrangement, although our own experience at trying to find out whom to interview did not, in 1996, indicate a smooth running arrangement.

37 Source: DCMS Annual Report 2005, www.culture.gov.uk/NR/rdonlyres/ 4260F578-4465-4B83-811F-DC7C50FDBA4E/0/DCMSAR2005fullreport.pdf, accessed on 7 November 2005.

38 We were told in 1996 that 'those responsible for Europe in the old Department of Education had difficulty in securing the attention of the wider ministry on EU issues'. Interview DfEE, 10 December 1996.

39 See www.dfes.gov.uk/aboutus/whoswho/lifelong.shtml, accessed 7 November 2005.

40 The E1/11 has been replaced by the European Health Insurance Card.

41 Policy lead on health and safety was with the DTI and previously the Department of Education and Employment.

42 Interview, Department of Health, 29 November 1996.

43 Interview, Department of Health, 29 November 1996.

44 Details are drawn from the DH's directory of events for the presidency's health programme: www.dh.gov.uk/PolicyAndGuidance/International/EuropeanUnion/ EUPresidency2005/fs/en, accessed 7 November 2005. Many of the regulator meetings were being organised by the Medicines and Healthcare products Regulatory Agency rather than the DH itself.

45 See the DH's 2007 Departmental Report, www.dh.gov.uk/en/ Publicationsandstatistics/Publications/AnnualReports/DH_074767, (p. 182), accessed 21 July 2007.

46 Interview, ODA, 25 November 1996.

47 Prior to the ODA's Fundamental Economic Review earlier in 1996 EC aid projects were all overseen in the EU Department, i.e. separately from national aid projects. The ensuing June 1996 re-organisation ended this organisational duplication.

48 September 2005 organisational plan, sourced at: www.dfid.gov.uk/aboutdfid/ organisation/organogram.pdf, accessed 9 November 2005; 2007 plan accessed at the same URL, 21 July 2007. Of the three large directorates-general one is geographically based, a second covers 'policy and international' and a third covers central functions. EU coordination is in the second of these DGs (the Europe, Trade and International Financial Institutions Division). One geographical division includes aid to Europe and Central Asia.

49 All data from 1996 derive from an interview in the Department of Transport, 25 November 1996.

50 Information here derives from an interview with a former DoT official, 31 October 2000.

51 Interview with a former DoT official, 31 October 2000.

52 The sequence of the upheavals is as follows: Department for the Environment, Transport and the Regions (May 1997–June 2001); the Department for Transport, Local Government and the Regions (June 2001–May 2002); Department for Transport (May 2002–).

53 www.dft.gov.uk/about/how/coll_organisationofthedft/howthedftisstructured1, accessed 21 July 2007. This directorate is responsible *inter alia*, for aviation and maritime transport.

54 See www.dft.gov.uk/about/eu/transportachievementsduringt5483, accessed 21 July 2007.

55 Interview, Department of Social Security, 3 December 1996.

56 Interview, DfEE, 10 December 1996.

57 Interview, Department of Social Security, 3 December 1996. In 1996 EU policy coordination and the oversight of social security obligations under the treaties were the responsibility of the DSS's International Relations and EU Branch, staffed by five officials.

58 See the DWP's Departmental Framework, available at www.dwp.gov.uk/ aboutus/DepartmentalFrameworkJune20071.pdf, accessed 21 July 2007.

59 See www.cabinetoffice.gov.uk/regulation/europe/, accessed 21 July 2007.

60 See www.dti.gov.uk/regional/regional-dev-agencies/index.html, accessed 21 July 2007.

61 For details, see Government Offices for the English Regions, 'Tasking Framework', available at: www.gos.gov.uk/common/docs/239393/ TaskingFramework, 13. For the review, see www.gos.gov.uk/common/docs/ reviewreport.pdf: both accessed 21 July 2007.

62 At this time a further lawyer advised the Lord Advocate on equivalent matters relating to the intersection of European law and Scottish legislation. This lawyer had the additional function of advising on the drafting of Scottish legislation to transpose European Directives.

63 In the *Factortame* case relating to the Common Fisheries Policy, the Attorney General represented the government. This case was important because it was the first instance when an act of parliament was overruled by the ECJ, thus challenging the constitutional principle of parliamentary sovereignty. The Solicitor General had attended in this capacity a BSE-related case on the beef export ban. Information from interview, Attorney General's Department, 14 January 1997.

64 Together with our collaborators Caitríona Carter, Patricia Hogwood and Andrew Scott we undertook two projects on devolution and European policy. One concerned the institutional transition in the UK, Wales and Scotland; the other, for which we were joined by Ricardo Gomez, examined its practice in specific policy areas and including the English regions. We acknowledge the ESRC for funding both projects and our research colleagues. The former project was published as Bulmer *et al.* (2002); the latter in numerous papers, many available in draft form at the project's legacy site: http://les.man.ac.uk/devolution/; also see Bulmer *et al.* (2006) for an overview. A total of 168 officials and politicians were interviewed – i.e. separately from the Whitehall project proper, which also included multiple interviews across the three territorial offices. We cannot reference all these interviews here, of course.

65 For a full account of the transition to devolution, and its impact on EU policy-making, see Bulmer *et al.* (2002).

66 For instance, the Welsh Office was only created in 1964, while the Northern Ireland Office's powers arose from the reinstatement of direct rule in 1972 because of the 'Troubles'. The Scottish Office dated from 1885.

67 Interviews: Scottish Office Development Department, 23 January 1997; Welsh Office, 22 January 1997.

68 Interview, Scottish Office, Department of Agriculture, Environment and Fisheries, 23 January 1997.

69 Interview, Scottish Executive Development Department, 30 November 1999. The first official tasked, at the instigation of John Major, with monitoring territorial discord was Kenneth Mackenzie. Mackenzie had come to the Cabinet Office from the SO's Agricultural Department, so was well placed.

70 This took place as part of the Government of Wales Act 2006, see: http://new.wales.gov.uk/gowasub/gowa/?lang=en, accessed 24 July 2007.

71 These notes are now hosted by the Ministry of Justice website: www.justice.gov.uk/guidance/devolutionguidancenotes.htm, accessed 26 July 2007.

72 See www.scotland.gov.uk/Resource/Doc/923/0051017.pdf, accessed 26 July 2007.

73 See www.scotland.gov.uk/Publications/2004/01/18759/31717, accessed 26 July 2007. At this time European policy was being run from the Finance and Central Services Department. The Northern Irish counterpart document (*Taking Our Place in Europe*) was published by the Office of the Minister and the Deputy First Minister in 2006, at a time when devolution was suspended, see: www.ofmdfmni.gov.uk/taking_our_place_in_europe.pdf, accessed 26 July 2007.

74 See, for one, 'Left out in Europe Scots ministers can't afford to be ignored', *The Herald*, 22 January 2007. The report was based on a leaked document written by Michael Aron, head of the SE's office in Brussels. According to *The Herald*, the 'document . . . gives examples of Scottish ministers being left out

of EU council meetings and having to sit in another room where they must listen, but cannot contribute, to the debate. Even when allowed access to the EU's commissioners, it is on condition that Scotland toes the Westminster line'. Thanks to Scott James for providing the press cutting.

75 Quoted at: http://news.bbc.co.uk/1/hi/uk_politics/272015.stm, accessed 26 July 2007.

8

Understanding the impact of Europe

This chapter returns to our concern with Europeanisation as manifested through a historical institutionalist analysis. In the first section of the chapter we use historical institutionalism as a way of taking stock of developments. We concentrate on the lessons to be drawn from the preceding four empirical chapters. The nature and dimensions of the changes that have taken place are examined and we isolate any critical moments and consider which of these might be defined as critical junctures when a new pathway was taken. We examine the extent of transformation at these points – whether the change is incremental or transformative (radical or incremental-transformative). We note that the story varies not only across time but also across Whitehall depending on whether we are analysing changes at the hub of the European network or in its inner and outer cores. We then move on to explain why these changes have taken place, before returning to our model of Europeanisation and adapting and refining it in the light of our findings. In helping to explain the changes that have taken place we consider the role of significant individuals as well as the effects of more impersonal influences.

Was change transformative or incremental?

Turning to the nature and dimensions of the changes in Whitehall it is noticeable that over the period since the UK's first application the impact of the EU upon Whitehall and the ways its personnel do business has been profound. Indeed the European policy-making network in Whitehall is now extensive and it draws together a larger grouping of civil servants and ministers than any other cross-departmental policy grouping that has existed on a long-term basis (Bulmer and Burch 2000: 58). The obvious competitor is the expenditure community which radiates out from the Treasury, but that is smaller, and more centred and contained. The EU network is, however, very varied in its operation and composition. Much depends on the exact business in hand as the content of policy determines who will be drawn in. In essence there are a core number of individuals in Whitehall who work on EU matters full-time and a much wider grouping of participants who are drawn into the network from time to time according to the issue being handled. Judged in the long term a pattern has emerged of slow and accretive change in the development and extension of the EU network throughout Whitehall. The overall effect, we argue, has been, over a fifty-year period, substantial and significant. This is a key finding and it corresponds with our notion of incremental transformative change as outlined in Chapter 2.

At this point it is worth remembering that our approach to judging the extent of change – whether it is substantial and significant – is to consider changes across our four institutional dimensions. That is, change in the overall *system*, in *organisations*, in *processes* and in *regulation* – as well as any *cultural* changes within or across any or all of these dimensions (see Chapter 2). According to this approach the degree of change reflects both the extent of change within a dimension and the extent of change across them. Such assessments need to be applied to the hub of the Whitehall EU network as well as its inner and outer cores.

Overall the very act of joining the European project in 1973 constituted the first significant *system* change. It involved formal acceptance of the condition that European law would have primacy over national law, that the legal structures and processes of government would be conditioned and circumscribed by the direct effect of European rules and obligations, and that in certain areas of domestic policy, for example, agriculture, important decisions would be shaped and determined in Brussels. Although this transformation was not emphasised at the time of entry, the act of accession in 1973 has been, at least until the devolution reforms of the late 1990s, the most important shift in the UK constitutional set-up in the postwar period. Moreover, since 1973 there has been a further deepening of European integration as embodied, for example, in the SEA and the Maastricht Treaty. This deepening has meant that the radical change of 1973 has slowly become more embedded in the UK system. Beyond accession, also, there has been a significant alteration in the framework of government brought about by the greater engagement of UK personnel in supranational fora at the EU level. This enhanced engagement has meant that the UK process of governance has increasingly involved participation in and awareness of extra-national pressures and involvement. This is a situation often summed up in the notion of multi-level governance which, while it may not be enshrined in UK constitutional understandings, is an unavoidable and highly consequential reality of being a member of the EU.

In terms of *organisations* the picture of change is less dramatic. So far as the hub of the network is concerned, there have only been two substantially new organisations created to deal with European business: COES and UKREP. And both of these were created in prototype prior to accession.

In addition, there have been substantial organisational changes in the FCO to reflect the fact of EU engagement notably the creation of new divisions to deal with EU matters both external and internal. Other departments have also created new sections to deal with the requirements of EU engagement as the need has arisen. This especially applies to the DTI and DEFRA and, more recently, the Home Office and the MoD. Notably, all Departments, with the exception of the DCMS, have established EU coordinating arrangements to handle issues across the department. In organisational terms the tendency throughout Whitehall has been to adapt and augment what was already in place. Alterations in the key positions in Whitehall and the authority attached to them as a result of EU engagement have also been slow and accretive but quite substantial in the long term. We have already noted the enhanced position of the PM (see Chapter 5), and wholly new positions have arisen concerning the coordination of business across central government (notably the posts in COES) and at departmental and intra-departmental levels. On the ministerial side one wholly new post has emerged, that of Minister of State Europe in the FCO, although existing ministerial posts in other highly Europeanised sectors have taken on more EU-related responsibilities and most ministers have had to attend EU meetings, even the Home Secretary. Indeed *organisational* change is most evident in the growth of positions dealing with EU business right across all parts of the EU network in Whitehall. There has also been a broader challenge to the traditional distribution of authority in Whitehall as a result of EU membership and that has been the gradual erosion of the FCO's monopoly over the conduct of external affairs. Of these changes, the growth in positions and activity is a direct EU effect, while other changes also have more domestic, UK, origins. Overall organisational change reflects a pattern of incremental transformation with few big dramatic shifts but a cumulative line of development which over time has proved to be substantial.

Turning to the *processes* for handling business, change is equally substantial but more dramatic. Engagement in Europe has, since the 1950s, seen the creation of a wholly new set of policy processes and distribution networks in Whitehall and beyond. Most of these centre on COES and the processes for the reception and digestion of business from the EU and the projection of the UK position into the EU. Notably change is to be found in the more evident elaboration of a system of formal meetings and committees; the creation of the Friday meeting to handle the input from UK-based processes into Brussels-based processes; and ultimately the shift to a more flexible structure of meetings and decision fora. As we have seen these policy processes vary somewhat according to the business in hand but they can be distinguished by the extent to which they are cross-departmental or contained within a department – such as the DCE in DEFRA. New processes and subsidiary networks have emerged to deal with new areas of cross-departmental business such as JHA, the CFSP and ESDP. While these new processes and networks have emerged, they have tended to be in keeping with the established Whitehall model of policy-making, but with one important difference; they are plugged into a timetable and policy-making process at EU level. The frequency of meetings attended by UK ministers over the period from the 1990s, as noted in Chapter 3 (see Tables 3.3 and 3.4), indicates the extent to which their working patterns have been changed by EU membership. The same generalisation holds for officials. The picture is one of a gradual increase in involvement, but which, if viewed over the long-term from pre-1973, is significant and substantial. So change here is adaptive, though in terms of the extent of the activity now engaged it is transformative and innovative. This greater involvement has been a direct result of EU membership as has the creation of the Friday meeting, internal departmental processes such as the DCE and subsidiary networks dealing with JHA and defence and foreign policy. The changes in the scale of the policy-making processes are a direct response to the growth in the quantity and complexity of European business, although the increased informality of the operation has reflected largely domestic causes and developments such as the adoption by Whitehall of IT and email and changes in management style leading to a move away from a highly formalised system of official standing committees.

Changes in *regulation* are not as dramatic as changes in process but are, if looked at over the whole period, substantial. Over time, rules, guidelines, operating codes and understandings have been established and inculcated about how to handle EU business and how to engage with the EU. In some cases, such as European Public Expenditure Survey (EUROPES), this has had an effect on the rules and practices governing other aspects of the operation of Whitehall. Within COES and in departments guidance has built up over the years about how to handle EU engagement. Some of this has been laid down in Notes of Guidance (as in COES); some exists less formally as 'good practice'. Changes in *regulation* have been both accretive and cumulative as the business of dealing with Europe has altered and expanded since 1973. Here the EU factor is the key driver, but the rules and understandings that have emerged to deal with it are usually based on traditional Whitehall approaches and formats. Strategic capacity to think and plan ahead on Europe remained problematic throughout the period up until 1997 especially at the ministerial level and mainly for domestic, party political reasons. From 1997 the Blair government benefited from less party and governmental division over Europe and has consequently been better able to address strategic questions and project initiatives at EU level. The EU-effect here has been to create the need for a strategic capacity, but the response has usually reflected UK shaping factors.

The *cultural* aspects of EU engagement across all our dimensions are harder to isolate. There is little change in attitudes towards the organisation of Whitehall or understandings about how business in Whitehall should be organised that is directly engendered by the EU. For example, creation of executive agencies and the greater emphasis on implementation, delivery and management within Whitehall in the period since 1979 are directly a product of international and domestic pressures rather than EU ones. There is, however, some change in views about how policy is best developed and the tactical and strategic considerations that need to be taken into account when dealing with EU-related business. A large number of home civil servants have through immersion in the EU and in working in tandem with FCO personnel developed negotiating skills more traditionally associated with the art of diplomacy. Some interviewees referred to the FCO style and its impact across Whitehall. To these participants the FCO's 'style of action' has had an evident influence on the way that Whitehall has operated since entry. The FCO's 'house characteristics' include 'a very effective negotiating approach':

> considering quite hard what should be the level and timing of involvement in a particular policy area, when is it useful to try and impact, at what level should we go in, when does it have to be topped up with some other form of intervention, who are going to be your friends, what are the key issues?[1]

In addition to the effect on the style of administration, there has been cumulatively an emergence of a substantial cadre of civil servants and, indeed, ministers who have, through dint of participation in EU policy-making, built up a substantial awareness of EU issues, tactics and procedures. These can simply be shared understandings about how the EU works through to skills in making it work such as building coalitions and alliances – a necessity in areas of policy-making increasingly subject to QMV. This awareness is in part a product of the slow 'socialising' effect that increased involvement with the EU has brought into play over four decades of membership, especially with the diffusion of expertise from officials who have had a tour of duty in the EU institutions or UKREP. It is also in part a product of the deliberate post-1997 effort by the Blair government to inculcate across the board more awareness of matters European. It is difficult to quantify the impact of this accumulation of know-how about EU matters on the operation of Whitehall, but it is undoubtedly a factor shaping the changing values and administrative culture of UK central government.

Thus we see substantial change of a cumulative nature across all our dimensions including some especially significant changes in *system* and *process*. On our criteria, with change registered within and across all dimensions, UK central government's adaptation to the EU provides an example of substantial change of the incremental transformative variety. Notably, while these changes have cumulatively amounted to a transformation in how and what Whitehall does, the responses to pressures from the EU have been more those of absorption and accommodation than a series of radically transformative steps. The general pattern is thus one of significant change in the long run, but on Whitehall's terms and largely in keeping with Whitehall's ways of doing things. Of course, not all the changes that have taken place can be directly ascribed to Europeanisation and this is a point we pick up later in this chapter. There are also, within the general pattern of incremental transformative change, moments of more sudden alteration. In the next section of this chapter we examine these critical moments and junctures.

What are the critical moments and critical junctures

In Chapter 3 we identified a number of critical moments following through from the UK's relationship with the EU. These we defined as moments when a *perceived opportunity* arises for significant change. That is, an event takes place which raises a general expectation that significant change will follow. Such a general expectation may reveal itself in a variety of ways. It may, for example, emerge within elite groups, it may come to dominate or define media debate, or it may register substantially among public opinion or indeed involve a mixture of these manifestations (Burch *et al.* 2002). In relation to UK/EU policy-making such expectations of significant change may be triggered by a treaty change or constitutional reform at EU level, or by events at the domestic level such as the entry into power of a new government with a distinctive EU programme. If the opportunities created by a critical moment are acted upon and *significant* changes follow (that is, changes within and across our four institutional dimensions), then we have a critical juncture: a significant shift in the way things are done which creates a new pathway that is followed through thereafter. Of course the opportunity arising at a critical moment may not be acted upon. So which were the critical moments and which of these led to critical junctures in the handling of UK European policy? The answers to these questions differ according to whether we are examining activities at the hub or at the inner and outer cores of the EU policy-making network.

The critical moments identified in earlier chapters (especially Chapter 3) opening up important opportunities for the core of Whitehall to respond to EU related matters are outlined in Table 8.1. In each of these cases there was a general expectation amongst elites, and/or the media, and/or public opinion that these were substantial events from which significant change in the operation of UK central government could be expected to follow. In earlier chapters we specified that only three of these can, at least if judged as having significant consequences for institutional change in Whitehall, be classified as critical junctures. These are the 1961 original application for entry which saw the creation of the basic machinery and approach to coordinating EU policy across Whitehall; the UK's accession to the EU in 1973 which saw a change in the emphasis and purpose of the machinery

Table 8.1 Critical moments and junctures relating to the hub of UK/EU policy-making network

Date	Critical moment	Critical juncture?
1957	Treaty of Rome	No
1961	UK application for entry	Yes
1967	Second UK application	No
1973	UK accession	Yes
1975	Referendum on re-negotiated terms of entry	No
1986	Single European Act	No
1992	Treaty on European Union (Maastricht)	Yes
1997	Amsterdam Treaty	No
1997–98	New Labour – Step Change initiative	Yes
1999	Devolution	Yes
2001	Treaty of Nice	No

and the extent of resource devoted to it; and the Maastricht Treaty which saw little immediate change but because of its three-pillared nature spawned a more fragmented structure within Whitehall with two subsidiary networks covering justice and home affairs and foreign and security issues. However, we also identified two critical junctures which arose principally from domestic dynamics. The first of these arose from the election of the Blair government and its Step Change programme launched in 1998, which saw a greater emphasis on projection into the EU. We also hold, on the basis of an earlier study we have undertaken (Bulmer *et al.* 2002: 170–3), that the special arrangements for UK EU policy-making that have followed on from devolution in Scotland, Wales and Northern Ireland constitute a critical juncture in UK EU policy-making and, more broadly, in the nature of UK governance. This is because the effect of devolution has been to re-order the institutional framework by creating directly elected assemblies and executives in the devolved territories which are able to engage in the process of UK EU policy-making. This re-ordering has created new opportunities for intervening in UK EU policy-making. Notably devolution has also already led to significant variations across the UK in EU related policies on agricultural, rural, and environmental matters. Opportunities for significant institutional change arose at all the other critical moments but were not exploited. In nearly all cases this was because the UK was able to accommodate any EU pressures into the established Whitehall ways of operating without significant changes.

Moving to the inner and outer cores of the network the picture is somewhat different. It also varies across departments and agencies and is much affected by the gradual extension of competences at the EU level. As new competences arose so departments and the relevant sections within them

Table 8.2 Illustrative critical junctures in the 'inner' and 'outer cores' of the EU network

Date	Department	Event
1970	MAFF	Departmental Committee on Europe (DCE) set up to handle CAP
1984	Treasury	Creation of EUROPES
1989–90/ 1993–97	DoE	Enhanced Europeanisation under Chris Patten and John Gummer
1991	Scottish Office	Europeanisation reforms under Ian Lang
1993	Home Office	Creation of Justice and Home Affairs cooperation
1993–94	DTI, DoE, territorials and GoRs	1988 reforms to structural funds necessitate stronger sub-national/regional involvement
1998–2001	MoD	Creation of European Security and Defence Policy
1999–	Devolveds	Re-calibration of in-house European policy-making following devolution

were drawn into EU matters either through participation in the Whitehall network or directly into Europe. In terms of institutional change we note some key critical junctures in Table 8.2.

All of these critical junctures entailed significant institutional adaptations and accommodation within departments. The handling of the CAP and fisheries led to the development of separate policy and negotiation machinery for each policy area within MAFF. In the case of CAP this was centred upon the Departmental Committee on Europe. The operation of EUROPES from 1984 to November 2003 impacted on the development of UK EU policy in areas of EU spending especially in relation to research and development. Significant reforms of the departmental approach to Europe took place following comprehensive reviews in the DoE and the Scottish Office (Jordan 2002; Smith 2001). New arrangements had to be set up in the Home Office in 1993 and the Ministry of Defence from 1998 to handle the EU aspects of JHA cooperation, and defence policy respectively. The structural funds required new mechanisms for bidding for and then distributing them which required involvement of the relevant regional offices of both the DTI and the DoE as well as representatives of regional interests. The impact of these initiatives on the further development of regional interests and machinery in the more peripheral parts of England has been profound (Burch and Gomez 2002). The creation of Scottish and Welsh assemblies and executives in 1999 allowed both countries to substantially re-order their approach to the EU, resulting in a more territorial focus (Bulmer *et al.* 2006).

The pattern that emerges is one in which critical moments, often instigated by EU initiatives, are usually responded to by adaptation or accommodation. Though as shown in Table 8.1 there are a small number of critical moments that became critical junctures in that they induced changes that go beyond adaptation and accommodation to bring in substantive institutional change. Of course, while changes have taken place in response to seeking and sustaining EU membership it does not follow that all these provide instances of significant Europeanisation. Responses may have been as much, or even primarily, the product of domestic or global pressures for reform. This is a matter we explore in the rest of this chapter.

Europeanisation: explaining the changes

What is clear from the material presented in preceding chapters is that while the relationship with the EU has had significant policy consequences for the UK its impact on the institutions and operation of Whitehall is less marked. Clearly there is a Europeanising effect and that is reflected over the long term, but if we wish to explore the nature of this effect more fully we need to do two things. First, we need to consider possible patterns of causation and, secondly, we need to refine our model of Europeanisation so as to cover both EU and other pressures for change.

In examining causation it is important to re-emphasise that institutional change is not only likely to occur in response to new developments at EU level. There are other competing sources of change deriving from the domestic level: whether party-political or political-administrative in nature; and whether Whitehall-wide or department-specific in nature. Examples include:

- putting into operation Labour's manifesto commitment to devolution (party-political, Whitehall-wide but with department-specific politico-administrative impact);
- the growth of 'agency government' by confining departments to policy issues and assigning tasks of policy implementation to agencies (politico-administrative, Whitehall-wide);
- constraints upon departmental spending, with implications for resources, training budgets and so on (politico-administrative, Whitehall-wide but with differential departmental responses);
- government re-organisation, such as the creation of the Department for Environment, Food and Rural Affairs in June 2001 at the start of the Blair government's second term (departmental, politico-administrative).

Each of these kinds of change has had a significant impact upon government's response to the EU even though the source of change has nothing to do with the EU itself. Devolution has created greater complexity in EU policy-making because of the need to interface with authorities which are no longer part of UK central government and are accountable to different political masters. Agency government creates longer chains of command where the implementation of EU law is concerned and may impede co-ordination. Cuts in resources or training budgets may impact upon a department's arrangements for handling of European policy; *or* it might offer an opportunity for unsatisfactory ones to be reformed. The key point, then, is that Europeanisation-effects cannot be isolated to developments in the EU and how they are received in the British political arena – something which has been contentious enough since the 1960s! – but also intersect with unrelated changes in British public administration. In addition to these domestic sources of change, alterations may also come about as a result of global pressures from beyond the EU which also may directly affect developments in the UK such as in the case of the challenges posed for government by climate change. We aim to be sensitive to these other sources of change and to avoid simplistic attribution of all change in EU policy-making to Europeanisation.

With these points about attribution in mind, we can distinguish a number of possible causation effects in relation to Europeanisation. First, there are those cases where there is a direct, exclusive and evident EU effect as in the case of an EU regulation which requires to be carried out by all member states as a matter of European law. Second, there are other cases where there is direct and evident effect, but the EU is not the sole source of that effect. In such cases, where there are multiple shaping factors, EU influences might be judged as either primary or secondary or tertiary (etc.) in a sequence of causation, or as of equal weight alongside pressures from other sources. So while the immediate cause of a response may not emanate from the EU, the cause of that non-EU stimulus might well be EU-related. This situation can be illustrated in the case of the creation of integrated government offices in the English regions in 1994 in response to pressures from regional businesses, who wanted a more coordinated approach by central government in the regions. Although the primary cause of the initiative, it was also shaped, indirectly and as a secondary cause, by mechanisms established in some of the English regions to make best use of the EU structural funds. Third, EU pressures can be indirect in the sense that they are context- and attitude-shaping so that any EU effect is expressed through its impact on the climate of opinion amongst governing elites or the engaged public more generally. For instance the general EU-related notion of a 'Europe of the Regions' and the EU emphasis upon the principle of subsidiarity, whereby powers should be placed at the most appropriate territorial level, helped to shape the thinking underlying Scottish and Welsh devolution even though the direct, immediate and primary causes of this change were domestic.

We need to adapt our initial model (see Figure 2.1) in order to accommodate these points. In our way of seeing the Europeanisation process, the pressures shaping change, whether direct or indirect, whether initiatory or developmental, whether derived from EU or domestic or global forces, are processed through various mediating factors at domestic level. These mediating factors involve both structure and agency – a shaping context and a dynamic element that animates activity within that context. In our revised model this shaping context is captured in both the established institutional structure of central government, and accountability to the wider domestic political environment (as manifested through party, public opinion and the media) in which central government is embedded. In addition we need to add, as the third element in our model, the facilitating role fulfilled by significant actors. The contextual factors place constraints on, and provide opportunities for, change, and actors operating within this framework are conditioned by political and organisational cultures that can further help or inhibit change. Significant actors not only operate within this framework but also may help to shape it. They play a crucial role in facilitating and bringing about change either by overcoming constraints or by exploiting opportunities, or by working within existing cultures or even by altering them. In other words, in many cases change would not happen, or not at that particular time, without their intervention.

Significant actors may bring about a new and enduring change in institutional structures arrangements and values. They may be the ones that respond to European and other pressures to act in the context of the established institutional framework. As we have seen in earlier chapters, important in the early days of EU engagement, for instance, were Edward Heath, Sir Frank Lee and John Robinson all of whom played significant roles in shaping the timing, content and pace of institutional change at the hub of the network. The critical distinction is that their actions did have a *lasting effect on the institutions for handling EU policy-making in Whitehall*. Defined in these terms significant actors are not to be distinguished simply as a consequence of the positions they hold. For example, Norman Lamont, Kenneth Clarke and Gordon Brown as successive chancellors of the exchequer were at the centre of EU policy-making in Whitehall, but none of these had a lasting institutional effect by bringing about significant changes in Whitehall's approach to handling EU policy. By contrast, Tony Blair as Prime Minister, provides an example of an individual in the inner core of the EU network who did have a lasting effect. Just as Ian Lang, Scottish Secretary under John Major, provides and example of an individual in the outer core who had a significant effect. His determination to reform the Scottish Office's approach to handling Europe had lasting effects. Two further examples of significant individuals in the outer core are Christopher Patten and John Gummer, who, as successive Secretaries of State for the Environment, facilitated the Europeanisation of the DoE, making it both more EU aware and more EU active (see Jordan 2002).

These considerations noted above are illustrated diagrammatically in Figure 8.1. This shows, in the light of the evidence we have presented in preceding chapters, a significant refinement of our original model of Europeanisation (outlined in Chapter 2 – see Figure 2.1). To that model we have added global pressures for reform. The significance of domestic reform pressures has become very evident in our empirical account. As shown in Figure 8.1, global pressures are sometimes manifested through the EU but they may also or solely be directed through the member state. We have also indicated that the impulses deriving from the EU are best seen as the 'duties of membership', that is, the need to be able to participate in downstream and upstream relations with the EU. The original formulation in Figure 2.1 refers to adaptational pressure but this expression is rather strong and arguably only applies at the time of accession. The term was influenced by the notions of fit and misfit that has been applied in the Europeanisation literature (see Risse *et al.* 2001). These notions seem inappropriate to adaptation of national institutional structures, since the EU imposes no institutional template, to which they should adapt.

The global, EU and domestic pressures are mediated at the domestic level through the established institutional framework of central government and its wider domestic political environment, both of which constrain or open up opportunities for change. Change is also shaped by entrenched political and organisational cultures. We also add a crucial facilitating role for significant actors who have a lasting effect on the way things are done. The process of institutional development is then examined within and across

Figure 8.1 Europeanisation and institutional adaptation

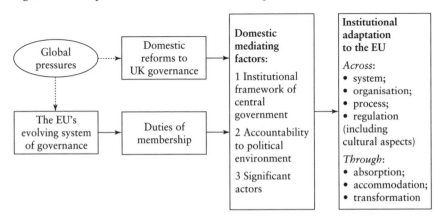

our institutional dimensions – system, organisation, process and regulation. By exploring changes in and across these categories we are able to get a sense of the spread and depth of institutional change and by these means determine the extent to which a change can be judged as significant and whether it involves absorption, accommodation or transformation.

In the next chapter we draw on features of our model in analysing the impact of the EU on the operation of central governments in other member states. This provides a point of comparison for the UK case, setting it in the context of what other states do.

Note

1   Interview, retired senior Cabinet Office official, 17 April 1997.

9

Whitehall in comparative context

Thus far in our study we have explored the impact of EU membership on UK central government in isolation from other member states. In this chapter we have two objectives. First, by comparing the experiences of other member states we seek to give a clearer profile to the distinctive features of adjustment in UK central government. Secondly, we aim to build on our framework (Chapter 2) and explanatory model (Chapter 8) to offer a comparative approach to exploring the Europeanisation of member state institutions. The chapter is divided into four sections. In the first, the UK response to Europeanisation is located in comparative perspective using France and Germany as comparisons. In a second section, we summarise the EU's impact on the working lives of civil servants and ministers across the EU. In a third section we step back further and seek to identify analytical patterns of adaptation in central governments and government institutions more widely. We then develop a set of propositions, drawn from our model in Chapter 8, which offer an explanation of institutional adaptation. We thus move step-by-step from the empirical to the analytical with a view to exploring what our findings may offer to the general study of institutional adaptation in member states in the face of Europeanisation.

The European challenge and national diversity

A particularly useful comparative perspective on executive adaptation has been offered by Hussein Kassim (2003; see also Kassim 2000b; 2005). He has sought to classify the different approaches to European policy co-ordination along two dimensions: coordination ambition and the extent of centralisation in the coordination machinery (Kassim 2003: 92–3). The intersection of these two parameters generates four categories within which to classify states: comprehensive centralised; comprehensive decentralised; selective centralised; and selective decentralised. Kassim's 2003 data identified no state in the last category but he plotted thirteen member states onto a grid reflecting the other three categories (Kassim 2003: 93).

The UK and France were classified as 'comprehensive centralised', since they share the ambition to engage actively in all areas of EU policy and have strongly centralised machinery to assist with this objective (see Table 9.1). By contrast, Spain and Ireland are examples of states which have been more selective in their coordination: in the case of Spain, focusing on the budget/ structural funds, the CAP and fisheries in particular. In other words, the policy areas of particular national interest have been strongly prioritised. Nevertheless, a centralised coordination system is practised.[1] Germany is an example of a member state which has comprehensive ambitions on European policy but its coordination system has to contend with fragmentation within the federal government as well as further decentralising tendencies stemming from the federal system of government (see Table 9.1).[2]

France and Germany offer useful reference points for highlighting what is distinctive about the UK. France has a centralised system of government like the UK but is distinguished by a presidential regime. Like the UK it has a wide-ranging coordination ambition. At the heart of French coordination was the SGCI (Secrétariat Général du Comité Interministériel), set up in 1948 as part of the Prime Minister's office (see Lequesne 1993; Menon 2000). The SGCI has been quite different from the COES in one key aspect, though: in 2000 it had a staff of some 150 (Menon 2000: 83). It is not, therefore, a 'light touch' coordination mechanism in the manner of the COES but a very large unit. In October 2005 the SGCI was re-designated SGAE: Secrétariat Général des Affaires Européennes.[3] The SGAE has the following tasks: inter-ministerial coordination and giving instructions to the French Permanent Representation; advice and expertise for government as a whole; oversight of transposition of European law; briefing members of the French parliament as well as MEPs; circulating information to French ministries; and 'monitoring the French presence in the European institutions'.[4] Only CFSP escapes the SGAE's responsibility for coordination; the Ministry of Foreign Affairs has the policy lead on that. The SGAE's

Table 9.1 Illustrative classification of national EU policy coordination systems

Comprehensive centralised	*Selective centralised*
United Kingdom	Spain
Sweden	Ireland
France	Portugal
Comprehensive decentralised	*Selective decentralised*
Italy	None
Germany	
Belgium	

Source: Data adapted from Kassim (2003: 93), Figure 4.

coordination functions are supported by the Interministerial Committee on Europe, which was set up in 2005 and is chaired by the prime minister. The then prime minister, Dominique de Villepin, held meetings on a monthly cycle. It should be noted that the creation of the interministerial committee and the re-naming of the secretariat were decisions taken in the aftermath of the May 2005 'no-vote' in the French referendum on the Constitutional Treaty.

The functions of the SGAE broadly resemble those of the COES, with two minor variations. First, 'monitoring the French presence in the European institutions' corresponds in part with the tasks previously undertaken by the Cabinet Office's EU Staffing Branch and now absorbed into its Civil Service Capability Group. Similarly, transposition of European law is a function undertaken in the UK by the Treasury Solicitor's Department, although the latter is closely linked with the COES. The striking comparison is that the SGAE is much larger, having no fewer than 19 specialist units. Part of this difference in size is accounted for by the fact that coordination is more difficult within French government because ministries have greater autonomy and information is less readily shared. In part, the size of the SGAE also arises from the wish to bring the whole of government on board with agreed policy. There can be much lobbying of SGCI/SGAE by political appointees located within ministerial *cabinets*, particularly prior to 2005 when inter-ministerial coordination was much less than today. There is no counterpart to this practice in the UK system. The SGCI has also found itself caught up in the differences between the prime minister and the president during periods of co-habitation when these two politicians have come from different sides of the political spectrum. Coordination within the French system is therefore deemed to require considerably more resources than in the UK. With a unified civil service, an orientation of officials towards active information-sharing, clear prime ministerial authority and a lack of ministerial *cabinets* to deal with, the COES can get by with a fraction of the staff of its French counterpart. The French arrangements reflect how the requirements of participation in the EU policy process have been translated into the specific national pattern of governance.

The German coordination system is particularly complex but the federal government has similarly comprehensive aspirations on European policy. First, it is decentralised as a result of being a federal system. Consequently, on policy areas for which the 16 federal states (Länder) hold domestic responsibility, they hold constitutional authority under Article 23 of the Basic Law in respect of European policy as well. The Länder not only have the right to participate in the making of some areas of EU policy but can also request to take over representation of the Federal Republic in working groups or even the Council. This right imposes clear limitations on the federal government's powers to coordinate policy. But even within the federal government in Berlin there are severe constraints on coordination. The individual ministries have considerable autonomy, and that is amplified by the fact that all governments since the creation of the Federal Republic in 1949 have been coalitions. Hence the institutional interests of individual departments may be compounded by coalition politics, not least because senior civil servants may be (party-)political appointees. If this were not sufficient decentralisation, there are two different ministries coordinating European policy. The Foreign Office and the Economics and Technology Ministry can both lay claim to coordinating functions. The Foreign Office can claim it is the more senior of the two because its remit covers integration policy and an overview across the board. The Economics and Technology Ministry is responsible for the preparation of COREPER I as well as economic and financial affairs matters that fall under COREPER II (see Figure 3.1 for the division of labour between the two). In practice, the Economics Ministry therefore chairs the meetings that prepare the larger part of day-to-day EU business. At higher levels of the coordination hierarchy, the Foreign Office has a greater role in assuring coordination – until the cabinet level, at which point the Chancellor's Office takes the chair (see Bulmer *et al.* 2001: 195–6). During the 2007 German presidency, which took on the task of trying to salvage key parts of Constitutional Treaty, the Chancellor's Office took on key coordination tasks, thus giving no fewer than three departments in the Berlin government with coordination functions.[5] Contrary to the UK's cabinet system, the principle in Germany is that inter-departmental coordination largely takes place in a reactive mode – once a difference of view has emerged and has not been resolved lower down the hierarchy. By this time it is not unusual for divergent views to have been articulated by different German representatives in EU-level arenas.

From a British perspective, the German approach to EU coordination is unusual; indeed, polyphonic diplomacy in Brussels would be regarded as a failure of the UK coordination system. At interviews in Whitehall the German approach was generally regarded as an anti-model, diametrically opposed to that of the UK. Single-party government, a unified civil service, collective cabinet responsibility, clear responsibility for European coordination in the COES, and central government's reserved status for European policy vis-à-vis devolved authorities, which in any case lack constitutional standing: these factors place the UK government at considerable distance from its German counterpart. For Germany the coordination of European policy can be very laborious and the procedures can impede the articulation of policy, for instance when treaty reform is under consideration (see Bulmer *et al.* 2000: 79–84). This situation also becomes acute where the EU is trying to mainstream policy objectives across government. Andrew Jordan and Adriaan Schout (2006) have explored this situation in connection with environmental policy integration: a European initiative which has to be acted on not just by those responsible directly for the policy area but requires mainstreaming across multiple government departments. Another similar policy, but outside their study, is the Lisbon strategy on economic competitiveness, which requires action on issues ranging from employment, innovation, economic policy and so on. On horizontal issues such as these, where one domestic ministry may serve as advocate for the policy across government, domestic coordination is critical to the success of the EU policy. Jordan and Schout argue convincingly that, on environmental policy integration, UK central government is much more successful at exploiting the capacities of networked governance than its German counterpart, which is hampered by reactive (rather than the UK's active) information sharing.

Despite these critical comparative remarks about Germany, it is very important to keep in mind that these complex policy-making circumstances obtain on non-EU policy as well, so politicians and officials are very familiar with the routines. As in the UK and France, the requirements of engagement with the EU policy process have been translated into the German pattern of governance. A second observation is necessary: the main German political parties and other key actors share a broadly positive approach to European policy. European policy has not been subject to the intra- and inter-party divisions that have prevailed since 1973 in the UK (see also Chapter 10). Finally, it has to be borne in mind that the chancellor has the constitutional authority to set the guidelines of government policy (*Richtlinienkompetenz*), and has utilised it to drive forward numerous European policy initiatives, such as monetary union and political unification under Helmut Kohl or, more recently, with seeking to recover key elements of the Constitutional Treaty during the 2007 presidency led by Chancellor Angela Merkel. Over many decades the German imprint on European integration has been considerable. This observation is made in order to underline that a smooth-running, 'Rolls Royce' system, such as that of UK central government, should not be translated into an indicator of effective influence in the EU. UK central government coordination is especially good for *tactical* considerations of European policy. Germany may have been weak on this aspect but, unlike the UK, it cannot be criticised for having an inconsistent European policy *strategy*. For the UK, European policy strategy has at important times – for example, following John Major's re-election in April 1992 and until his electoral defeat in May 1997 – been submerged beneath the need to maintain party unity on Europe. France has displayed a less consistent European policy strategy than Germany, with President de Gaulle's resistance to supranational integration during the 1960s being at odds with the method pioneered by his own countrymen, Jean Monnet and Robert Schuman, a decade earlier. Nevertheless, the importance of the latter as architects of supranational integration (and even, in a different sense, of de Gaulle) highlights French centrality to the

EU. Moreover, the long-standing Franco-German bilateral relationship has bolstered the two states' influence in the EU. For example, the abolition of bilateral border controls was an initiative by these two states that eventually led to the Schengen Accord, which itself was a kind of pioneering exercise ahead of JHA cooperation, introduced in the Maastricht Treaty. This is just one example of many Franco-German initiatives that have enabled both states to have a strong projection capacity at EU level and a significant imprint upon the character of the EU (see Bulmer *et al.* 2000: 55–60; Cole 2001). For the UK, however, the Anglo-French initiation of the ESDP is one of a limited number of examples of projection and imprint. UK governments have developed no long-standing bilateral alliance/s of a comparable nature.

From this brief empirical comparison we can see that the UK's organisational response to the EU is distinctive but closer to France than to Germany. The comparison also confirms arguably the key finding of the comparative literature on EU policy-making in the member states, namely that distinctive national patterns of adaptation are evident (Harmsen 1999; Kassim *et al.* 2000a; Wessels *et al.* 2003; see Laffan 2007 and Bursens 2007 for literature reviews, and in particular Rometsch and Wessels 1996a). This finding does not in fact depart from that made in a pioneering study undertaken by Helen Wallace in the early 1970s: 'There are deep rooted differences in administrative traditions and political style which account for significant variations in the adaptation of individual governments to Community membership' (Wallace 1973: 86). Johan Olsen has summarised the situation in more detail:

> European level developments do not dictate specific forms of institutional adaptation but leave considerable discretion to domestic actors and institutions. There are significant impacts, yet the actual ability of the European level to penetrate domestic institutions is not perfect, universal or constant. Adaptations reflect variations in European pressure as well as domestic motivations and abilities to adapt. European signals are interpreted and modified through domestic traditions, institutions, identities and resources in ways that limit the degree of convergence and homogenization. (Olsen 2002: 936)

National governments have found translator devices for incorporating the European challenge within existing patterns of public administration (Bulmer and Burch 2001: 94).

Impacts below the surface

Beneath this macro level of analysis there are some other important consequences of Europeanisation that risk being overlooked. These consequences are common to adaptation in all member governments. A first impact is the obligation for national officials – principally but not exclusively from central government – to participate in the EU's multi-level administration.

The emergent 'European administrative space' (Olsen 2003; Egeberg 2006) has transformed national officials' patterns of behaviour. Thus, the work pattern of many home civil servants has become increasingly Europeanised. Of course, this development has also occurred independently of Europeanisation as a result of increased global exchange on technical issues, such as telecommunications or technology policy. Nevertheless, the EU has the most intensive networks for interaction of this kind and the distinctive policy-making structures of the EU place larger responsibilities on the participating officials. More broadly, of course, this development highlights how international relations are no longer the preserve of diplomats from ministries of foreign affairs. EU policy is much more 'intermestic' in character: a fusion of the international and the domestic.

There is, in consequence, a sub-group of UK officials who may be seen as boundary managers and boundary spanners between the EU and central government (Laffan 2005: 16–17). Establishing a precise delineation of the group is quite difficult in the absence of any quantitative studies of the EU's impact on the work of civil servants. Even so, it is clear that officials in the COES and UKREP form a cadre of boundary *managers*, as do a number of senior officials in the key ministries (the FCO, DEFRA, DTI, the Treasury and, more recently, the Home Office). In the other ministries this group is smaller and largely confined to coordination units. Boundary *spanners* comprise a larger group of officials from across the whole of government. Their engagement in the European administrative space represents a secondary activity that follows on from their domestic responsibilities. The precise make-up and size of these groups vary from one member state to another, reflecting amongst other things the domestic pattern of (de-) centralisation of EU policy-making (Laffan 2005: 16–17).

A second impact is that most cabinet ministers (and many junior ministers as well) must now reckon with negotiations in the EU as part of their duties. The book by former Labour minister Gerald Kaufman – *How to Be a Minister* – includes a full chapter on 'how to be communautaire' (Kaufman 1997: 141–50). Apart from its amusing account of his experiences as a participant in European negotiations when a minister in the DTI, Kaufman's book illustrates precisely the point that Council meetings, bilateral meetings with counterparts or meetings with European commissioners are part of the political routine for many ministers. The EU has thus changed the job description of many UK ministers; it is no longer the Foreign Secretary and his ministerial team which exclusively represent the UK's interests abroad. The title 'Home Secretary' or its typical continental counterpart (minister of the interior) has almost become a misnomer in this era of intensive EU cooperation in home affairs. The increased Europeanisation of ministerial work is also striking for the Prime Minister, although once again as part of a wider pattern of increased summit diplomacy.

A third area of impact is on the balance of authority within government. Buller and Smith observe that 'as EU business increases the FCO and the Cabinet Office are losing control' (1998: 172). It is indeed no longer possible for the FCO and the COES to act as information gatekeepers between central government and the EU (although the SGAE in France is perhaps more successful). However, what of the EU's impact on the broader power balance within government? In all member states the head of government (or in presidential systems, the head of state) has found his or her powers strengthened by virtue of the key role played at EU level by the European Council. Ministers of foreign affairs have generally found their authority reinforced. Even if much EU business is conducted by 'domestic ministers', foreign ministers are very intensively involved in the EU. There have been times when they have appeared to be eclipsed, for example by finance ministers during the negotiation and planning of monetary union, but this phase passed once much of the policy responsibility passed into the hands of the European Central Bank.

In comparative terms the impact of the EU on the position of individual ministries of foreign affairs within their respective system is tied up with whether it has a coordinating role. In those cases where it is coordinator, the ministry of foreign affairs may have *increased* its power within the government. This situation obviously does not apply in the UK context. In order to know whether the FCO has lost out as a result of EU membership we need to consider how central government would operate if the UK were outside the EU. Paradoxically, if the UK were a member of the European Economic Area, like Norway, the single market would still be a major concern for central government officials but ministerial meetings would be much reduced. EU ministers meet frequently on such issues but EEA ministers do not. On the other hand, the FCO would lose all its intensive engagement with fellow member states on the CFSP and ESDP. So under this scenario it is unlikely that the FCO would be more influential within Whitehall, although the influence of the prime minister and of the COES would surely be much less than at present. Thus the real conclusion is arguably that the *globalisation* of domestic economies has brought about changes to the working patterns of central government. The EU is simply a particularly strong manifestation of that.

Comparing the EU's impact on core executives and national governance

Hitherto we have identified that the impact of the EU on central government is nationally differentiated but that there are some common features below the surface. In reviewing the literature on the Europeanisation of core executives Brigid Laffan has identified four key empirical findings and we locate the UK within each of these parameters (2007: 133–5). First, she distinguishes between central coordinators, an inner core and an outer circle of ministries and highlights how some ministries have moved, with the passage of time and increase of EU business, from the outer circle to the inner core (Laffan 2007: 133). She mentions environment and interior ministries as examples of those moving from the outer circle to the inner core. The Europeanisation of the (then) Department of the Environment was outlined in Chapter 6 (see also Jordan 2002) and has been underpinned by its incorporation into DEFRA. Although we located the Home Office in the outer core, this was a marginal decision; from our analysis, there can be no doubt about the transformation of its work in the aftermath of the Maastricht Treaty.

A second finding relates to the responsibility for leading coordination within central government. Some states place coordination under the prime minister; others have a foreign ministry-led system of coordination (Laffan 2007: 133). The UK fits the former model, as does France. The Finnish and Swedish coordination machineries were re-positioned under the respective prime ministers in 2000 and 2005 respectively (see Laffan 2007: 133–4). Examples of states where the ministry of foreign affairs leads on coordination include Denmark, Portugal and Spain (see Kassim 2005: 292–6). Germany's dual system of coordination is highly distinctive. Laffan also identifies the common feature of inter-ministerial committees to assist coordination (Laffan 2007: 134). Apart from different institutional characteristics of the committees concerning their composition and level of seniority, a distinction can be made between those which operate pro-actively, such as in the UK system with the Friday meeting, and those which operate in a more routinised manner, and only engage at senior levels at a later, problem-solving stage, such as in Germany. Not all member states have something approaching the UK's cabinet committee, EP. France, as noted, only created such a body in 2005. According to Laffan (2005: 12) Greece has no interministerial committee at all for coordinating European policy.

Laffan's third observation relates to the boundary managers between the domestic and European political arenas (2007: 135). She indicates that there is cross-national variation in the size and training of this group. As a large member state, the size of this group is relatively substantial in the UK. The comparative position of the UK in regard to the level of training is more difficult to judge. The European Fast Stream has been a striking feature in the UK but has been geared primarily to training up civil servants to enter the EU institutions.[6] Whilst some of the European Fast Streamers have become diplomats or home civil servants in the UK, we doubt whether they amount to a significant proportion of the boundary managers. We found European training amongst UK boundary managers to be rather haphazard. For the typical boundary manager there would be a fairly common pattern that would include a period in UKREP or a Commissioner's *cabinet* and/or in the COES. Another factor that is often overlooked is the fact that British civil servants are part of a unified system, whereas the pattern is more fragmented in some other states, where there may be competing allegiances, such as to *grand corps* in France or to individual ministries, which often do their own recruitment in other states. The integrated British system is important in the context of the willingness of civil servants and, indeed, the expectation to participate in active information-sharing across government. British bureaucratic culture is quite distinctively attuned to coordination when seen in comparative perspective.

Brigid Laffan's final observation relates to change in coordination systems (Laffan 2007: 135). In reviewing the adjustment to Europe in six smaller EU member states she found that pressures for change, especially for enhanced capacity, emerged from two exogenous and two endogenous sources (see Laffan 2005: 21–2).[7] The identified exogenous sources were 'the demands of engagement with the EU', that is, the initial need to adjust in preparation for accession, and 'regime change in the EU', such as the renewed dynamics of European integration or preparations to join the Euro. The endogenous variables were change in the domestic government or a major EU-related domestic event, notably the Irish people's initial rejection of the Nice Treaty in the 2001 referendum. These findings are broadly compatible with our explanatory model of adaptation (see Figure 8.1), based on the UK experience.

Beyond these impacts of Europeanisation upon core executives of the member states there are two broader consequences of adaptation that are frequently recognised: the strengthening of the executive branch vis-à-vis national parliaments; and some re-configuration of the balance of authority between national and sub-national government.

National parliaments – and the UK Houses of Parliament are no exception – have faced a major problem in that they are not direct participants in EU decision-making, whereas national governments are 'more embedded in the Union's policy and political networks than any other actors' (Laffan 2007: 130). With growing EU legislation arising from the single market as well as burgeoning policy activity (often non-legislative) in two new policy pillars following the Maastricht Treaty, parliament has had major problems in seeking to maintain oversight and control. Occasional lapses by government in providing timely information to Westminster have not helped the situation.[8] Subsequent reforms have reduced some of the impact of these problems but the underlying one of absence from the EU negotiations remains (see Giddings and Drewry 2004). National parliaments have not only been losers from the domestic impact of the EU but they have also been slower in adjusting to new realities (see Maurer and Wessels 2001; Kassim 2005: 297–303).

As for the territorial dimension of governance, the broad debate is about whether European integration has strengthened the state (by which is meant the national government) (see Moravcsik 1994). Alternatively, has integration promoted multi-level governance, as argued by Gary Marks and others (Marks *et al.* 1996)? These seemingly diametrically opposed positions can be reconciled in subtle ways. The multi-level governance argument is most plausible in the context of territorially sensitive policies, such as the European structural funds. Even here the argument can be intense between those analysts who posit that it is national governments which determine the budgetary resources for the structural funds and which shape their policy content, and other analysts who place emphasis on sub-national government's exploitation of funding opportunities to enhance their position vis-à-vis central government *at the implementation stage*. In the UK context there is certainly evidence that the structural funds can explain the emergence of English regions and the creation of government offices in the regions (Burch and Holliday 1993; Burch and Gomez 2002). Under the Labour governments these offices were strengthened and given further authority on the implementation of structural funds. Where under the Thatcher governments there was centralised control over the structural funds, consistent with the position of Moravcsik, there is now much greater acceptance of the need for a multi-levelled approach. The EU may also have had some impact on the momentum towards UK devolution but it was far from the principal factor. A parallel and persuasive argument has been that the structural funds have encouraged the growth of partnership approaches to governance by bringing in socio-economic actors at the regional level. These characteristics took hold in England before the Blair government, but have been significantly extended since 1997.[9]

Temporality and the analysis of domestic institutional change

In Chapter 8 we set out a model to explain institutional adaptation in UK central government. What contribution can our analysis make to the comparative understanding of some of the empirical developments outlined above?[10] We offer four propositions and relate them to the model outlined in the previous chapter and seek to extend thereby the analytical toolkit for understanding the Europeanisation of member state institutions. We also offer some brief empirical illustration of how they may shed light on comparative experience.

Proposition 1: The timing of accession matters.

As of 2007 no fewer than 27 member states have had to go through a process of adjusting to EU membership. The exact circumstances of the adjustment faced by institutions in each of the 27 states (and, specifically, their central governments) have varied quite considerably. For the original six member states, Europeanisation was not an issue in the 1950s, since the priority was on the upstream flow from central government to the supranational level as part of the construction of the European Communities. Member governments were more concerned with shaping the

Communities than with the nature of the impact that might subsequently flow in the opposite direction. Europeanisation (and its study) really only gained momentum as a result of the growth of the single market and further reform in the 1992 Maastricht Treaty.

Proposition 2: Domestic reform pressures derive from the duties of engagement with the EU policy process.

Upon accession to the EU, and depending on the timing (proposition 1), member state institutions will search for the most suitable way to attend to the duties arising from membership. These duties are downstream (reception, for example by transposing European legislation) and upstream (projection, namely engagement in the EU policy process). The precise duties of engagement depend on the timing of integration.

One obvious comparative observation arising from these two propositions is that the later that member states have joined the EU, the greater the impact of accession, since the EU's institutional and policy density has increased over the 55-year period since the establishment of the European Coal and Steel Community (ECSC). This adjustment was an especial challenge for ten of the recent accession states because it followed quite recent democratic transitions in the aftermath of the end of the Cold War and the break-up of the Soviet Union (Goetz 2005). The later that a member state joined the EU, the greater will be the pressure for major domestic reform upon accession.

Rather than reflecting on how these two propositions have an impact at the macro level, we consider them in relation to comparative engagement of subnational authorities (SNAs) in EU policy-making. The EU's main effect on territoriality came with the creation and development of the structural funds from the mid-1970s onwards (indeed, initially as a result of pressure from two states which acceded in 1973: Ireland and the UK). For the founding member states and those joining in 1973 there had been no significant impact on the territoriality of the state. Consequently, incremental adjustment took place using informal arrangements (for instance, see Bulmer and Paterson 1987: 191–5 for the informal arrangements developed between the federal and Länder governments in Germany). However, with the growth of the structural funds in the late 1980s the impact of the EU on the territorial nature of German government was such that the Maastricht Treaty became an opportunity for a 'fight back' (Jeffery 1994). The Länder (with support from Belgian authorities) projected demands into the Maastricht negotiations for greater sensitivity to SNAs and secured the creation of the Committee of the Regions as well as the right of subnational ministers to sit in the Council. At the same time the domestic ratification of the Maastricht Treaty gave the Länder governments leverage so that they could achieve a domestic constitutional reform (Article 23, Basic Law), enabling them to have formalised domestic participation rights where European policy impacted on their powers (see Bulmer *et al.* 2000: 33–40). Hence, German (and Belgian) SNAs used institutional opportunity structures to strengthen their domestic position. Another federal state, Austria, which only joined in 1995, was able to benefit from the experiences of its German and Belgian counterparts and develop internal territorially sensitive coordination mechanisms *upon accession.*[11] The Spanish experience has been characterised by a growing empowerment of the authorities beyond Madrid, but under different circumstances. When Spain acceded in 1986 it was a new democracy and its own internal territorial distribution of authority was not strongly embedded. Over the period since membership the historic nationalities, especially in Catalonia and the Basque country, have sought to strengthen their authority, including over European policy. The key opportunities in respect of the latter have not come at the time of new developments at EU level but as a result of domestic opportunities arising from government-formation in Madrid. These opportunities have derived from the fact that the different Catalan and Basque political parties have on occasion occupied a crucial role in ensuring a majority to the governing party in Spanish parliament. The asymmetrical decentralisation within Spain has resulted in the historic nationalities (Basque country, Catalonia and Galicia) securing not only an important role for themselves but also for the other autonomous communities (Morata 2007).

These cases show how the timing of the EU's developing territorially redistributive powers impacted differentially on different member states. For Germany the territorial challenge confronted the Länder well after accession and it was necessary to find allies, notably in Belgium, and convince the federal government to take up their cause during the Maastricht Treaty negotiations for strengthened participation rights for SNAs. In the case of Austria, when it acceded the territorial implications of the EU were clear and its SNAs could consider the practices of its German and Belgian counterparts when identifying an optimal way for its Länder to engage with the EU. In the case of Spain, however, the domestic territorial reforms were taking place more or less at the same time as changes at EU level. Reform to the autonomous communities' role in EU policy-making came as a result of domestic electoral timing and domestic dynamics rather than from timing at EU level. The SNAs in Spain had to catch up with the implications of Europeanisation once internal territoriality had stabilised. In the UK the centralising tendencies of Mrs Thatcher's governments ran in the opposite direction to developments at EU level. Some initial adaptation to the EU structural funds took place in England under John Major's government and then across the whole UK as a result of the domestic reforms brought about by devolution. The broad conclusion here, then, is that the timing of accession is a key factor in explaining domestic adaptation, although domestic dynamics are also key (see proposition 4b below).

Proposition 3: The member state's initial institutional response is determined by a particular set of embedded national circumstances.

Proposition 4: After accession, adjustment is then a function, either of new challenges arising from the path taken by European integration (proposition 4a) or of reforms to domestic governance that may have no direct origin in integration (proposition 4b).

We consider these propositions together. The pattern of adjustment upon accession and subsequently, we argue, is characterised by translating the duties of engagement into the pre-existing domestic institutional context. This context comprises the formal and informal institutional structure of domestic governance and the culture embedded within it; the opportunities and constraints for significant political actors to shape it; and accountability to the political environment (see Figure 8.1). An alternative proposition – which we reject – would be that the member state's initial response is guided simply by identifying the optimal way to contend with participation in the EU policy process and then reforming the domestic institutions accordingly. This alternative proposition implies openness to major domestic dislocation, with the duties of EU membership trumping other considerations: an unlikely scenario, in our view.

How do the three factors identified in Figure 8.1 (the institutional framework, significant actors and accountability to the political environment) explain comparative experience either upon accession or subsequently? Because member state patterns of governance are more embedded than those of the EU, our assumption is again that adjustment to the EU will normally take the form of translating new duties into pre-existing domestic patterns of governance. For long-standing member states the duties of engagement are re-calibrated with each major reform of the EU itself. For example, by adding Justice and Home Affairs to the EU's policy portfolio and raising foreign policy aspirations with the creation of the CFSP, existing member states were presented with new duties of engagement arising from the Maastricht Treaty. Several states, including the UK, undertook reforms to their coordination machinery as a result. However, as we have seen the institutional framework may be subject to change with implications for EU policy as a result of predominantly domestic initiatives, such as UK devolution.

As regards our second mediating factor – accountability to the political environment – we find plenty of empirical evidence. Upon accession the Danish parliament, the Folketing, utilised the contested nature of the European issue to assure for itself the right to *mandate* ministers attending the Council (see Kassim 2005: 300). Now termed the Europaudvalget, this committee arguably offers the strongest example of domestic parliamentary control over the executive in domestic EU policy-making across all 27 member states. That it was able to achieve this remarkable power demonstrates how wider accountability can be an important determinant of the domestic institutional response. This mediating factor can equally come into play in the period after accession. In Ireland the rejection of Nice Treaty led to reform in the domestic machinery (Laffan and Mahoney 2003). In France the rejection of the Constitutional Treaty in 2005 has had a similar consequence. In Germany the electoral process and subsequent coalition negotiations led to the transfer in 1998 of the Economics Ministry's coordination role to the Finance Ministry (Bulmer *et al.* 2001). In Spain, as noted earlier, the rights of the autonomous communities (or regions) to participate in domestic EU policy-making have derived from the power-brokering role that Catalan and Basque political parties have had in the formation of national governments in Madrid (see Morata 2007). Political accountability matters, therefore, and in the UK the periods of division over European policy within governments – under Major or at times during the 1974–79 Labour governments – have certainly impacted on the EU policy machinery's work if not its organisation.

The role of significant actors is not to be under-estimated. In the UK case we have seen how Edward Heath set the tone with his pronouncement in 1971 that all ministries should think and act European. Similarly, Prime Minister Blair was instrumental in re-focusing the domestic machinery towards the goal of better projecting British interests in Brussels. In Greece the very characterisation of the system has been described as 'the dominance of individuals over structure' because the system is not formalised (Spanou 2003: ix). Thus it was Prime Minister Kostas Simitis who set the tone in prioiritising Greek preparations for joining the Eurozone and the necessary organisational preparations (Spanou 2003: 2).

The empirical analysis of adjustment can be measured in three ways. First, the dimensions of adaptation may be captured by our classification framework (system, organisation, process, regulation and the cultural dimension).[12] Secondly, the extent of adjustment to the EU can be judged according to the categories of absorption, accommodation and transformation. Finally, the trajectory of adjustment over time may be examined according to the contrasting rhythms of incremental change and occasional critical junctures when a major reform ensues. As our summary of findings indicated in connection with the UK, the timing of critical junctures may differ depending on whether the research focus is upon the system as a whole or upon individual ministries. How do our propositions stack up when applied to the temporal dimension of institutional adaptation in the member states?

In Chapter 8 we identified several critical junctures in the UK central government's response to Europeanisation. These were: the application in 1961, accession in 1973, following the 1992 Maastricht Treaty, and under Blair (the Step Change initiative and devolution) at the end of the 1990s (see Box 8.1). The latter case highlighted the fact that endogenous variables can explain a critical juncture as much as the (exogenous) EU. We find a similar combination of critical junctures interspersed with incremental change if we examine the German system of coordination (see also Bulmer and Burch 2001: 87–91). The shape of the original machinery can be traced to the creation of the European Coal and Steel Community. Coordination on the substance of policy was located in the Federal Economics Ministry. This location was attributable to a number of factors including the technical nature of the ECSC and the weakness of the Foreign Office owing to limitations on German external sovereignty. Codification of the system came in 1958 when the Treaties of Rome came into force. The Economics Ministry was given formal responsibility for coordinating day-to-day business and set up a European Division. The Foreign Office was given responsibility for integration policy (Koerfer 1988; Hesse and Goetz 1992). Other federal ministries, such as agriculture and finance, developed responsibilities for European policy within their own domain.

The period thereafter witnessed incremental change until the challenge of the Maastricht Treaty. The Länder governments utilised their ability to block ratification in the upper house of parliament, the Bundesrat, to force through a constitutional amendment giving them specific rights to consultation on those aspects of European policy that affected their domestic powers (Knodt 1998). At the same time the system became more fragmented, with the significant impact of JHA business on the federal interior and justice ministries as well as on the Länder. The Foreign Office revamped its internal organisation by creating a European Division in 1993. The Maastricht Treaty thus constituted a second critical juncture.

A third critical juncture came about in 1998, at almost the same time as change in the UK, and for similar generic reasons, namely the election of a new government. The incoming coalition under Social Democrat (SPD) Chancellor Gerhard Schröder took the decision to move the Federal Economics Ministry's coordination role to the Federal Finance Ministry. The key explanation was that the SPD party chairman, Oskar Lafontaine, was an influential figure in the coalition negotiations and wanted to strengthen his ministry's portfolio. In the event Lafontaine resigned as finance minister in March 1999. However, the coordination function was restored in 2005 to the Economics Ministry in the interests of coalition balance between the Christian Democrats (who supplied the Chancellor, Angela Merkel) and the SPD. As SPD ministers led both the Foreign Ministry and Finance Ministry, the latter's coordination functions were moved back to the (itself re-organised) Economics and Technology Ministry, suggesting another critical juncture (Beichelt 2007).[13]

Thus the dual dynamics of incremental change and critical junctures, where significant new procedural pathways are pursued, also coexist in the German case. This terminology was similarly used by Brigid Laffan and her collaborators in a six-country study of adaptation. For Ireland the critical juncture was created by the 'no-vote' on the Nice Treaty, resulting in 'increased attention to the management of EU affairs in the core executive and in the national parliament' (Laffan 2005: 21). Both components were subject to significant reform. In the case of Greece the critical juncture came as result of a concerted effort, assisted by a committee of outside academic experts, to ensure the political and economic system was able to meet the criteria for accession to the Euro (Laffan 2005: 22). The re-organisation of the Finnish coordination system (in 2000) reflected the wider shift from a presidential to a parliamentary political system.

Conclusion

We have reviewed the experience of several other member states in this chapter and expanded our analytical framework to provide better applicability to comparative analysis. What this brief comparison suggests is threefold. First, the model for explaining domestic change arising from Europeanisation (Figure 8.1) stands up to evidence from beyond the UK. Second, the set of propositions regarding the intersection of timing with this model deserves greater exploration. Third, it is clear that the UK system is well coordinated and efficient in the sense that a relatively light-touch group unit in the Cabinet Office oversees coordination. However, efficiency and effectiveness are two different things. We will return to the latter in our concluding chapter.

Notes

1 As will be seen below, there have been some decentralising reforms within the Spanish coordination system in recent times.

2 Kassim uses a grid system for plotting the precise location of national coordination systems (see Kassim 2003: 93). However, such a presentation encounters the problem that the exact location will change over time. For example, following recent reforms in Spain to extend the engagement of the autonomous communities and the historic nationalities or with the introduction of devolution in the UK these two states have somewhat less centralised coordination systems than in the past. But they remain in the same respective box in Table 9.1.

3 See the online presentation of the SGAE, www.sgae.gouv.fr/, accessed 24 September 2007. Thanks to Emiliano Grossman for drawing our attention to the change. We are also grateful to Christian Lequesne and Philippe Rivaud for briefing us on the SGCI system.

4 See 'An Overview of the General Secretariat for European Affairs', www.sgae.gouv.fr/presentation/docfiles/textesofficiels/present_sgae_uk.pdf, accessed 17 September 2007.

5 Presentation by senior official of the Federal Chancellor's Office at conference of the Institut für Europäische Politik, Berlin, 28 September 2007; interview Federal Chancellor's Ofice, 19 December 2007. See also the very thorough

analysis of the conduct of the German presidency in the contributions to Kietz and Perthes (2008).

6   As noted earlier, the European Fast Stream is suspended at the time of writing owing to the lack of openings in the European institutions, since recruitment is skewed towards nationals of recent accession states.

7   For further papers arising from this cross-national project covering Ireland, Finland, Greece, Estonia, Hungary and Slovenia, see the homepage: www. oeue.net.

8   Interview, House of Commons, 12 December 1997.

9   This argument has been developed by Ian Bache, for instance at a Jean Monnet Café, Manchester, 27 February 2007: 'The EU structural funds: have they promoted multi-level governance in the UK?'. See also Bache (2008) and Burch and Gomez (2002). A more partnership-based approach was in evidence in the UK before the Conservative governments lost office in 1997.

10 It should be noted that we have refined this model somewhat beyond an earlier version that was set out in Bulmer and Burch (2005).

11 Whilst states joining later face a greater adjustment challenge, they do have the possibility to undertake institutional learning from the experience of comparable states which joined earlier.

12 Quantitative studies of impact are also a potential research method (see Laffan and Mahoney 2003: 20 for the findings of a quantitative survey of the EU's impact on the work of Irish civil servants).

13 We refrain from defining 2005 as a critical juncture owing to a lack of sufficient data at this stage.

10

Conclusion

In Chapter 1 we set out our research aims and prospectus. Our primary objective has been to provide an authoritative account of the impact of EU membership on the practice of government in Whitehall. In order to achieve this we have examined EU related changes in Whitehall from the events surrounding the first application to join in 1961 through to the end of the Blair premiership in 2007. Our time-frame of more than 45 years has enabled us to address the temporality of UK central government's adaptation to the EU – both across Whitehall and more specifically within individual departments. Our examination of change has been facilitated by the development of tools of analysis derived from two approaches: Europeanisation and historical institutionalism. In particular we have drawn on historical institutionalism as a way of isolating key moments of change and of judging the pattern, degree and extent of adaptation by UK central government. We have used Europeanisation to help us understand the factors driving these changes and the extent to which EU influences can be isolated from other causes of change both domestic and international. Our conclusions on these matters were set out in Chapter 8. We also highlighted the importance of significant individuals in facilitating change and the importance of exploring matters concerning the effectiveness of the UK approach to the EU (see Chapters 2 and 8; Figure 8.1). The question of effectiveness remains to be addressed and it forms a large part of the subject matter of this concluding chapter. However, before moving on to examine the strengths and weaknesses of the UK approach and its effectiveness more broadly, the chapter begins with a summary of the main findings arising from the study.

The characteristics of Whitehall's changing approach to the EU

The Whitehall approach to handling European policy is now well established having emerged in a largely piecemeal fashion over a period of more than 40 years. There is an established network which has as its hub the

COES (and No. 10), the FCO and UKREP. The exact scope of this network and who is drawn into it varies in accordance with the business in hand. The hub of the network relates to and is supplemented by a number of subsidiary networks which have emerged in the period since the 1990s as EU competences have expanded – notably sub-networks dealing with JHA and foreign and defence policy. Beyond this, the penetration of the EU now applies to every department and many of the executive agencies connected to them. Not all departments are drawn into EU business to the same extent, however, with DEFRA (dealing with agriculture, environment and rural affairs) and the DTI (dealing with trade and internal market issues) still being the most involved of the line departments. The Treasury maintains an influential position in shaping the business of the hub as well as that of the wider EU networks. The span of the EU policy-making network now stretches out beyond the central state to include the devolved Scottish, Welsh and Northern Irish executives.

The key features of the ways in which Whitehall has adapted to the EU varies according to which aspects of the EU policy-making network are being examined whether it is the hub of the network (as explored in Chapter 5), or its inner core (as explored in Chapter 6) or its outer circle (as explored in Chapter 7).

At the hub of the European policy-making network there have been eight key changes. First, the projection aspect of EU policy-making has been significantly augmented. This is most evident in the period since 1997. Prior to that, much of the emphasis and effort was placed on reception. A primary concern was to ensure a speedy and efficient response to EU initiatives and to achieve full consultation and an agreed line within Whitehall. Arguably reception was greatly refined over the period from accession onwards to produce the 'Rolls Royce' machine that is sometimes referred to. In contrast, largely because of party political difficulties and disagreement amongst ministers, effective projection of UK interests within the EU was neglected. Generally the UK did not seek to set the EU agenda but tended to be reactive rather than pro-active. The most obvious exception to this was the single market initiative in which the UK was very active.

This greater emphasis on projection has entailed developing more effectively the means to shape EU policy through active engagement beyond the national context. Central to this has been an increasing exploitation of bilateral relationships with other member states at an early stage in policy development so as to condition the climate surrounding, and the content of, decision-making in the EU. This increasing reliance on bilateralism and a more engaged approach to the EU is the second key change in the ways in which Whitehall has adapted to the EU. Again in its most developed form, this is a post-1997 development.

The third key change has been the fragmentation of the network around subsidiary hubs, notably those sub-networks covering JHA and foreign and defence policy. These began to emerge prior to the 1992 Maastricht Treaty in 1992 and they have crystallised and become established as EU policy competences in these areas have expanded.

The fourth key change has been the growing importance of the office of the PM in the EU policy-making network. This began in 1975 with enhancement of the PM's formal position in EU policy-making through creation of the European Council. It developed intermittently thereafter, depending on the character, objectives, and opportunities available to particular prime ministers, though there is a long-term trend of strengthening PMs' links with, and usage of, the COES. These links were, however, significantly formalised post-1997 with COES and its leading personnel becoming more closely drawn into the ambit of No. 10, and with a more evident remit to service the PM on EU matters. This also coincided with a weakening of the FCO's position at the hub of the network.

The fifth key change has been in the ways information is handled and decisions are reached. These have been greatly affected by the advent and extensive uses of video-conferencing and by the shift to IT and email throughout Whitehall. Again this is a mid-1990s phenomenon which has had a profound effect on the way the system works. It has speeded up the process of handling EU matters and made it easier to transact business over distance, but it has also made the business of keeping control over the flow of information far more difficult.

These developments in the technologies of communication have been one of the factors contributing to the sixth key change: a shift to more informal and fluid policy-making structures at the hub and inner core of the network. This is especially reflected in the move away from the established, tiered system of official standing committees and the greater use of ad hoc committees and more informal meetings. This is a trend affecting coordination across Whitehall which can be traced back to the mid-1980s.

The seventh key change shaped by EU membership has been the breakdown of the foreign and domestic policy division which characterised the structure of Whitehall since the middle of the nineteenth century if not earlier. This change is reflected in the increasing domestication of the way in which policy is formulated and carried through into Brussels, usually by the relevant departmental division without much, if any, engagement of the FCO. It is also evident in the change in the distribution of staffing in UKREP to draw in more officials on secondment from home departments.

The final key change which has followed on from EU membership has been a significant alteration in the roles and activities of ministers and civil servants. This is an evident point, but it needs emphasising. Ministers have been drawn into the processes of policy-making in Brussels and into discussions and agreements with counterparts in other member states. They have been confronted with new negotiating challenges which ideally

means they learn new skills and become aware of tactical and strategic considerations that follow on from the EU's decision rules and the necessity
of coalition building. Not all ministers and civil servants do in fact learn
these skills. Even when developing policy in the domestic context, ministers
and officials have to be aware of the possible EU aspects of policy. It is
a condition which was recognised in the machinery of government as
early the mid-1970s when it was required that all cabinet and committee
papers should spell out the possible implications for the UK's EU policy
of any new policy proposal (Burch and Holliday 1996: 58). This increased
involvement and the need to learn new skills of negotiation, alliance-
building and tactical decision-taking has also applied to civil servants.

Moving down to the inner and outer core of the network across
departments and the agencies attached to them the over-riding trend is
the expansion of EU business so as to engage many more sections of
Whitehall. However, this increasing pervasiveness of EU business across
Whitehall is patchy. There is much variety in the degree of engagement at
departmental level. As already noted, the original, most involved departments remain at the heart of the system – the FCO, DEFRA, DTI and the
Treasury, but others are now extensively drawn in. Part of this spread across
Whitehall can be measured in terms of increasing EU competences and
the growth in the number of staff engaged in them. As noted in earlier
chapters, for example, there has been a marked degree of Europeanisation
of UK policy responsibilities in the areas of environmental regulation
(these have grown incrementally since 1973), regional policy (from 1975),
research and technology policy (from the mid-1980s), market regulation
(the internal market) (especially from 1986), food standards (from the late-
1990s), asylum and immigration and 'home affairs' (especially from 1993),
foreign affairs (also especially from 1993 onwards), transport and civil
aviation (especially from 1986), employment policy (from 1998), defence
(from 1998), and rural development (from 1999). These expanding EU
competences have drawn in the relevant sections of Whitehall either for
the first time or on a more substantial basis.

In addition to these objective measures, a critical distinction concerns
how central EU business is to the core brief of the department. For example, for Culture, Media and Sport, the Department of Health (DH), and
the Treasury EU business is not at the very core of the organisation, but
it is in the cases of DEFRA and DTI. This distinction can also be applied
within departments or in relation to the work of the agencies attached to
them. For instance, EU business is the very core of the agricultural and
rural development side of DEFRA, it is also important on the environmental
policy side of the department but in this case other international involve-
ments are also relevant. In the DH EU business is not core, but it is at
the centre of the work of one of its executive agencies, the Medicines and
Health Care Products Regulatory Agency which oversees the development

and implementation of UK and EU regulations concerning pharmaceuticals (Department of Health 2006: 141).

Strengths and weaknesses of the UK approach

When asked a set of open-ended questions about the strengths and weaknesses of the UK approach to organising for Europe, our interviewees – ministers and civil servants in UK and Brussels – proved to be remarkably united in response. The two main strengths emphasised were good coordination and the ability to agree a coherent and united negotiating line. Good coordination involves comprehensive coverage of Whitehall departments and beyond to include devolved administrations and to ensure that all who need to be consulted are. A clear strength is seen as having effective mechanisms at the core to achieve this, notably COES. As one senior practitioner with experience in both UK and EU institutions since accession put it – 'the mechanism is admirable . . . that has worked pretty well'.[1] This is a general view endorsed by others who speak of the UK being 'better co-ordinated than any other member state',[2] that the UK approach is 'comprehensive and systematic' and that very little 'escapes its grasp',[3] and that, unlike some other member states, 'information is automatically circulated'.[4] Good coordination is one of the factors that assists the development of an agreed negotiating position, thus ensuring 'consistency and coherence across the board'.[5] This ability, as the cliché has it, to 'sing from the same hymn sheet' is often highlighted. Of course, as we have seen, the bulk of issues are very often handled and coordinated in the relevant department without the involvement of the 'hub'.

This sense of being fully prepared is illustrated very well in the words of an official dealing with major cross-departmental issues right at the hub of the UK system.

> The strengths are that we are presenting a united front across Whitehall and any position that has been worked up has taken into account every department's concerns so that no department has been overlooked . . . In the process of coordination, you have thought out everything, the pros and cons and have really tried to work it out. So, once a position is agreed, departments are ready to accept it because they have had their say and they can see it's a fair process . . . Also, each department reinforces each other, which is also good, which means that . . . once you have got an agreed position, there is no argument over briefing, it is more a question of how do you marshal your arguments. But the substance of the briefing doesn't provoke rows. So, in terms of establishing a policy, I think the system works really, really well.[6]

A pragmatic approach to business and a high level of professionalism are also seen as major strengths of the UK approach.

Turning to weaknesses it is notable that while the UK may be good at establishing a policy to the satisfaction of Whitehall, it is not considered quite so good at negotiating that policy in the EU. In particular practitioners highlighted three main problems with the UK approach to organising for Europe: its inflexibility, a lack of vision and strategic thinking, and weakness of political will. Inflexibility is the deficit side of having a well coordinated machine and an agreed policy line. Matters may be determined in the UK at too early a stage and then become inflexible. There is a tendency not to allow for the ebb and flow of negotiations. This issue has become increasingly pertinent as the use of QMV has been extended. Positions agreed in Whitehall may easily become hard to un-pick in negotiations in Brussels. This situation was especially the case during the Major government due to the political sensitivity of European policy. A typical criticism from UKREP at this point was that the Whitehall brief 'doesn't give any room for manoeuvre'.[7] This was a view put forward by most of our interviewees and is summed up in the quotes below from two senior officials – one in the Commission and one in a major EU involved department in the UK.

> [The main] weakness is . . . its rigidity, there is very little improvisation or flexibility within the British structure . . . the sheer consistency with which everybody answers the same question at every level. This doesn't make for a very creative diplomacy . . . People cannot shift from their instructions without going back to yet another discussion . . .[8]

> We tend to coordinate at too early a stage when a proposal first appears from the Commission, we will then have a well ordered Cabinet Office discussion . . . that tends to lead us into positions that are over-defined in the early stages and reduce our flexibility for doing the other thing which . . . is useful and that is being open and flexible to the views of other member states and seeing what alliances you can form from what modest shifts you can make from what you first thought of and what other people are thinking of.[9]

A lack of strategic thinking and planning and a lack of visionary thinking about Europe also register as weaknesses highlighted by practitioners. The lack of strategic capacity is seen by some practitioners as a general problem of British central government and not peculiar to the European field.[10] However, the problem is arguably more acute in the EU area owing to the political sensitivity of the issue. As we have seen attempts have been made to overcome the problem of strategic thinking and forward planning on the big issues over the years at official and ministerial level. Much of this is seen as having been bedevilled by a lack of vision on Europe and political will and leadership – again given the sensitivity of EU issues. This criticism is clear in the words of a member of the European cadre:

> the UK tends not to be very creative, e.g. through kite-flying. The UK is less good at coming up with proposals of its own; more reactive. Also in being reactive, positions may become a bit inflexible, even in a different political environment. The UK may have things 'too cut and dried early on'. Whitehall finds it difficult to have a view and not articulate it early on, when

that might be advantageous tactically. On strategy, the political level has to think things through . . . there is a British cast of mind that is critical/ reactive and wary of the grand visionary scheme . . . The Treasury and the Cabinet Office would be unwilling to fly such kites without us having thought through all the angles first. This situation is more deeply embedded than the current political situation.[11]

The contested nature of the European issue in domestic politics has tended to limit the amount of political willingness to present bold initiatives at EU level that serve British interests. Strikingly, the single market initiative of Mrs Thatcher's government and the initiatives made under the Blair governments were undertaken at a time when strong parliamentary majorities prevailed. However, even the Blair governments failed to change the domestic political climate on European policy, particularly in the print media (see Daddow 2007).

How effective is the UK approach?

In addition to the evaluations of practitioners, how well does the UK approach measure up in terms of our criteria for judging the effectiveness of member states' approaches to reception, projection and pro-active engagement? In Chapter 2 we argued that a member state's approach to reception is effective when a national government is able to absorb, handle and reach decisions on material transmitted from the EU. This can be manifested through a series of indicators as summarised below:

- speed of response to EU initiatives;
- how widely information is distributed to relevant players within government;
- how comprehensive that information is;
- the extent of the capacity to examine and analyse the input received;
- the effectiveness of procedures for scrutiny and oversight both within the bureaucracy and within parliament;
- the ability to reach a coordinated and agreed view in preparation for negotiations with other member states.

On all these indicators UK central government's approach to reception of EU initiatives can be judged to have been effective. Capacity and performance in relation to reception is not in doubt. Matters are handled speedily, the information net is wide and comprehensive, analytical capacity is substantial, and the ability to reach an agreed view is a characteristic of the UK approach even though the agreed view may be somewhat insular and focused on the concerns of Whitehall. There is some weakness when it comes to scrutiny and oversight. Parliamentary scrutiny has been tightened in recent years, though bureaucratic oversight has been weakened somewhat as the increase in the flow and extent of business has meant some fragmentation of the hub of the system and as departments handle more day to day business in-house. The UK also has a good record on transposing EU legislation (see Armstrong and Bulmer 1996; 2003). Thus the UK can be rated high on reception capability. Traditionally it has been much weaker insofar as projection is concerned.

In Chapter 2 we argued that the effectiveness of a member state's projection can be evaluated in terms of two central criteria: dependability and calculability. In practice these cover a number of factors including:

- the smoothness with which business is conducted by the member state within the EU context and the clarity with which positions are presented;
- the extent to which a member government has an effective strategic capacity to think ahead;
- its general reputation for positive and constructive action in the EU; and
- its capacity to adopt and pursue tactics commensurate with effective bargaining in the multi-governmental context of the EU.

Here the UK scores well on the first factor but not so well on others, although there was a concerted effort to address these areas of weakness under the Blair government. However, our analysis of reception and projection has to be placed in the wider context of political opportunities and constraints within which policy-makers in Whitehall work. What has been the impact of this policy: its effectiveness at EU level? Under the Blair governments some important achievements were made in placing a British imprint on the EU. The Lisbon Strategy for European competitiveness and the ESDP were notable examples. The government was also quite successful at getting its views incorporated into the failed Constitutional Treaty, even if domestically it seemed to be very defensive in the face of a Eurosceptic print media, failing to secure public acceptance for its achievements (Kassim 2004; Menon 2004b). It obtained further objectives when the more limited Lisbon Treaty was negotiated in 2007. However, the decision to support President George W. Bush's invasion of Iraq in 2003 had a divisive effect with major partners. The previous major positive impact on the EU had been Mrs Thatcher's support for the single market in the early to mid-1980s. The list of instances when the UK government sought the re-negotiation of EU policies (the CAP, the budget) or blocked policy developments before then opting out of them (Social Charter, Social Chapter, European Monetary System, EMU, some aspects of home affairs cooperation) tended to dominate its diplomacy prior to Labour's election in 1997. The efficiency of the coordination machinery thus cannot be disentangled from the wider political context. If ministers do not want to engage with the EU, the presence of efficient machinery is not necessarily a major strength of British politics. Indeed, if the government pursues a hostile diplomacy in the EU, most graphically during the policy of non-cooperation pursued by the Major government in 1996, an efficient machinery might actually make matters worse (Westlake 1997). Europeanised it may be, but the UK's public administration is in the service of political leaders who have rarely been able to escape domestic constraints, which have included a sceptical print media and, at times, intra-party and inter-party dissent.

Vivien Schmidt has shed important comparative light on this situation that chimes with our findings in Chapter 9. She distinguishes between *simple* national polities, such as France and the UK, where policy is the preserve of a single national authority, and *compound* polities, such as Germany or Italy, where a more decentralised or polyphonic approach is present. Her argument is that simple polities are more easily able to handle what we term the reception and projection responses of Europeanisation because of the greater concentration of power (Schmidt 2006: 33–4).[12] However, she argues that compound polities' more diffuse power structures have placed a premium upon corporatist policy processes and consensus politics. Consequently, these polities are better able to build a domestic consensus around the benefits that Europeanisation may bring. To put it in stronger profile, the UK's majoritarian electoral system, its competitive parliamentarism, a conflictual political style and polarised party politics place major constraints on creating a wider consensus on European policy, such as would enable the policy machinery not only to be efficient but also much more *effective* at EU level. By contrast, Germany's proportional party system, its parliamentary politics of compromise, consensual political style and so on generate a highly supportive European consensus, even if it is harnessed to a less efficient machinery (see Schmidt 2006: 155–218 for fuller discussion). Hence the failure of even the Blair government – with its manifesto commitments to a constructive approach to European policy – to create a more positive *domestic* discourse around European policy highlights the real problems associated with a Europeanisation of political parties and public opinion.

European policy-making under Gordon Brown

The above conclusions pose the obvious question: what has changed under Prime Minister Gordon Brown? Brown succeeded Blair in June 2007, so we have under a year of his premiership as evidence when the book went to press. Significantly, some organisational changes relevant to European policy-making came with the transition. We note these changes below, although it is early to assess whether these and his premiership will result in any significant long-term changes to the organisational response in Whitehall to the EU.

The first changes to note concern those associated with 'the hub'. Kim Darroch, the Head of the COES and EU Adviser to Tony Blair moved to take up the post of Ambassador to the EU/Head of UKREP. Gordon

Brown appointed Jon Cunliffe, formerly second permanent secretary and Managing Director, Macroeconomic Policy and International Finance in the Treasury, as his successor. Cunliffe has been given the designation 'Head of the European Secretariat and International Economics and EU Adviser to the Prime Minister'.[13] The inclusion of the international economics responsibility was a novelty and presumably resulted from the way in which the former chancellor wishes to prioritise economic diplomacy as well as from having established good working relations with Cunliffe in the Treasury. The COES itself now also includes international economic issues in its remit.[14] A set of questions is posed by this innovation associated with the change of PM. First, how will the combination of international economic diplomacy and the extensive EU workload integrate within the COES? Will it lead to a downgrading of European policy? Secondly, in view of the recruitment of Cunliffe from the Treasury, with its relatively defensive posture towards the EU (see Chapter 6), will the emphasis under Blair's premiership upon strengthening UK central government's projection of policy ideas at EU level, become a lower priority?

In part, these questions will be answered by the lead given by Gordon Brown himself. He took office at a time when there were opportunities and threats. The opportunities arose from the election of Nicolas Sarkozy as French president, with his greater Atlanticist orientation and a preparedness to re-think French European policy. In addition, the German Chancellor, Angela Merkel, had gained prestige in the EU from her quiet diplomacy, not least during the German presidency in the first half of 2007, when she was able to craft the basic principles of the Lisbon Treaty. Like Brown, Merkel lacks the charisma of Blair even if Sarkozy has clearly been influenced by it. Merkel is a potential ally for Brown on the issues of combatting global poverty and climate change.[15] The threats arose in the first instance from the 2007 Lisbon Treaty, where Brown proved able to secure its ratification through parliament. The mid-term review of the EU budget, scheduled for 2008–9, is a potential opportunity for reforming its priorities away from the CAP towards a more forward-looking agenda. However, it is also a threat in that Brown has made his views known on the budget as chancellor, and an inflexible pursuit of that position might simply fuel further dispute with partners (see O'Donnell and Whitman 2007: 259–60).

Some aspects of Gordon Brown's European policy are known from his 12-month tenure as chancellor. First, he was much less adept at inter-personal relations with EU counterparts than his predecessor, Kenneth Clarke, and he was expected to be even less so as PM than Tony Blair. His principal policy reference-points have been Atlanticist. His lack of priority for EU business was reflected in his tendency to send other ministers to represent the Treasury in the Council. A review of his past European policy statements led O'Donnell and Whitman to the view that a failure to compromise on his existing positions was likely to lead to the UK resuming the role of an 'awkward partner' (2007: 262). However, another interpretation might be that, as chancellor, he took on the institutional persona of head of the Treasury, with its well-established defensive European policy. Accordingly, he might then adopt a new persona as PM and respond to the new circumstances of that office. This interpretation would be more convincing if Gordon Brown had confined himself to mainstream Treasury advice. However, his reliance on advisers such as Ed Balls and Ed Miliband, now ministers in his government, suggested little change in this position.

The Lisbon Strategy and the environment are amongst the issues where Gordon Brown could pursue a more pragmatic policy by working with counterparts (see O'Donnell and Whitman 2007: 263–6; Bulmer and Parkes 2007). Also supporting a more pragmatic approach was the appointment of David Miliband, one of the rising stars of the Labour Party and a pro-Europeanist, to the position of Foreign Secretary. Brown has left his Foreign Secretary greater (but not complete) independence to pursue a positive agenda at EU level. He stepped back from the more 'presidential' approach of Blair, whose strong role in foreign policy was a product of his own interests as well as the fact that there was a clear domestic division of labour on economic matters with Gordon Brown. The decision by Brown to arrive late on 13 December 2007 to sign the Lisbon Treaty separately from his counterparts neither played well domestically nor with EU partners.

In short, the balance of probablities appeared to lie with Gordon Brown taking a less pro-active approach to European policy than that of his predecessor. Nevertheless, he and Miliband launched an important agenda-setting paper in October 2007, immediately after the Lisbon Treaty was agreed. The paper, entitled *Global Europe* – was an attempt to define a positive European policy agenda in the period following the negotiation of the new treaty (Cabinet Office/FCO 2007). Consistent with Blair's Step Change, the paper took seriously the need actively to present a positive British agenda for the EU's development. The real tests for the Brown premiership's European policy therefore are the pursuit of this 'Global Europe' agenda, the fate of the Reform Treaty, and the UK's diplomacy on the mid-term budget review.

In the meantime Brown introduced a number of other changes to the structure of the government that impact upon the conduct of European policy. One of the core ministries – the DTI – was re-structured into the Department for Business, Enterprise and Regulatory Reform (BERR). The BERR includes the DTI's responsibilities for productivity, business relations, energy, competition and consumers, and combines them with the Better Regulation Executive (BRE), previously part of the Cabinet Office. The Office of Science and Innovation was merged with the higher education and skills functions of the former DfES to create the Department for Innovation,

Universities and Skills. Meantime, the remaining part of the DfES's functions are the Department for Children, Schools and Families: a ministry which looks likely to have negligible European business.

All the above changes are the result of an endogenous change, namely the resignation of Tony Blair. The arrival of Gordon Brown formed an important test of the robustness of the Step Change reforms to European policy-making under Tony Blair and the extent to which these had been built into Whitehall's ways of doing business. We have suggested earlier in our conclusion that the effectiveness of the UK's machinery is contingent upon the wider political environment. Here was another opportunity to see that contingency in play. For UK civil servants and ministers, despite the continuities highlighted in this book, the challenge of responding to the EU was once again renewed.

Notes

1 Interview, former senior UKREP official, 15 January 1997.
2 Interview, DTI, 8 April 1997.
3 Interview, former senior Cabinet Office official, 17 January 1997.
4 Interview, FCO, 3 December 1996.
5 Interview, former senior Cabinet Office official, 17 April 1997.
6 Interview, Cabinet Office, 28 September 1997.
7 Interview, UKREP, 20 March 1997.
8 Interview, EU Commission, 17 March 1997.
9 Interview, MAFF, 6 December 1996.
10 Interviews, former senior Cabinet Office officials, 17 April 1997 and 16 April 1997 respectively.
11 Interview, DTI, 2 December 1996.
12 Schmidt uses the terminology of downloading and uploading.
13 The No. 10 website gives the European part of his portfolio an even lower profile by designating his role in the PM's Office as 'Head of International Economic Affairs, Europe and G8 Sherpa', see www.number10.gov.uk/output/page12.asp, accessed 15 October 2007.
14 See www.cabinetoffice.gov.uk/secretariats/european_secretariat.aspx, accessed 15 October 2007.
15 For more on the potential for British–German cooperation in the EU, see Bulmer and Parkes (2007).

References

Allen, D. (1988), 'Britain and Western Europe', in M. Smith, S. Smith and B. White (eds), *British Foreign Policy: Tradition, Change and Transformation*, London, Unwin Hyman, 168–92.

Allen, D. (2005), 'The United Kingdom: A *Europeanized* Government in a *Non-Europeanized* Polity', in S. Bulmer and C. Lequesne (eds), *The Member States of the European Union*, Oxford, Oxford University Press, 119–41.

Allen, D. and Oliver, T. (2006), 'The Foreign and Commonwealth Office', in I. Bache and A. Jordan (eds), *The Europeanization of British Politics*, Basingstoke, Palgrave, 52–66.

Argyris, C. and Schön, D. (1978), *Organizational Learning*, Reading, MA, Addison-Wesley.

Armstrong, K. and Bulmer, S. (1996), 'United Kingdom', in D. Rometsch and W. Wessels (eds), *The European Union and Member States*, Manchester, Manchester University Press, 253–90.

Armstrong, K. and Bulmer, S. (1998), *The Governance of the Single European Market* Manchester, Manchester University Press.

Armstrong, K. and Bulmer, S. (2003), 'The United Kingdom: Between Political Controversy and Administrative Efficiency', in W. Wessels, A. Maurer and J. Mittag (eds), *Fifteen into One: The European Union and Member States*, Manchester, Manchester University Press, 388–410.

Aspinwall, M. (2000), 'Structuring Europe: Powersharing Institutions and British Preferences on European Integration', *Political Studies*, 48:3, 415–42.

Aspinwall, M. and Schneider, G. (2001), 'Institutional Research on the European Union: Mapping the Field', in G. Schneider and M. Aspinwall (eds), *The Rules of Integration: Institutionalist Approaches to the Study of Europe*, Manchester, Manchester University Press, 1–18.

Bache, I. (1998), *The Politics of European Union Regional Policy*, Sheffield, Sheffield Academic Press.

Bache, I. (2004), 'Multi-level Governance and European Union Regional Policy', in I. Bache and M. Flinders (eds), *Multi-level Governance*, Oxford, Oxford University Press, 165–78.

Bache, I. (2008), *Europeanization and Multi-level Governance*, Lanham, MD, Rowman and Littlefield.

Bache, I. and Jordan, A. (eds) (2006a), *The Europeanization of British Politics*, Basingstoke, Palgrave Macmillan.

Bache, I. and Jordan, A. (2006b), 'Europeanization and Domestic Change', in I. Bache and A. Jordan, *The Europeanization of British Politics*, Basingstoke, Palgrave Macmillan, 17–33.

Baker, D. and Seawright, D. (eds) (1998), *Britain For and Against Europe: British Politics and the Question of European Integration*, Oxford, Clarendon Press.

Barnett, J. (1982), *Inside The Treasury*, London, Deutsch.

Beichelt, T. (2007), 'Over-efficiency in German EU Policy Coordination', *German Politics*, 16:4, 421–33.

Borrás, S. and Greve, B. (eds) (2004), 'Special Issue: The Open Method of Co-ordination in the European Union', *Journal of European Union*, 11:2, 181–336.

Börzel, T. (1999), 'Towards Convergence in Europe? Institutional Adaptation to Europeanization in Germany and Spain', *Journal of Common Market Studies*, 39:4, 573–96.

Börzel, T. (2002), 'Pace-setting, Foot-dragging, and Fence-sitting: Member State Responses to Europeanization', *Journal of Common Market Studies*, 40:2, 193–214.

Börzel, T. and Risse, T. (2003), 'Conceptualising the Domestic Impact of Europe', in K. Featherstone and C. Radaelli (eds), *The Politics of Europeanisation*, Oxford, Oxford University Press, 57–80.

Buller, J. (1995), 'Britain as an Awkward Partner: Reassessing Britain's Relationship with the EU', *Politics*, 15:1, 33–42.

Buller, J. and Smith, M. (1998), 'Civil Service Attitudes towards the European Union', in D. Baker and D. Seawright (eds), *Britain For and Against Europe: British Politics and the Question of European Integration*, Oxford, Clarendon Press, 165–84.

Bulmer, S. (1993), 'The Governance of the European Union: A New Institutionalist Approach', *Journal of Public Policy*, 13:4, 351–80.

Bulmer, S. (2007), 'Theorizing Europeanisation', in P. Graziano and M. Vink (eds), *Europeanization: New Research Agendas*, Basingstoke, Palgrave Macmillan, 46–58.

Bulmer, S. and Burch, M. (1998), 'Organising for Europe: Whitehall, the British State and the European Union', *Public Administration*, 76:4, 601–28.

Bulmer, S. and Burch, M. (2000), 'The Europeanisation of British Central Government', in R. A. W. Rhodes (ed.), *Transforming British Government; Volume 1: Changing Institutions*, London, Macmillan, 46–62.

Bulmer, S. and Burch, M. (2001), 'The "Europeanisation" of Central Government: The UK and Germany in Historical Institutionalist Perspective', in G. Schneider and M. Aspinwall (eds), *The Rules of Integration*, Manchester, Manchester University Press, 73–96.

Bulmer, S. and Burch, M. (2005), 'The Europeanization of UK Government: From Quiet Revolution to Explicit Step-change', *Public Administration*, 83:4, 861–90.

Bulmer, S. and Burch, M. (2006), 'Central Government', in I. Bache and A. Jordan (eds), *Europeanisation in the UK*, Basingstoke, Palgrave Macmillan, 37–51.

Bulmer, S. and Parkes, R. (2007), 'The Berlin–London connection: From "No Frills" to "Full Service"', SWP Comments 2007/C 21, Berlin, Stiftung Wissenschaft und

Politik, December, available at: www.swp-berlin.org/en/common/get_document. php?asset_id=4550, accessed 31 January 2008.

Bulmer, S. and Radaelli, C. (2005), 'The Europeanisation of National Policy', in S. Bulmer and C. Lequesne (eds), *The Member States of the European Union*, Oxford, Oxford University Press, 338–358.

Bulmer, S., Jeffery, C. and Paterson, W. (2000), *Germany's European Diplomacy: Shaping the Regional Milieu*, Manchester, Manchester University Press.

Bulmer, S., Maurer, A. and Paterson, W. (2001), 'The European Policy-making Machinery in the Berlin Republic: Hindrance or Hand-maiden?', *German Politics*, 10:1, 177–206.

Bulmer, S., Burch, M., Hogwood, P., and Scott, A. (2006), 'UK Devolution and the European Union: A Tale of Cooperative Asymmetry?', *Publius*, 36:1, 75–94.

Bulmer, S., Dolowitz, D., Humphreys, P. and Padgett, S. (2007), *Policy Transfer in European Union Governance: Regulating the Utilities*, Abingdon, Routledge.

Bulmer, S., Burch, M., Carter, C., Hogwood, P. and Scott, A. (2002), *British Devolution and European Policy-making: Transforming Britain into Multi-level Governance*, London, Palgrave.

Burch, M. and Gomez, R. (2002), 'The English Regions and Europe', *Regional Studies*, 36:7, 767–78.

Burch, M., and Gomez, R. (2004), 'The Reform of the EU Common Agricultural Policy in a Devolved UK', paper presented at ESRC Seminar on Rural Policy in a Devolving UK, Cardiff University, April 30, available at: www.cardiff.ac.uk/euros/Rural%20conference%20notes/CAPReformCardiff300404.doc, accessed 26 July 2007.

Burch, M. and Holliday, I. (1993), 'Institutional Emergence: The Case of the North West Region of England', *Regional Politics and Policy*, 3:1, 29–50.

Burch, M. and Holliday, I. (1996), *The British Cabinet System*, London, Prentice Hall.

Burch, M. and Holliday, I. (1999), 'The Cabinet and Prime Minister's Offices: An Executive Office in All But Name', *Parliamentary Affairs*, 52:1, 32–45.

Burch, M. and Holliday, I. (2004), 'The Blair Government and the Core Executive', *Government and Opposition*, 39:1, 1–21.

Burch, M., Gomez, R., Hogwood, P., and Scott, A. (2005), 'Devolution, Change and European Union Policy-making in the UK', *Regional Studies*, 39:4, 465–75.

Burch, M., Hogwood, P., Bulmer, S., Carter, C., Gomez, R. and Scott, A. (2003), 'Charting Routine and Radical Change: A Discussion Paper', Manchester Papers in Politics, Devolution and European Policy Making Series, no. 6.

Bursens, P. (2007), 'State Structures', in P. Graziano and M. Vink (eds), *Europeanization: New Research Agendas*, Basingstoke, Palgrave, 115–27.

Butt Philip, A. (1992), 'British Pressure Groups and the European Community', in S. George (ed.), *Britain and the European Community: The Politics of Semi-detachment*, Oxford, Clarendon Press, 149–71.

Cabinet Office (1971), *The United Kingdom and the European Communities*, Cmnd 4715, London, HMSO.

Cabinet Office (1996), *Review of the European Fast Stream Scheme*, London, Office of Public Service.

Cabinet Office (1997), *Ministerial Code: A Code of Conduct and Guidance on Procedures for Ministers*, London, Cabinet Office.

Cabinet Office (1999a), *The Guide to Better European Regulation*, London, Cabinet Office Regulatory Impact Unit.

Cabinet Office (1999b), *Memorandum of Understanding and Supplementary Agreements: Between the United Kingdom Government, Scottish Ministers and the Cabinet of the National Assembly for Wales*, Cm 4444, London, Stationery Office.

Cabinet Office (2005), *Departmental Report 2005: Cabinet Office*, Cm 6543, London, Stationery Office.

Cabinet Office/FCO (2007), 'Global Europe: Meeting the Economic and Security Challenges', available at: www.fco.gov.uk/Files/kfile/FCO_BEU_DOC_GlobalEurope71022.pdf, accessed 24 October 2007.

Camps, M. (1964), *Britain and the European Community: 1955–1963*, Oxford, Oxford University Press.

Carter, C. (2001), 'The Parliament of the United Kingdom: From Supportive Scrutiny to Unleashed Control?', in A. Maurer and W. Wessels (eds), *The European Parliament and National Parliaments after Amsterdam*, Baden-Baden, Nomos, 395–424.

Charlton, M. (1983), *The Price of Victory*, London, BBC Publications.

Checkel, J. (1999), 'Social Construction and Integration', *Journal of European Public Policy*, 6:4, 545–60.

Civil Service Fast Stream (2005), *European Fast Stream*, accessed at: http://european.faststream.gov.uk, website now closed.

Cockfield, (Lord) A. (1994), *The European Union: Creating the Single Market*, Chichester, Chancery Law Publishing.

Cole, A. (2001), *Franco-German Relations*, Harlow, Longman.

Collier, R. and Collier, D. (1991), *Shaping the Political Agenda: Critical Junctures, the Labor Movement, and Regime Dynamics in Latin America*, Princeton, NJ, Princeton University Press.

Colman, D. (1992), 'Agricultural Policy', in S. Bulmer, S. George and A. Scott (eds), *The United Kingdom and European Union Membership Evaluated*, London, Pinter Publishers, 29–39.

Council of the EU (2002), 'Seville European Council 21 and 22 June 2002: Presidency Conclusions', Annex 1, p. 23, available at: http://ue.eu.int/ueDocs/cms_Data/docs/pressdata/en/ec/72638.pdf, accessed 5 July 2007.

Cowles, M. G., Caporaso, J. and Risse, T. (eds) (2001), *Transforming Europe: Europeanization and Domestic Change*, Ithaca, NY, Cornell University Press.

Cram, L. (1997), *Policy-making in the EU: Conceptual Lenses and the Integration Process*, London, Routledge.

Daddow, O. (2007), 'Playing Games with History: Tony Blair's European Policy in the Press', *British Journal of Politics and International Relations*, 9:4, 582–98.

Dehousse, R. (1998), *The European Court of Justice*, Basingstoke, Macmillan.

Denman, R. (1996), *Missed Chances: Britain and Europe in the Twentieth Century*, London, Pinter.

Department of Health (2006), *Departmental Report 2006*, Cm 6814, London, Stationery Office.

Dickie, J. (2004), *The New Mandarins: How British Foreign Policy Works*, London, I. B. Tauris.

Diez, T. (1999a), 'Speaking "Europe": The Politics of Integration Discourse', *Journal of European Public Policy*, 6:4, 598–613.

Diez, T. (1999b), *Die EU lesen: Diskursive Knotenpunkte in der britischen Europadebatte*, Opladen, Leske & Budrich.

Docksey, C. and Williams, K. (1994), 'The Commission and the Execution of Community Policy', in G. Edwards and D. Spence (eds), *The European Commission*, Harlow, Longman, 117–45.

Donnelly, M. (1993), 'The Structure of the European Commission and the Policy Formation Process', in S. Mazey and J. Richardson (eds), *Lobbying the European Community*, Oxford, Oxford University Press, 74–81.

Dyson, K. and Featherstone, K. (1999), *The Road to Maastricht: Negotiating Economic and Monetary Union*, Oxford, Oxford University Press.

Edwards, G. (1992), 'Central Government', in S. George (ed.), *Britain and the European Community: The Politics of Semi-detachment*, Oxford, Clarendon Press, 64–90.

Egeberg, M. (ed.) (2006), *Multilevel Union Administration: The Transformation of Executive Politics in Europe*, Basingstoke, Palgrave.

Egeberg, M., Schaefer, G. and Trondal, J. (2006), 'EU Committee Governance between Intergovernmental and Union Administration', in M. Egeberg (ed.), *Multilevel Union Administration: The Transformation of Executive Politics in Europe*, Basingstoke, Palgrave Macmillan, 66–85.

European Council (2000), 'Presidency Conclusions – Lisbon European Council: 23 and 24 March 2000', available at: http://europa.eu.int/ISPO/docs/services/docs/2000/jan-march/doc_00_8_en.html#A, accessed 5 July 2005.

Featherstone, K. and Radaelli, C. (eds) (2003), *The Politics of Europeanisation*, Oxford, Oxford University Press.

Fligstein, N. and McNichol, J. (1998), 'The Institutional Terrain of the European Union', in W. Sandholtz and A. Stone Sweet (eds), *European Integration and Supranational Governance*, Oxford, Oxford University Press, 59–91.

Foreign and Commonwealth Office (1999), *FCO Departmental Report 1999*, available at: www.fco.gov.uk, accessed 18 September 2008.

Foreign and Commonwealth Office (2000), *FCO Departmental Report 2000*, available at: www.fco.gov.uk, accessed 18 September 2008.

Foreign and Commonwealth Office (2001), *FCO Departmental Report 2001*, available at: www.fco.gov.uk, accessed 18 September 2008.

Foreign and Commonwealth Office (2005), *FCO Departmental Report 2005*, available at: www.fco.gov.uk, accessed 18 September 2008.

Forster, A. and Blair, A. (2002), *The Making of Britain's European Foreign Policy*, Harlow, Pearson Education.

Franklin, M. (1988), 'Metamorphoses of the MAFF', *Journal of the Royal Agricultural Society of England*, 149, 52–7.

Galloway, D. (2001), *The Treaty of Nice and Beyond*, Sheffield, Sheffield Academic Press.

Gamble, A. (1998), 'The European Issue in British Politics', in D. Baker and D. Seawright (eds), *Britain For and Against Europe: British Politics and the Question of European Integration*, Oxford, Clarendon Press, 11–30.

Genschel, P. (2001), 'Comment: "The Europeanisation of Central Government"', in G. Schneider and M. Aspinwall (eds), *The Rules of Integration*, Manchester, Manchester University Press, 97–100.

George, S. (1994), *An Awkward Partner: Britain in the European Community*, 2nd edn, Oxford, Oxford University Press.

George, S. (1995), 'A Reply to Buller', *Politics*, 15:1, 43–7.

George, S. (1998), *An Awkward Partner: Britain in the European Community*, 3rd edn, Oxford, Oxford University Press.

Giddings, P. and Drewry, G. (eds) (2004), *Britain in the European Union: Law, Policy and Parliament*, Basingstoke, Palgrave Macmillan.

Goetz, K. (2001), 'European Integration and National Executives: A Cause in Search of an Effect', in K. Goetz and S. Hix (eds), *Europeanised Politics? European Integration and National Political Systems*, London, Frank Cass, 211–31.

Goetz, K. (2005), 'The New Member States and the EU: Responding to Europe', in S. Bulmer and C. Lequesne (eds), *The Member States of the European Union*, Oxford, Oxford University Press, 254–80.

Graziano, P. and Vink, M. (2007), *Europeanization: A Handbook for a New Research Agenda*, Basingstoke, Palgrave.

Greenwood, S. (ed.) (1996), *Britain and European Integration since the Second World War*, Manchester: Manchester University Press.

Gregory, F. (1983), *Dilemmas of Government: Britain and the European Community*, Oxford, Martin Robertson.

Griffiths, R. T. (1997), 'A Slow One Hundred and Eighty Degree Turn: British Policy towards the Common Market, 1955–60', in G. Wilkes (ed.), *The Brussels Breakdown: Britain and the First Failure to Enlarge the European Community 1961–63*, London, Frank Cass.

Haas, P. (1992), 'Introduction: Epistemic Communities and International Policy Coordination', *International Organization*, 46:1, 1–36.

Hall, P. (1986), *Governing the Economy: The Politics of State Intervention in Britain and France*, Cambridge, Polity Press.

Hall, P. (1993), 'Policy Paradigms, Social Learning and the State: the Case of Economic Policy-making in Britain', *Comparative Politics*, 25:3, 275–96.

Hall, P. and Taylor, R. (1996), 'Political Science and the Three New Institutionalisms', *Political Studies*, 44:5, 936–57.

Hanf, K. and Soetendorp, B. (1998a), 'Small States and the Europeanization of Public Policy', in K. Hanf and B. Soetendorp (eds), *Adapting to European Integration: Small States and the European Union*, Harlow, Addison, Wesley, Longman Limited, 1–13.

Hanf, K. and Soetendorp, B. (eds) (1998b), *Adapting to European Integration: Small States and the European Union*, Harlow, Addison, Wesley, Longman Limited.

Harmsen, R. (1999), 'The Europeanization of National Administrations: A Comparative Study of France and the Netherlands', *Governance*, 12:1, 81–113.

Haverland, M. (2000), 'National Adaptation to European Integration: The Importance of Institutional Veto Points', *Journal of Public Policy*, 20:1, 83–103.

Hay, C. and Rosamond, B. (2002), 'Globalisation, European Integration and the Discursive Construction of Economic Imperatives', *Journal of European Public Policy* 9:2, 147–67.

Hayes-Renshaw, F. and Wallace, H. (1997), *The Council of Ministers*, Basingstoke, Palgrave Macmillan.

Hayes-Renshaw, F. and Wallace, H. (2006), *The Council of Ministers*, 2nd edn, Basingstoke, Palgrave Macmillan.

Heath, E. (1998), *The Course of My Life: My Autobiography*, London, Hodder and Stoughton.

Heclo, H. and Wildavsky, A. (1974), *The Private Government of Public Money*, London, Macmillan.

Héritier, A. (2007), *Explaining Institutional Change in Europe*, Oxford, Oxford University Press.

Héritier, A. and Knill, C. (2001), 'Differential Responses to European Policies: A Comparison', in A. Héritier, D. Kerwer, C. Knill, D. Lehmkuhl, M. Teutsch and A.-C. Douillet (eds), *Differential Europe: The European Union Impact on National Policymaking*, Lanham, MD, Rowman and Littlefield, 257–94.

Hesse, J.-J. and Goetz, K. (1992), 'Early Administrative Adjustment to the European Communities: The Case of the Federal Republic of Germany', in E. Heyen (ed.), *Jahrbuch der Europäischen Verwaltungsgeschichte*, Baden-Baden, Nomos, 181–205.

Hix, S. and Lord, C. (1997), *Political Parties in the European Union*, London, Macmillan.

HM Treasury (1996), 'EC Spending and Public Expenditure Control: EUROPES', undated EU Finances Team unclassified document supplied in correspondence to the authors, 19 December.

HM Treasury (1998), *Public Services for the Future: Modernisation, Reform, Accountability: Public Service Agreements 1999–2002*, Cm 4181, London, Stationery Office.

Holden, R. (2002), *The Making of New Labour's European Policy*, Basingstoke, Palgrave.

House of Commons (2005), *The European Scrutiny System in the House of Commons*, London, available at: www.parliament.uk/documents/upload/TheEuroScrutinySystemintheHoC.pdf, accessed 18 September 2008.

Howe, G. (1994), *Conflict of Loyalty*, London, Macmillan.

Humphreys, J. (1996), *A Way through The Woods: Negotiating in the European Union*, London, Department of the Environment.

Jeffery, C. (1994), 'The Länder Strike Back: Structures and Procedures of European Integration Policy-making in the German Federal System', Leicester, Leicester University Discussion Papers in Federalism no. FS 93/2.

Jeffery, C. (ed.) (1997), *The Regional Dimension of the European Union: Towards a Third Level?*, London, Frank Cass.

Jeffery, C. (2000), 'Sub-national Mobilization and European Integration', *Journal of Common Market Studies*, 38:1, 1–23.

Jordan, A. (2002), *The Europeanization of British Environmental Policy: A Departmental Perspective*, Basingstoke, Palgrave Macmillan.

Jordan, A. (2003), 'The Europeanization of National Government and Policy: A Departmental Perspective', *British Journal of Political Science*, 33:2, 261–82.

Jordan, A. and Schout, A. (2006), *The Coordination of the European Union: Exploring the Capacities of Networked Governance*, Oxford, Oxford University Press.

Kassim, H. (2000a), 'The United Kingdom', in Kassim *et al.* (eds) (2000a) 23–53.

Kassim, H. (2000b), 'The National Coordination EU Policy: Confronting the Challenge', in Kassim *et al.* (eds) (2000a), 235–64.

Kassim, H. (2001), 'Representing the United Kingdom in Brussels: The Fine Art of Positive Co-ordination', in H. Kassim *et al.* (eds) (2001), 47–74.

Kassim, H. (2003), 'Meeting the Demands of EU Membership: The Europeanization of National Administrative Systems', in K. Featherstone and C. Radaelli (eds), *The Politics of Europeanisation*, Oxford, Oxford University Press, 83–111.

Kassim, H. (2004), 'The United Kingdom and the Future of Europe: Winning the Battle, Losing the War', *Comparative European Politics*, 2:3, 261–81.

Kassim, H. (2005), 'The Europeanization of Member State Institutions', in S. Bulmer and C. Lequesne (eds), *The Member States of the European Union*, Oxford, Oxford University Press, 285–316.

Kassim, H., Peters, G. and Wright, V. (eds) (2000a), *The National Co-ordination of EU Policy*, Oxford, Oxford University Press.

Kassim, H., Peters, G. and Wright, V. (2000b), 'Introduction', in Kassim *et al.* (eds) (2000a), 1–21.

Kassim, H., Menon, A., Peters G. B. and Wright, V. (eds) (2001), *The National Co-ordination of EU Policy: The European Level*, Oxford, Oxford University Press.

Kaufman, G. (1997), *How to Be a Minister*, 2nd edn, London, Faber and Faber.

Kavanagh, D. and Seldon, A. (1999), *The Powers Behind the Prime Minister*, London, Harper Collins.

Kietz, D. and Perthes, V. (2008), *The Potential of the Council Presidency: An Analysis of the German Chairmanship of the EU, 2007*, Berlin: Stiftung Wissenschaft und Politik. Also available at: www.swp-berlin.org/en/common/get_document.php? asset_id=4656, accessed 31 January 2008.

Kitzinger, U. (1973), *Diplomacy and Persuasion: How Britain Joined the Common Market*, London, Thames and Hudson.

Knill, C. (2001), *The Europeanisation of National Administrations: Patterns of Institutional Persistence and Change*, Cambridge, Cambridge University Press.

Knodt, M. (1998), 'Auswärtiges Handeln der deutschen Länder', in W.-D. Eberwein and K. Kaiser (eds), *Deutschlands neue Außenpolitik: Band 4 Institutionen und Ressourcen*, München: R. Oldenbourg Verlag, 153–66.

Koerfer, D. (1988), 'Zankapfel Europapolitik. Der Kompetenzstreit zwischen Auswärtigem   Amt   und   Bundeswirtschaftsministerium', *Politische Vierteljahresschrift*, 29:4, 552–68.

Krasner, S. (1988), 'Sovereignty: An Institutional Perspective', *Comparative Political Studies*, 21:1, 66–94.

Laffan, B. (2005), 'Impact of the EU on Executive Government: A Comparative Analysis', Dublin: Dublin European Institute, available at: www.oeue.net/ papers/acomparativeanalysis-theimpact.pdf, accessed 17 September 2007.

Laffan, B. (2007), 'Core Executives', in P. Graziano and M. Vink (eds), *Europeanization: New Research Agendas*, Basingstoke, Palgrave Macmillan, 128–40.

Laffan, B. and Mahoney, J. (2003), 'The Europeanisation of the Irish Core Executive', Dublin: Dublin European Insititute, available at: www.oeue.net/ papers/ireland-theeuropeanisationofth.pdf, accessed 5 October 2007.

Larsen, H. (1997), 'British Discourses on Europe: Sovereignty of Parliament, Instrumentality and the Non-mythical Europe', in K. E. Jørgensen (ed.), *Reflective Approaches to European Governance*, Basingstoke, Macmillan, 109–27.

Lavenex, S. and Wallace, W. (2005), 'Justice and Home Affairs: Towards a "European Public Order"?', in H. Wallace, W. Wallace and M. Pollack (eds), *Policy-making in the European Union*, 5th edn, Oxford, Oxford University Press, 457–80.

Leader of the House of Commons (1998), *The Scrutiny of European Union Business*, Cm 4095, London, Stationery Office.

Lee, M. (1990), 'The Ethos of the Cabinet Office: A Comment on the Testimony of Officials', *Public Administration*, 68:3, 235–42.

Lequesne, C. (1993), *Paris–Bruxelles: Comment se fait la politique européenne la France*, Paris, Presses de la Fondation Nationale des Sciences Politiques.

Lequesne, C. (2000), 'The Common Fisheries Policy: Letting the Little Ones Go?', in H. Wallace and W. Wallace (eds), *Policy-making in the European Union*, 4th edn, Oxford, Oxford University Press, 345–72.

Lewis, J. (1998), 'Is the "Hard Bargaining" Image of the Council Misleading?', *Journal of Common Market Studies*, 36:4, 479–504.

Ludlow, P. (1982), *The Making of the European Monetary System*, London, Butterworths.

Ludlow, P. (1997), *Dealing with Britain: The Six and the First UK Application to the EEC*, Cambridge, Cambridge University Press.

Ludlow, P. (1998), 'The 1998 UK Presidency: A View from Brussels', *Journal of Common Market Studies*, 36:4, 573–83.

McDonagh, B. (1998), *Original Sin in a Brave New World*, Dublin, Institute of European Affairs.

MAFF (1996), 'Guide to the Institutions of the European Union', European Union Division, Branch II, May.

Maitland, D. (1996), *Diverse Times, Sundry Places*, Brighton, Alpha Press.

March, J. and Olsen, J. (1989), *Rediscovering Institutions: The Organizational Basis of Politics*, New York, The Free Press.

March, J. and Olsen, J. (1996), 'Institutional Perspectives on Political Institutions', *Governance*, 9:3, 247–64.

Marcussen, M., Risse, T., Engelmann-Martin, D., Knopf, H. J. and Roscher, K. (1999), 'Constructing Europe? The Evolution of French, British and German Nation State Identities', *Journal of European Public Policy*, 6:4, 614–33.

Marks, G., Hooghe, L. and Blank, K. (1996), 'European Integration from the 1980s: State-centric v. Multi-level Governance', *Journal of Common Market Studies*, 34:3, 341–78.

Marsh, D. and Rhodes, R. (eds) (1992), *Policy Networks in British Governments*, Oxford, Clarendon Press.

Maurer, A. and Wessels, W. (eds) (2001), *National Parliaments on Their Ways to Europe: Losers or Latecomers?*, Baden-Baden, Nomos.

Maurer, A. and Wessels, W. (2003), 'The European Union Matters: Structuring Self-made Offers and Demands', in W. Wessels, J. Mittag and A. Maurer (eds), *Fifteen into One? The European Union and Its Member States*, Manchester, Manchester University Press, 29–65.

Mazey, S. and Richardson, J. (1996), 'EU Policy-making: A Garbage Can or an Anticipatory and Consensual Policy Style?', in Y. Mény, P. Muller and J.-L. Quermonne (eds), *Adjusting to Europe: The Impact of the European Union on National Institutions and Policies*, London, Routledge, 41–58.

Menon, A. (2000), 'France', in Kassim *et al.* (eds) (2000a), 79–98.

Menon, A. (2004a), 'European Puzzle', *Prospect*, 104, November: available at: www.prospect-magazine.co.uk/article_details.php?id=6496, accessed 27 July 2007.

Menon, A. (2004b), 'Leading from Behind: Britain and the European Constitutional Treaty', Notre Europe, Research and European Issues, no. 31, Paris: Notre Europe, available at: www.notre-europe.eu/uploads/tx_publication/Etud31-en-2_01.pdf, accessed 8 October 2007.

Milward, A. (1992), *The European Rescue of the Nation State*, London, Routledge.

Mittag, J. and Wessels, W. (2003), 'The "One" and the "Fifteen"? The Member States between procedural adaptation and structural revolution', in W. Wessels, J. Mittag and A. Maurer (eds), *Fifteen into One? The European Union and Its Member States*, Manchester, Manchester University Press, 413–54.

Morata, F. (2007), 'The European Union and the Spanish State of the Autonomies', paper given at CONNEX Research Group conference, 7–9 June, available at: www.mzes.uni-mannheim.de/projekte/typo3/site/fileadmin/BookSeries/Volume_Three/chapter14.pdf, accessed 31 January 2008.

Moravcsik, A. (1993), 'Preferences and Power in the European Community: A Liberal Intergovernmentalist Approach', *Journal of Common Market Studies*, 31:4, 473–524.

Moravcsik, A. (1994), 'Why European Integration Strengthens the Nation-state', Working Paper no. 52, Cambridge, MA, Harvard Center for European Studies.

Moravcsik, A. (1998), *The Choice for Europe: Social Purpose and State Power from Messina to Maastricht*, London, UCL Press/Ithaca, NY, Cornell University Press.

Naughtie, J. (2001), *Rivals – Blair and Brown: The Intimate Story of a Political Marriage*, London, Fourth Estate.

Newman, K. (1997), 'Legal Problems for British Accession', in G. Wilkes, (ed.), *The Brussels Breakdown: Britain and the First Failure to Enlarge the European Community 1961–1963*, London, Frank Cass, 120–32.

Norman, P. (2003), *The Accidental Constitution: The Story of the European Convention*, Brussels, EuroComment.

Nugent, N. (1992), 'British Public Opinion and the European Community', in S. George (ed.), *Britain and the European Community: The Politics of Semi-detachment*, Oxford, Clarendon Press, 172–201.

Nugent, N. (2006), *The Government and Politics of the European Union*, 6th edn, Basingstoke, Macmillan.

O'Donnell, G. (2004), 'The Modern Treasury: Macro Good, Micro Better?', speech to the 51st Annual Dinner of the Society of Business Economists, available at: www.hm-treasury.gov.uk./newsroom_and_speeches/speeches/perm_sec_speeches/speech_pst_050204.cfm accessed September 2005.

O'Donnell, C. M. and Whitman, R. (2007), 'European Policy under Gordon Brown: Perspectives on a Future Prime Minister', *International Affairs*, 83:1, 253–72.

Office of the Deputy Prime Minister (ODPM) (2001), *Memorandum of Understanding and Supplementary Agreements: Between the United Kingdom Government Scottish Ministers and the Cabinet of the National Assembly for Wales and the Northern Ireland Executive Committee*, Cm 5420, London, Stationery Office.

Olsen, J. (1995), 'European Challenges to the Nation State', Arena Working Paper no. 14/95, Oslo, University of Oslo.

Olsen, J. (1996), 'Europeanization and Nation-state Dynamics', in S. Gustafsson and L. Lewin (eds), *The Future of the Nation-state*, London, Routledge, 245–85.

Olsen, J. (2002), 'The Many Faces of Europeanization', *Journal of Common Market Studies*, 40:5, 921–52.

Olsen, J. (2003), 'Towards a European Administrative Space?', *Journal of European Public Policy*, 10:4, 506–31.

O'Neill, Sir Con (2000), *Britain's Entry into the European Community: Report of the Negotiations of 1970–72*, ed. David Hannay, London, Frank Cass.

Page, E. (1997), *People Who Run Europe*, Oxford, Oxford University Press.

Page, E. (1998), 'The Impact of European Legislation on British Public Policy-Making: A Research Note', *Public Administration* 76:4, 803–9.

Page, A. (2004), 'Balancing Supremacy: EU Membership and the Constitution', in P. Giddings and G. Drewry (eds), *Britain in the European Union: Law, Policy and Parliament*, Basingstoke, Palgrave Macmillan, 37–59.

Parrish, R. (2003), *Sports Law and Policy in the European Union*, Manchester, Manchester University Press.

Pickering, C. (2002), ' "Sir Douglas in Euroland": Treasury Officials and the European Union, 1977–2001', *Public Admnistration*, 80:3, 583–99.

Pierson, P. (2004), *Politics in Time: History, Institutions and Social Analysis*, Princeton, NJ, Princeton University Press.

Pollitt, C. (1984), *Manipulating the Machine: Changing the Pattern of Ministerial Departments, 1960–83*, London, Allen and Unwin.

Powell, W. and DiMaggio, P. (eds) (1996), *The New Institutionalism in Organisational Analysis*, Chicago, University of Chicago Press.

Radaelli, C. (2000), 'The Europeanization of Public Policy: Notes on Theory, Methods and the Challenge of Empirical Research', European Integration on-line paper, available at: www.eiop.or.at, accessed 18 September 2008.

Radaelli, C. (2003), 'The Europeanization of Public Policy', in K. Featherstone and C. Radaelli (eds), *The Politics of Europeanisation*, Oxford, Oxford University Press, 27–56.

Risse, T. (2000), ' "Let's Argue!" Communicative Action in International Relations', *International Organization*, 54:1, 1–39.

Risse, T., Cowles, Maria G. and Caporaso, J. (2001), 'Europeanization and Domestic Change: Introduction', in M. G. Cowles, J. Caporaso and T. Risse (eds), *Transforming Europe: Europeanization and Domestic Change*, Ithaca, NY, Cornell University Press, 1–20.

Rometsch, D. and Wessels, W. (eds) (1996a), *The European Union and Member States*, Manchester, Manchester University Press.

Rometsch, D. and Wessels, W. (1996b), 'Institutions of the EU System: Models of Explanation', in D. Rometsch and W. Wessels (eds), *The European Union and Member States*, Manchester, Manchester University Press, 20–36.

Rosamond, B. (1998), 'The Integration of Labour? British Trade Union Attitudes to European Integration', in D. Baker and D. Seawright (eds), *Britain For and Against Europe: British Politics and the Question of European Integration*, Oxford, Clarendon Press, 130–47.

Rosamond, B. (2000), *Theories of European Integration*, Basingstoke, Macmillan.

Ross, G. (1994), 'Inside the Delors Cabinet', *Journal of Common Market Studies*, 32:4, 499–523.

Ross, G. (1995), *Jacques Delors and European Integration*, Oxford, Polity Press.

Rothstein, B. (1992), 'Labor-market Institutions and Working Class Strength' in K. Thelen, S. Steinmo and F. Longstreth (eds), *Structuring Politics: Historical Institutionalism in Comparative Analysis*, Cambridge University Press, Cambridge, 33–56.

Sabatier, P. (1998), 'The Advocacy Coalition Framework: Revisions and Relevance for Europe', *Journal of European Public Policy*, 5:1, 98–130.

Schmidt, V. (2006), *Democracy in Europe: The EU and National Politics*, Oxford, Oxford University Press.

Scott, A. (2001), 'The Role of Concordats in the New Governance of Britain', *Edinburgh Law Review*, 5, 21–48.

Scott, D. (2004), *Off Whitehall: A View from Downing Street by Tony Blair's Adviser*, London, I. B. Tauris.

Scottish Office (1991), *The Scottish Office and the European Community – A Review: Summary of the Main Findings and Recommendations*, Edinburgh, Scottish Office Industry Department.

Scottish Office (1997), *Scotland's Parliament: A White Paper*, Cm 3658, 07–97, London, Stationery Office.

Skowronek, S. (1982), *Building a New American State: The Expansion of National Administrative Capacities, 1877–1920*, New York, Cambridge University Press.

Smith, James (2001), 'Cultural Aspects of Europeanisation: The Case of the Scottish Office', *Public Administration*, 79:1, 147–65.

Smith, James (2006), 'Government in Scotland', in I. Bache and A. Jordan (eds), *The Europeanization of British Politics*, Basingstoke, Palgrave Macmillan, 67–81.

Smith, Julie (2005), 'A Missed Opportunity? New Labour's European Policy 1997–2005', *International Affairs*, 81:4, 703–21.

Smith, Julie and Tsatsas, M. (2002), *The New Bilateralism: The UK's Relations within the EU*, London, Royal Institute of International Affairs.

Smith, M. (1999), *The Core Executive in Britain*, London, Macmillan.

Spanou, C. (2003), 'The Europeanisation of the Greek Core Executive', OEUE Occasional Paper 09.03, Dublin: Dublin European Institute, available at: www.oeue.net/papers/greece-theeuropeanisationofthe.pdf, accessed 5 October 2007.

Stack, F. (1983), 'The Imperatives of Participation', in F. E. Gregory, *The Dilemmas of Government: Britain and the European Community*, Oxford, Martin Robertson.

Steiner, J. (1992), 'Legal System', in S. Bulmer, S. George and A. Scott (eds), *The United Kingdom and EC Membership Evaluated*, London, Pinter Publishers, 124–37.

Stephens, P. (1997), *Politics and the Pound: The Tories, the Economy and Europe*, London, Macmillan.

Stevens, A. and Stevens, H. (2001), *Brussels Bureaucrats? The Administration of the European Union*, Basingstoke, Palgrave.

Study of Parliament Group (2005), *Newsletter*, no. 38.

Tallberg, J. (2007), 'Bargaining Power in the European Council', paper given at European Union Studies Association biennial conference, Montreal, 19 May 2007, available at: www.unc.edu/euce/eusa2007/papers/tallberg-j-12c.pdf, accessed 4 July 2007.

Teasdale, A. (1993), 'The Life and Death of the Luxembourg Compromise', *Journal of Common Market Studies*, 31:4, 567–79.

Teasdale, A. (1998), 'Britain's Successes in the European Union 1973–98', in M. Fraser (ed.), *Britain in Europe: The Next Phase*, 2nd edn, London, Stratagems Publishing, 157–9.

Thain, C. and Wright, M. (1995), *The Treasury and Whitehall: The Planning and Control of Public Expenditure, 1976–1993*, Oxford, Clarendon Press.

Thelen, K. and Steinmo, S. (1992), 'Historical Institutionalism in Comparative Politics', in K. Thelen, S. Steinmo and F. Longstreth (eds), *Structuring Politics: Historical Institutionalism in Comparative Analysis*, Cambridge, Cambridge University Press, 1–32.

Tratt, J. (1996), *The Macmillan Government and Europe: A Study in the Process of Policy Development*, London, Macmillan.

Treasury (1966), *Negotiations with the European Community 1961–1963*, Treasury Historical Memorandum, no. 10, T267/14, PRO.

Treasury Solicitors (2005), *European Law*, available at: www.tsol.gov.uk/Pdfs/European%20Law.pdf, accessed 18 September 2008.

UKREP (2005), *UK Presidency of the EU: 2005 UKREP Guide*, Brussels: UKREP, available at: www.UKREP.be/UKREP%20Guide.pdf, accessed 18 September 2008.

Walker, N. (ed.) (2004), *Europe's Area of Freedom, Security, and Justice*, Oxford, Oxford University Press.

Wallace, H. (1973), *National Governments and the European Community*, London, Chatham House/PEP.

Wallace, H. (2005), 'An Institutional Anatomy and Five Policy Modes', in H. Wallace, W. Wallace and M. Pollack (eds), *Policy-making in the European Union*, 5th edn, Oxford, Oxford University Press, 49–90.

Wallace, W. (1986), 'What Price Interdependence? Sovereignty and Interdependence in British Politics', *International Affairs*, 62:3, 367–89.

Wallace, W. (2005), 'Foreign and Security Policy: The Painful Path from Shadow to Substance', in H. Wallace, W. Wallace and M. Pollack (eds), *Policy-making in the European Union*, 5th edn, Oxford, Oxford University Press, 429–56.

Wallace, H. and Wallace, W. (1973), 'The Impact of Community Membership on the British Machinery of Government', *Journal of Common Market Studies*, 11, 243–62.

Weiler, J. (1991), 'The Transformation of Europe', *Yale Law Journal*, 100:8, 2405–83.

Welsh Office (1997), *A Voice for Wales: The Government's Proposals for a Welsh Assembly*, Cm 3718, London, Stationery Office.

Wessels, W., Maurer, A. and Mittag, J. (eds) (2003), *Fifteen into One? The European Union and Its Member States*, Manchester, Manchester University Press.

Westlake, M. (1995), *The Council of the European Union*, London, Cartermill.

Westlake, M. (1997), 'Keynote Article: "Mad Cows and Englishmen" – the Institutional Consequences of the BSE Crisis', in N. Nugent (ed.), *The European Union 1996: Annual Review of Activities*, Oxford, Blackwell, 11–36.

Westlake, M. and Galloway, D. (2004), *The Council of the European Union*, 3rd edn, London, John Harper Publishing.

Whitman, R. (2006), 'The UK Presidency: In the Hot Seat', *Journal of Common Market Studies*, 44:annual review, 57–62.

Wilkes, G. and Wring, D. (1998), 'The British Press and European Integration 1948 to 1996', in D. Baker and D. Seawright (eds), *Britain For and Against Europe: British Politics and the Question of European Integration*, Oxford, Clarendon Press, 185–205.

Wilson, H. (1974), *The Labour Government 1964–70: A Personal Record*, Harmondsworth, Penguin Books.

Wright, V. (1996), 'The National Coordination of European Policy-making: Negotiating the Quagmire', in J. Richardson (ed.), *European Union: Power and Policy-making*, London, Routledge, 148–69.

Young, H. (1998), *This Blessed Plot: Britain and Europe from Churchill to Blair*, London, Macmillan.

Young, S. (2000), 'New Labour and the Environment', in D. Coates and P. Lawler (eds), *New Labour in Power*, Manchester, Manchester University Press, 149–68.

Index

Note: 'n.' after a page number indicates the number of a note on that page.